FREEDIVING FUNDAMENTAL GUIDE
The Freediver's Ultimate Handbook: Your Essential Guide from Beginner to Pro

By

Bassel Ounah

Grosvenor House
Publishing Limited

All rights reserved
Copyright © Bassel Ounah, 2025

The right of Bassel Ounah to be identified as the author of this
work has been asserted in accordance with Section 78
of the Copyright, Designs and Patents Act 1988

The book cover is copyright to Bassel Ounah

This book is published by
Grosvenor House Publishing Ltd
Link House
140 The Broadway, Tolworth, Surrey, KT6 7HT.
www.grosvenorhousepublishing.co.uk

This book is sold subject to the conditions that it shall not, by way of
trade or otherwise, be lent, resold, hired out or otherwise circulated
without the author's or publisher's prior consent in any form of
binding or cover other than that in which it is published and
without a similar condition including this condition being
imposed on the subsequent purchaser.

A CIP record for this book
is available from the British Library

Paperback ISBN 978-1-83615-221-7
Hardback ISBN 978-1-83615-220-0
eBook ISBN 978-1-83615-222-4

Dedication

This is to bold explorers, never afraid to go into the silent depths and push human capability to its limits, show the world that impossible is but uncharted; to those who found their solace in the ocean's embracing touch and shared its profound lessons of resilience, humility, and connection.

This book is dedicated to the legendary freedivers who turned their passion into a purpose: teaching generations to look beneath the surface and find a world of wonder- a world of the underwater and themselves. May your courage, determination, and respect for the ocean always light the way for dreamers, explorers, and guardians of the sea.

To the ocean: timeless teacher, endless fountain of wonder. We always respect its secrets and preserve its splendor for generations to come.

And to all who seek the deep, may you find adventure and a deeper connection to the world and yourself.

About the Author

Bassel Ounah is a certified freediving instructor trainer, a freediving coach, a visionary innovator, and an impassioned storyteller. His life in and around water is dedicated to the mysterious and wondrous underwater world. He has been in the water for over many years now, professionally building a career around exploring the meeting of human potential with the ocean's timeless depths. He founded Apnea Zone, a PADI Mermaid Instructor Trainer, and has taught countless freedivers-developing their physical skills, mental resilience, and spiritual connection to the sea.

Bassel's work extends far beyond the water's edge. As one of the pioneers in underwater virtual reality experiences with Neptune's Submerge VR, he has redefined how people connect with marine environments. His projects include immersive virtual campaigns to raise awareness about plastic pollution, which have gained international recognition for an innovative environmental education and conservation approach. Merging technology with the natural world, Bassel empowers people to witness the beauty and fragility of the ocean in ways that foster action and advocacy.

Author Bassel combines his love for history, exploration, and storytelling in his celebrated book series, The Pavlopetri Chronicles. His novels, such as The Depths of Pavlopetri and The Siren of Pavlopetri: Love Beyond Worlds, blend historical mystery with the allure of the ocean, taking the onlooker through an underwater realm of magic and mystery. His tales call upon the audience to dream beyond the surface and look toward the sea as a wellspring of inspiration, adventure, and introspection.

An avid marine conservationist, Bassel inspires and raises awareness about the many challenges the world's oceans and seas constantly face. Using education, environmental campaigns, or on-site restoration, he is devoted to safeguarding a healthy ocean for the generations that come after him. In this sense, his works epitomize the principle of sustainable practices, community engagement, and the inextricable link that binds humans and the sea together.

When Bassel is not plunging into the depths or crafting stories, he dedicates his time to empowering the next generation of ocean stewards. He encourages others to adopt the ocean as a site of adventure and a teacher of resilience, humility, and wonder. This book testifies to this mission—to take human beings more profoundly into the ocean, deeper inside themselves, courageously and respectfully, by unflinchingly illuminating the beauty of our blue planet.

Prologue

It is not simply a body of The ocean that represents a womb in life, one full of secrets and human exploration with no border. It has captured our fancy through the ages, beckons even today, and plunges deep inside, offering vistas of discovery- even a connectedness with something over and above us. The ocean is the haven for freedivers, teachers, and an endless well of inspiration; it's that place where breathing meets silence, and the limits of human potential are being rewritten.

Under the sea, there exists a world unknown to the turbulence of the atmosphere. Here, gravity loosens its grip, the sound drowned into stillness, and light fractures into an eternal kaleidoscope of blue. It is a world of contrasts: enormous strength yet utter delicacy, vast expanses, and, at the same time, a richly woven tapestry of life. On one breath, the descent into such a world is a surrender- a moment of trusting harmony with elements much more significant than ourselves. Inward as much as down.

This book is a tribute to the legends who have dared heed the ocean's call. These pioneers and champions have been pushing the limits of what we thought possible deeper into meters and the very substance of human potential. They taught us that freediving is not a sport but a way of life—a discipline that unites the physical, mental, and spiritual. Their stories are woven with triumphs, sacrifices, and a shared reverence for the underwater world.

Yet the ocean is calling, and not solely to the privileged and daring, reminding us of our shared responsibility to care for our Earth's blue heart lifeblood, and just as it gives so much, we depend on its treasures, nurtures, and are responsible for safeguarding its beauty. To dive into its depths is to bear witness to its fragility and assume its steward's position.

Through the stories in these pages, allow yourself to be submerged in the magic of the underwater world. Let them inspire you to explore new frontiers that will teach you patience, resilience, and respect. May these tales inspire you to protect the wonders beneath the surface and discover unknown depths in yourself.

The ocean awaits, as always, ready to expose its secrets to the brave ones desiring to dig them out and wisdom enough to accord respect to them. Indeed, its Mystery holds not only the world's secrets but also the truths about our own being human. Dive in. The journey starts here.

Table of Contents

1. Dedication iii
   a. A tribute to freedivers, the ocean, and the pursuit of inner and outer exploration.
2. About the Author v
   a. Bassel Ounah's biography highlights his achievements, passion for freediving, and commitment to marine conservation.
3. Prologue vii
   a. Introduction to the allure of the ocean and the transformative power of freediving.
4. Introduction to Freediving 1
   a. History, Mythology, and Cultural Significance of Apnea
   b. Evolution and Records in Freediving
   c. Freediving as Recreation, Sport, and Self-Exploration
   d. Freediving Disciplines Overview (STA, DYN, DNF, FIM, CWT, CNF, VWT, NLT)
5. Preparing for Freediving 19
   a. Equipment: Mask, Fins, Snorkel, Weight Belt, Wetsuit, Freedive Buoy Nose Clips, fluid Goggles, Dive Computers, Neck Weights, EQ Tools
   b. Importance of Physical and Mental Preparedness
   c. Basics of Safety and Risk Management
6. Freediving Breathing and Relaxation Techniques 37
   a. The Freedive Breathing Cycle: Relaxation, Full Breath, Breath Hold, Recovery
   b. Breathing Techniques: Yoga, Diaphragmatic Breathing, Pranayama
   c. CO_2 Tolerance, Hypoxia, and Hypercapnia Training
   d. Breathing Exercises for Relaxation and Mindfulness

7. **Understanding the Body's Adaptations to Water**   56
   a. Physiology of Immersion: Oxygen Cycle, Cardiovascular Adaptations
   b. Mammalian Dive Response (MDR), Blood Shift, and Bradycardia
   c. Vision, Heat, and Buoyancy Control in Water
   d. Mechanics of Breathing and Cardiovascular Responses
8. **Freediving Techniques and Equalization**   94
   a. Equalization Techniques (Frenzel, Mouthfill, Valsalva, Handsfree)
   b. Advanced Equalization for Depth: Sequential and Wet Equalization
   c. Body Positioning: Duck Dive, Finning, Free Fall, and Body Streamlining
   d. Stretching for Better Equalization and Lung Health
9. **Safety Protocols and Rescue Skills**   100
   a. The Buddy System and Static Buddying
   b. Identifying Signs of Distress (LMC, Blackouts)
   c. Rescue Techniques for Loss of Motor Control and Blackouts
   d. Risk Reduction, Safety Practices, and Decompression Sickness Prevention
   e. Essential Life Support (BLS) and CPR Techniques
10. **Confined and Open Water Training**   127
    a. Apnea Games and Training in Confined Water
    b. Open Water Diving Techniques and Safety Protocols
    c. Surface and Recovery Techniques in Open Water
    d. Recovery and Rescue Skills in Confined and Open Water Settings
11. **Freediving Physiology and Pathologies**   151
    a. Respiratory and Circulatory Systems in Depth
    b. Hypoxia and Blackout Prevention: Causes, Signs, and Intervals
    c. Barotrauma: Ear, Sinus, and Lung Protection Techniques

    d. Freediving-Related Pathologies (Haemoptysis, Pulmonary Edema, Taravana)
    e. Otorhinolaryngologic Considerations and Reverse Block Management

12. **Freediving Training and Physical Preparation**   181
    a. Annual Training Programs and Periodization
    b. Dry and Water-Based Training: Static, Dynamic, and Cross-Training
    c. Techniques for Motor Coordination and Physical Fitness
    d. Hypoxia and Hypercapnia Workouts and Pyramid Training

13. **Advanced Freediving Techniques and Training**   206
    a. Dynamic Apnea Training: Warm-Ups, Speed, and Contractions Management
    b. Static Apnea Training: Series, Psychological Blocks, and Breath Holds
    c. Deep Freediving Techniques: Free Fall, Lung Packing, Equalization
    d. Technical Information for Various Depth Disciplines

14. **Nutrition and Recovery for Freedivers**   234
    a. Dietary Recommendations and Hydration
    b. Managing Nutrition During Physical Exercise and Apnea
    c. Metabolism Considerations for Freediving
    d. Recovery Techniques and Overtraining Prevention

15. **Connection with Marine Environments**   261
    a. Ecological Awareness and Conservation Role of Freedivers
    b. Marine Biodiversity and Environmental Responsibility

16. **Future of Freediving and Technological Innovations**   275
    a. Freediving's Influence on Ocean Science and Conservation
    b. Technological Advancements in Freediving Equipment and Techniques
    c. Ethical Considerations for Future Freediving

17. Freediver Code of Conduct and Ethical Practices   304
    a. Safety, Ethics, and Responsibility in Freediving
    b. Freediving Community Code and Ethical Practices
18. Inspiring Biography & Achievements   319
    a. Male Freedivers Champions
    b. Female Freedivers Champions
    c. Historic Legends in Freediving
19. Appendix   338

Introduction to Freediving

History, Mythology, and Cultural Significance of Apnea

Freediving, or apnea, is this strange sport of diving down into the depths with one breath and without breathing apparatus, where the sole reliance is upon the physical and mental conditioning of the freediver. It is not just a sport but more of a specific, change-inspiring experience that allows freedivers to get familiar with the secrets of the underwater world with minimal environmental impact. While scuba diving involves depending on an apparatus to keep them underwater, one must draw on inner strength, control over breathing, and immense body awareness in freediving. It's like striking the right balance between physical endurance and mental tranquility.

A free freediver learns to extend his breath-hold time and descend to remarkable depths by slowing the heart rate, calming the mind, and managing oxygen and carbon dioxide levels. In a sense, the quiet and stillness of freediving lend it a meditative aspect, enabling freedivers to be in tune with nature, which no other water sport can provide. It is recreationally done to enjoy the beauty of coral reefs and marine life or competitively by pushing the limits in-depth, time, or distance-testing the full potential of the human body. History, Mythology, and Cultural Significance of Apnea

History can be traced back thousands of years to the roots of many freediver cultures worldwide.

As far back as ancient Greece, there were freedivers, known as "urinators" or "wet freedivers," who would descend to the bottom to retrieve natural sponges, which were highly prized. These freedivers had spent many years in training to achieve their breath-holding capabilities, and therefore, sponge diving was an esteemed and essential part of Greek coastal economies. Likewise, in Japan and Korea, the **Ama** and **Haenyeo** freedivers-female "sea women" have established more than two thousand years old freediving traditions. These women have traditionally gained great acclaim for their stamina and endurance to dive into the deep waters to harvest abalone, sea urchins, and many other underwater treasures that provide sustenance and significant income to the local economies. At the same time, freediving holds a mythological and spiritual place within many cultures.

Ancient Greek mythology also includes stories of freedivers favored by **Poseidon,** the god of the sea, who could stay underwater for hours without apparent ill effects of lack of oxygen. They were also thought to have a privilege with the ocean and to protect the secrecy of the sea. In Polynesia, folklore often mentions deep-sea freedivers in stories interwoven with reasons of bravery, recognition of the life-giving ocean, and respect for its forces, portraying freedivers as people with a holy connection with the sea. The most telling spiritual and cultural significance concerning freediving occurs when the sport is utilized as a rite of passage in various cultures.

As a rule, small **Ama** and **Haenyeo** freedivers start to be taught this kind of art when they are very young by older generations, who teach their knowledge and techniques. Intergenerational training like this is one aspect of continuing the family tradition and deeply implanting respect for the ocean. In many cultures, freediving is the link between man and the marine environment, proclaiming sustainable use and a deep commitment to taking responsibility for ocean conservation. In modern times, the sport has evolved into both a recreational and an extreme sport as freedivers continue to push the limits of human endurance. Some competitive freedivers have attained global recognition, reaching depths of over 100 meters and holding their breath for over 10 minutes. This modern resurrection of the sport of freediving, promoted through advances in technique, physiology, and safety, has also sparked new interest in the history and cultural practices associated with apnea.

Freediving remains an activity of much more than a sport; freediving is the means to explore personal limits, find profound calmness, and develop a special bond with the underwater world. Brought together through ancient and modern contexts, freediving is a massive mixture of tradition, discipline, and respect for the ocean's mysteries, which reminds us that the fascination between man and sea is timeless.

Evolution and Records in Freediving

Freediving is a sport that has undergone an incredible transformation- from a survival skill to a globally recognized sport that tests and expands the boundaries of human endurance and physiology. What in the past was a necessary activity for seaside people, done either to collect food and other goods or to satisfy some rite, nowadays has become a sport that challenges freedivers to achieve unmatched depth, length, and time without breathing, using only the physiological response of the body to the underwater environment. Nowadays, it embraces several specialized disciplines, each with its methodology in techniques, training methods, and competitive standards. These ever-increasing records in the disciplines testify to human potential and encourage a new generation to strive for sports excellence.

Historical Roots - Development of Modern Freediving

Freediving has its deep historical roots across a lot of cultures around the world. Thousands of years ago, this was an essential survival skill, especially among those coastal communities who relied on the sea. The first recorded instances are the Ama of Japan and the Haenyeo of Korea. Their women freedivers entered the ocean for abalone, pearls, and seaweed, acquiring excellent breath-holding capabilities with extensive training since childhood and years of practice later on. In ancient Greece, sponge freedivers plunged to the ocean's depths to gather sponges off the bottom. These freedivers would later be referred to as "urinators"; over time, they garnered an excellent reputation for holding their breath, which found their place in coastal communities' identities and economic life.

Freediving as an organized sport of the modern era thus took shape in the mid-20th century, created by scientific curiosity and the bravery of pioneering individuals ready to venture into human limits underwater. Records of the first recorded freediving depth started to be established in the 1940s by Italian freedivers like **Raimondo Bucher** and **Enzo Maiorca**. Performances that took the general public's imagination and the scientists' toll lit a torchlight on the astonishing human body and what it can go through with the intense pressures exerted by great water depths. Their successes launched the sport of freediving, inspiring others worldwide to see how far their bodies would take them. The bravery and devotion of these early pioneers foreshadowed a global freediving movement that would come complete with formalized training programs, competitions, and a strong emphasis on safety.

The Emergence of Freediving Organizations

As more and more people became interested in freediving, the sport also grew more competitive; thus came a growing need for an officially recognized body that could control standards and rules by ensuring safety. In 1992, the now more known acronym for the International Association for the Development of Apnea, **AIDA**, was born, and it rapidly became one of the most prominent governing bodies in the world when it came to the sport of freediving. **AIDA** was instrumental in establishing the official freediving disciplines, standardized global rules, and organizing international competitions, allowing freedivers to compete on equal terms. **AIDA** has been instrumental throughout this sport's history, with strict guidelines concerning safety, training, and record verification, thus allowing athletes to push their limits while inspiring future generations of freedivers safely. Other organizations, such as **CMAS**, or in a native English translation, Confédération Mondiale des Activités Subaquatiques, have contributed to regulating and popularizing this sport. Building up a strong community of amateur and professional athletes has made this discipline gain immense popularity over the years.

Freediving Disciplines and World Records

Modern freediving havens have different aims, such as skill and aspect of breath-hold diving. The principal freediving disciplines are listed below, along with some notable world records:

1. Constant Weight (CWT and CNF): At CWT, using fins, while at CNF, which is Constant Weight without Fins, the freedivers perform a downward-upward dive with the help of their body strength. **Alexey Molchanov** holds the record in CWT with 130 meters, while William Trubridge does so with 102 meters in CNF, revealing an astonishing sight of power and control.

2. Free Immersion (FIM): In this event, a rope is used for the descent and ascent without fins, allowing the freediver to focus on equalization and effective breath-hold. **William Trubridge** holds the world record in FIM at 124 meters.

3. Static Apnea (STA): This is the discipline concerning the time a freediver can hold his breath and has been in a position to remain entirely still underwater. It concerns mental focus and relaxation. The current world record by **Branko Petrovic** lies at 11 minutes 54 seconds, really demanding regarding control of one's body and mind.

4. Dynamic Apnea (DYN and DNF): In DYN, freedivers can perform a horizontal swim with fins, while in DNF, they do so without fins. Mateusz Malina holds the DYN and DNF records, which are 300 and 244 meters, respectively; thus, they constitute proof of great endurance and efficiency of motion.

5. No Limits (NLT): This is the most extreme discipline in which freedivers use a sled for descent and an inflatable device for ascending. **Herbert Nitsch** from Austria holds the world record at an unbelievable 214 meters in NLT. After that, he had to recover for a long time due to decompression sickness.

Each competitive discipline of freediving requires different skills, techniques, and physical and mental stamina; freedivers devote themselves to honing their approach. Over time, each discipline has undergone significant development in training methodology, equipment technology, and scientific knowledge of human physiology, which allows the freediver to push the limits more and more.

The following sections thoroughly examine each discipline and explore specific techniques, training regimens, and physiological adaptations. From mastering breath control during static apnea to dealing with the intensification of pressure during deep, no-limits dives, each discipline offers unique challenges and remarkable insights into what a human can achieve underwater. In this chapter, we will discuss the disciplines in more depth.

Scientific Advances and Training Techniques

As freediving evolved, there was a continued understanding of the body's physiological adaptations regarding breath-hold diving. The most critical adaptations include the mammalian dive response. These adaptations allow the freedivers to deal with the physical stresses associated with an extended breath-hold and extreme pressures. Hypoxic tolerance research, the body's ability to function on low levels of oxygen, and techniques for CO_2 training have made available training programs that can safely allow the freediver to increase depth and breath-hold times.

The training methods now range from high-intensity interval training for cardiovascular conditioning to breath-hold drills to build up hypoxia tolerance and all sorts of mental conditioning practices, including visualization. These days, freedivers pursue periodized training programs directed at their endurance, flexibility, and lung capacity with an unyielding feeling of control. Mental conditioning, consisting of meditation and various relaxation techniques, is equally important as it allows freedivers to overcome psychological problems accompanying extreme depths and breath-holding.

Records of Competitive Freediving - What Does the Future Hold?

The continuous coming-up of new athletes keeps pushing the limits of human endurance, and records in this sport of freediving continue to fall. Advances in training, equipment, and safety protocols have made modern freedivers dive deeper and longer underwater, succeeding in endeavors considered impossible a few years ago. At the exact moment, global competitions such as the **AIDA World Championships** position freediving not only as a competitive discipline but also as a kind of art: a combination of physical prowess with mental toughness.

Records set by pioneering freedivers like **Alessia Zecchini, Alenka Artnik,** and **Alexey Molchanov** continue to push the boundaries and inspire a new generation of freedivers. Thus, every record will keep freediving the boundaries of what has been known about the human body and prove that the quest for underwater exploration is not an individual journey but a shared adventure.

Modern evolution and freediving records strongly remind us of humanity's potential and the timeless appeal of the ocean. With further developments in technology and training techniques, these athletes-freedivers can break through barriers and find more depth inside themselves in the waters they dive into.

Freediving as Recreation, Sport, and Self-Explorations

Freediving is an adventure that plunges into the peculiar world of physical limitations and mental endurance, where the ocean plays a space of recreation and self-challenge. Diving underwater with a single breath links different elements: connection with nature, athletic performance, and a meditative exploration of one's capabilities and fears. The transformative potential of freediving has made it cater to a broad spectrum of enthusiasts, from casual recreational freedivers to those aiming for relaxation to the athlete competitors who push the limits of what human flesh and blood can endure. This sport is appealingly alluring because self-discovery opens avenues that test the limits one has imposed on oneself and create a feeling of deep inner peace. Each dive is an experience as unique as the freediver but simultaneously universally rooted in themes of courage, exploration, and harmony with the underwater world.

Freediving as Recreation

To many, this form of diving represents a tranquil escape from the fast-paced world above. In recreational freediving, freedivers seek to connect with nature at a much personal level by entering this weightless, silent, watery world where the only faint sounds could be that of water and marine life noises. Besides, unlike scuba diving, it requires minimal equipment: freedivers usually wear only masks, snorkels, fins, and sometimes a wetsuit to move freely and as unobtrusively as possible. This simplicity is the core of its attractiveness- the freedivers can slip beneath the surface without any, or minimal, disturbance of life around them. It engages the freediver to such an extent that mindfulness is one guaranteed dimension that makes an experience meditative, where every movement, breath, and sensation is heightened. Besides, for the recreational freediver, the accessibility of the sport lies at the heart of beauty.

Freediving does not require training to dive in shallow waters and view sceneries underwater; hence, it attracts amateur and professional freedivers. Due to its first contact with marine ecosystems, it has also found an increasing appeal with outdoor enthusiasts, snorkeling, and underwater photography. They will also get freediving to observe brilliant coral reefs and different fish species, swim with dolphins, and be among more enormous sea creatures like mantas and sharks in their natural environment and discreet manner. Each dive becomes a journey through the alien world, fluid in their movements- a human body becoming one with the water. Apart from the simplicity and accessibility, the sport of freediving has also become a way to embrace environmental mindfulness. During a dive, freedivers reach an appreciation for marine life and ocean ecosystems; it instills deep respect in them for taking good care of it.

Most freedivers get inspired by the unfiltered beauty of the underwater world and usually take up some associated causes in its conservation by motivating freedivers to take action in ocean health, beach cleanups, and awareness about the impacts on marine life due to pollution and climate change. It is in this silent companionship with the sea, its creatures, and its landscapes that one finds a source of great joy while at the same time acting as a powerful reminder of our role as stewards of the planet.

Freediving as a Sport

Freediving has developed into a highly regarded competitive sport rather than a recreational activity. It requires serious training, discipline, and a well-tuned balance between body and mind. By pushing athletes to their physical and mental limits, competitive freedivers are challenged to achieve extraordinary performances in depth, distance, and time in every discipline.

Competitions often attract competitors worldwide, joining them in one community through a common pursuit of excellence and furthering new records.

The sport is divided into several disciplines: constant weight with fins, dynamic apnea, free immersion, and static apnea. Each discipline favors different techniques and skills, requiring a different combination of physical fitness and mental endurance. To be competitive, the freediver must develop a physiology that will tolerate extreme stress underwater while perfecting the technical aspects of motion, breathing, and equalization. It is not all training by holding one's breath, but it involves cardiovascular conditioning, flexibility stretching, strength-building exercises, and special techniques for equalizing the middle ear and sinus pressures. One should also consider the control of breathing because there are exercises on slow and controlled breathing that optimize oxygen consumption and spare energy.

Most competitions in this sport are not about pure speed or strength but are more inclined to efficiency, control, and being composed under pressure. However, the most critical aspect of competitive freediving is mental training. The athletes must be psychologically developed to a certain level to remain calm at extreme depths, in darkness, under pressure, and sometimes even wholly alone. Such mental strength is achieved using exercises in visualization, meditation, and even controlled exposure to stressful situations. Visualization techniques allow the athletes to mentally rehearse their dives, preparing their minds to handle each discipline's demands.

Meditation reduces anxiety and controls the body's stress response, which creates a relaxed mental condition- an essential factor for success in the water. Deep concentration and focus help a freediver maintain clarity and control during his dives; any momentary lapse may affect performance and safety. Competitions testify to how much a man can endure and be determined. Records set by freedivers like **William Trubridge, Alessia Zecchini,** and **Alexey Molchanov** have shattered what once seemed impossible. Impossible only a decade ago. In 2019, **Alessia Zecchini** reached 113 meters in constant weight and set a new world record, inspiring freedivers worldwide. With each new record, it is not only a push toward the limits of this sport but also an extension of the understanding of human physiology and our relationship with the ocean.

These competitions are physical challenges and, in many ways, journeys into the mind. They show an athlete's capability to overcome fear, control extreme pressure, and realize serenity in a hostile environment.

Freediving as Self-Exploration

The most powerful transformation in freediving is its potential for self-exploration. Diving into the depths in one breath and understanding the limits of body and mind make freediving as much an inner journey as an outer one. For many freedivers, each dive is a chance to face their fears, test their stubborn will, and find peace within themselves.

Freediving invites the participant to explore the relationship between the breath and the body in a vulnerable state and to remain "awake" in situations that require control over thoughts and emotions.

Freediving requires participants to get used to sensations they would find somewhat uncomfortable or unnatural at the surface, such as the feeling of rising carbon dioxide levels or the pressure exerted by water. Through dive training, freedivers learn to quieten the inner voice; as does the musculature, the heartbeat slows, reaching a state of stillness whereby they can embrace the experience. This comfort with discomfort often puts them into other areas where the freediver finds their resiliency helpful in stresses, anxieties, and other land-based issues. The reflective process of the sport nurtures the development of self-awareness in the freediver, allowing them to respond to stress and learn to count their emotions with patience and calmness.

Many find it spiritual, even transformational. The big, volatile ocean is a mirror and teacher, revealing inner strengths and limitations. For this reason, freedivers approach the water respectfully and humbly, recognizing it's a realm out of human control. Its depths and darkness resonate with the unknown, forcing the freedivers to abandon their fears and surrender.

This process of letting go gives way to a unique kind of growth in which the freediver learns to embrace vulnerability, confront the ego, and acknowledge their limitations. The sense of release during a deep dive is emotionally powerful for many and allows them a newfound appreciation for life and its transient beauty. Equally, freediving feeds the intense relationship with nature and respect for the underwater world, further wanting to protect it. The ocean is no longer a place for recreation and sport but also a sanctuary for personal growth. Many are inspired by this kind of vulnerability when diving to commit themselves to protecting the environment, as diving can provide a personal realization of the beauty and fragility of the ocean. They directly witness the results of pollution, climate change, and overfishing, instilling a deep, empathetic view of the underwater world.

By freediving, they become athletes, adventurers, and ambassadors for ocean health and environmental sustainability.

The Convergence of Recreation, Sport, and Self-Exploration

The freediving within itself makes it so unique. It is the practice whereby people find and connect with the underwater world in their own way, whether leisurely dives in clear waters, competitive events pushing limits, or even personal journeys of self-discovery. These three elements of freediving- recreation, sport, and self-discovery interlink to further complement each other, offering anyone willing to take the plunge a well-rounded and enriching experience. The simplicity and peace of freediving can develop a want to improve technique or go deeper, placing the recreational freediver on the path to becoming a competitive freediver. For a competitive freediver, the beauty and tranquility of the underwater environment may remind them that there is more to freediving than just setting new records but taking time to enjoy the ocean and respect its mysteries.

For those who perceive freediving as a kind of self-adaptation, every dive provides insight and growth, building a bridge between athletic achievement and personal transformation.

Finally, freediving is holistic in its very nature. It combines the joy of underwater exploration with athletic discipline challenges and the reflective benefits of mindful practice. This activity teaches humility, respect for nature, and inner peace. Whether one dives to relax, for a sporting event, or self-discovery, freediving allows each person to find deep connections with the ocean and themselves.

That freedom at depth, however, is not just about the physical liberty in each dive into the silent depths of one's soul but also a journey whereby new layers can be revealed at each dive, continuing to grow and reach more profound levels of understanding.

Disciplines Overview

Freediving is a multi-disciplined sport, all with different challenges, skills, and physical demands. These disciplines test the freediver's ability to breathe, distance, and depth achieved in one breath. Each one requires a different skill and way of thinking, pushing freedivers to new frontiers within themselves and in the ocean. From static apnea to no-limits diving, each one invites the freediver into the underwater world for a unique experience, blending skill, toughness in the head, and great respect for the ocean. Below is an in-depth look into the primary disciplines of freediving as recognized by the freediving community and major governing bodies like **AIDA** and **CMAS**.

1. Static Apnea (STA)

Static Apnea is a discipline purely related to breath-holding duration. In this event, the freediver stays in the pool and stays in place. Other than this, the only concern is that he has to breathe longer. Since there is no need to move or change depth, static apnea provides the challenge of staying calm, conserving oxygen, and handling psychological stress from a long breath hold.

Mental Control and Serenity: STA is commonly called the "mental game." Unlike other sports requiring physical exertion, STA requires a freediver to be in complete mental quiet. Doing so slows down his heartbeats and advances him into the stage of meditation, reducing his body's oxygen intake and allowing him to extend the length of time he holds his breath.

Physiological Adaptations: When holding a static breath, the body makes several internal adaptations to use oxygen more efficiently. These include the mammalian dive response, in which the heart rate drops and blood vessels constrict to allow blood flow to only the brain and heart.

Training Techniques: Freedivers use various techniques to train themselves in STA, such as breath-hold exercises, mental training, and relaxation techniques. Standard visualizations, meditation, and mindfulness practices help freedivers cope with the discomfort and anxiety that arise during extended breath holds.

World Record: Branko Petrovic's current world record for static apnea is the unbelievable 11 minutes and 54 seconds. This clearly shows the brain's resilience and ability to hold one's breath.

2. Dynamic Apnea with Fins (DYN)

Dynamic Apnea with Fins is a pool event where freedivers are expected to cover the maximum possible distance by swimming horizontally on one breath. This requires intense, energetic, and 'economic' finning technique, streamlined positioning, and preserving oxygen while moving through the water.

Efficiency in Movement: During the DYN, the freediver must adopt a streamlined position and engage fins much more efficiently to conserve energy. A good finning technique enables the freediver to glide through the water with lesser resistance, supporting a more extended breath hold.

Breathing and endurance control: Unlike STA, DYN is a physical exercise. Freedivers must learn to regulate effort and relaxation by managing oxygen consumption and delaying the accumulation of carbon dioxide in the body.

Mental Endurance: While DYN is a physically active sport, it is also mentally exhausting. A freediver has to work against the human body's urge to breathe as he swims further, requiring determination and control over the body's reactions to high carbon dioxide levels.

World Record: Mateusz Malina set the record for dynamic apnea with fins at 300 meters. This great distance shows how a freediver can use good technique and save oxygen to provide a graceful and long underwater journey.

3. Dynamic Apnea without Fins (DNF)

Dynamic Apnea without Fins is conducted like DYN but without fins. DNF freedivers use their arms more strongly, using a modified dolphin kick to move forward, making this discipline more challenging and technical.

Body Movement Mastery: DNF delivery lacks fin assistance, so the driver must master a highly efficient body movement to ensure maximum propulsion. The typical technique involves a breaststroke-like arm movement followed by a dolphin kick, which helps minimize resistance to the maximum effect of forward movement.

Technical Precision: DNF requires a perfect balance between techniques and strength. Movement should be ideally conducted; otherwise, improper forms result in energy loss and enhanced oxygen consumption.

Streamlining and Hydrodynamics: To minimize drag, streamlining may be essential during DNF diving. A freediver must hold a streamlined body position to maximize distance while using less energy.

World Record: The current world record DNF is 244 meters from **Mateusz Malina,** which shows the freediver can secure an efficient and sustainable movement without fins.

4. Free Immersion (FIM)

Free Immersion is an open-water discipline in which freedivers use a rope to pull themselves down and back up without fins. This gives the freediver more control over descents and ascents, making it an excellent discipline for perfecting equalization techniques.

Rope-Guided Method: In FIM, the rope provides a fixed contact point, allowing freedivers to conserve energy by pulling themselves down. This method benefits equalization, as the freediver can stop and work on equalization without the additional swimming effort.

Equalization focus: FIM provides the perfect setting for equalization, especially in deeper dives. The rope allows the freediver to descend at a metered pace, focusing on pressure changes and managing them as one descends.

Mind-Body Connection: FIM requires both physical strength for the pulls and a focused mind. The cadence of the rope pulls has a soothing effect, allowing freedivers to focus on their bodies and manage their breath hold.

World Record: William Trubridge holds the FIM world record at 124 meters. This depth emphasizes how well FIM maintains controlled deep dives.

5. Constant Weight with Fins (CWT)

Constant Weight with Fins is one of the most popular competitive disciplines today. In CWT, the freedivers make the descent and ascent using fins and their power without touching the rope or changing weights. It is considered one of the most honest tests that require a freediver's physical strength and technique.

Controlled Descent and Ascent: CWT requires great finning technique and body control. The position of the body and good buoyancy are necessary for a freediver's streamlined descent and ascent.

Attention to Equalization: A freediver must equalize much more at greater depths. For pressures to be overcome effectively, the CWT freediver may undergo frequent and extensive training in equalization techniques, such as Frenzel or mouthful.

Physical Conditioning: CWT is a heavy discipline that demands solid lower body development. Indeed, the most essential propulsion is made with the legs. Freedivers often train in exercises that strengthen their legs and boost stamina.

World Record: Alexey Molchanov holds the record for CWT, reaching 130 meters. This record illustrates the strength, skill, and endurance needed in this heavy discipline.

6. Constant Weight without Fins (CNF)

Constant Weight without Fins: As the name suggests, CNF is the same as CWT, except that no fins are used. CNF is among the most physically and psychologically demanding of these disciplines because freedivers need to go up and down using only their arms and legs.

Mastering Movement: CNF requires exceptional efficiency and expertise in movement. For locomotion in the water, freedivers usually combine arm pulls with a kicking style similar to breaststroke.

Strength and Mental Focus: freedivers have to engage without the assistance of fins, which means relying on body strength and mental toughness. This energy-intensive diving requires taking good care of one's oxygen supply with much awareness to avoid early exhaustion.

Equalization and buoyancy: The CNF freediver faces added challenges regarding buoyancy during an ascent or descent. Maintaining such a shift in buoyancy and keeping cool is vital for successful CNF dives.

World Record: William Trubridge has the CNF record at 102 meters, which is the ultimate dedication and skill required to go to such depths without fins.

7. Variable Weight (VWT)

Variable Weight is another discipline in which freedivers use a weighted sled in descent and swimming upwards; most resort to performing this discipline with fins. This allows freedivers to reach deeper depths faster because the sled saves energy during the descent.

Sled-Assisted Descent: With VWT, a sled may be utilized for speedy descent, saving freediver energy for the ascent. Accelerating the descent through the utilization sled means equalization and breath control must also date the stroke pace. The Ascent: Most dive swim back to the surface under their posing fins. Ascent requires vigorous finning and cardiovascular endurance.

World Record: Stavros Kastrinakis's VWT world record of 146 meters exemplifies the depth potential of this sled-assisted discipline.

8. No Limits (NLT)

No Limits represents perhaps the most extreme and adventurous freediving disciplines. In this discipline, the freedivers can use any method for descending and ascending. Most freedivers would use a weighted sled for descent and an inflatable lift bag to return to the surface, reaching incredible depths.

Depth Maximization: NLT is all about the most profound possible dive. The sled goes down fast, and the lift bag quickly rises. This fast drop also means freedivers have to be exceptionally good at equalization.

Mental and Physical Demands: NLT requires superior mental resilience to cope with the high pressures at depth, supported by physical preparation for the rapid pressure changes.

Preparing for Freediving

Freediving is a sport that needs perfect combinations of technique, physical training, mental discipline, and equipment. Whether it is a relaxing, recreative dive, a training session for a competition, or setting personal records in-depth, proper dive equipment everything in freediving gear is specifically designed to support particular needs during breath-hold diving and allow freedivers to increase comfort, safety and efficiency while exploring the underwater world. Every device has a purpose that helps with an overall structure that enables freedivers to get things done comfortably. The primary and advanced gears in freediving are discussed extensively below, providing information for each piece's purpose, features, and advantages.

1. Essential Freediving Equipment

Mask

The mask is most likely one of the most primitive pieces of freediving equipment. Compared to ordinary scuba diving masks, it has a lower internal volume—that is, a smaller volume of air must be used to equalize as the freediver descends.

Purpose: A mask keeps an air pocket in front of the eyes to ensure transparency underwater. In freediving, when one changes depth very rapidly, the air volume in the mask is minimized to conserve invaluable air and facilitate easy equalization.

Features: Freediving masks are designed with low-profile frames and low volume. The lenses are closer to the eyes, reducing drag and requiring less air to equalize the mask at depth. A high-quality freediving mask is also made of soft, hypoallergic silicon, which creates a tight and comfortable seal around the face to prevent leakage and let the freediver focus on the dive.

Fitting Tips: When choosing a mask, check for a proper fit. Put the mask on your face without using the strap, breathe slowly through your nose, and let the mask work by creating a partial suction seal. If it doesn't leak, it's a good one to wear. A properly fitted mask helps avoid discomfort and fiddling with it during a dive.

Fins

Fins provide the propulsion freedivers need to descend and ascend as efficiently as possible. Freediving fins are significantly longer and more flexible than snorkeling or scuba diving fins, allowing freedivers to cover greater distances with each kick while expelling much less energy.

Purpose: Fins' primary role is to enable a freediver to transit the water using minimal energy wastage. Using fins expands the foot's surface area; hence, the freediver has enough force per kick to travel further into depths and quickly return to the surface.

Types: Freediving fins are made from different materials, such as plastic, fiberglass, and carbon fiber. Plastic fins are cheap and robust, making them very good for beginners. Fiberglass fins achieve the perfect balance between good performance and cost. Carbon fiber-free fins are referred to by avid amateur freedivers as light and super efficient, providing the best energy-to-propulsion ratio. However, they are also gentler. They may break if they are not carefully handled.

Technique: freedivers must use finning to swim efficiently. They must do slow, fluid kicks from the hip and not rapid ones from the knee. Thus, less energy will be used, and their descent and ascent will remain in reasonable control.

Snorkel

The snorkel is relatively rudimentary but of paramount importance in freediving equipment. It allows freedivers to breathe comfortably at the surface, saving them from all efforts connected with lifting their heads out of the water. It is helpful during surface intervals and in pre-dive preparations.

Purpose: Snorkel allows a freediver to relax while breathing at the surface with face immersed, conserving energy and keeping the freediver in a streamlined position and ready to start the dive with minimal motion.

Features: Freediving snorkels are designed to be lightweight, flexible, and streamlined to travel through the water with the least drag. They do not have the same design sophistication as scuba snorkels, such as purge valves or other features that might reduce underwater resistance. Some freedivers prefer a slightly curved snorkel for maintaining proximity to the head, thus further reducing drag.

Breathing Technique: Under the snorkel, freedivers take slow, regulated breaths to oxygenate their bodies before entering the water. This way, it avoids much stress, and this relaxation condition helps prolong the breath-holding time.

Weight Belt

These belts control a freediver's buoyancy, making it much more accessible to dive to depth and keeping him in control while underwater. Freediving weight belts differ from their scuba counterparts in that they are flexible, comfortable, and designed to meet freedivers' needs.

Purpose: The weight belt eliminates the buoyancy of the wetsuit and other equipment to enable the freediver to have neutral buoyancy at the desired depth. Proper weighting saves energy as they don't have to fight their buoyancy continuously.

Features: Freediving weight belts are usually made of rubber, which enables them to sit naturally on the freediver's hips and not slide up during descent or ascent. These belts expand and contract with the body's movement, giving a far more comfortable and secure fit. Freedivers use small weights, adding or removing them according to the desired depth and buoyancy.

Safety Tip: Proper weighting is necessary for the freediver's safety. At about 10 meters, a freediver will try to remain neutrally buoyant and quickly ascend by exerting minimal work.

Wetsuit

A wetsuit for free diving was fashioned for flexibility, warmth, and drag reduction. However, chemoprotection, or preventing the loss of body temperature, would be crucial for prolonged dives in deeper seas or waters.

Purpose: The wetsuit will keep the body warm, helping preserve the freedivers' heat while diving into cold waters. A well-fitted wetsuit ensures minimal drag and provides mobility comfort, making the freediver feel comfortable and streamlined.

Features: Open-cell neoprene Wetsuits are usually performed in this sport, with tiny air bubbles providing excellent insulation. Most of these suits are very smooth, not contributing to friction as they pass through the water. A two-piece suit is typical, and some people prefer the hood entirely to cover their body; indeed, one needs to put a lubricant on because this type of wetsuit is more snugly fitted, although it is much warmer than closed-cell wetsuits.

Thickness: Wetsuits vary in thickness. There are 2mm up to 5mm of thickness. The thicker the wetsuit, the better insulation is achieved; however, a little bit of comfort will be constrained movement; therefore, the choice would be based on water temperature and preference.

Freedive Buoy

A buoy is an aquatic floating platform that allows freedivers to hold themselves and their gear above water. It is also a point of reference and safety when undergoing depth training.

Purpose: The buoy is attached to a line for depth training. It allows the freediver to practice their descents and ascents in a very controlled manner. It is also a rest point and visual marker for safety support.

Features: The buoys are primarily round and brightly colored, making them more visible while freediving. They have handles for carrying the buoys, special pockets for the gear, and attachments for connecting the descent line. A good-quality buoy is resistant to sun, saltwater, and multiple uses.

2. Advanced Freediving Equipment

Advanced freedivers can use specialized equipment to optimize their sports techniques further.

Nose Clips

Small devices pinch the nose closed, allowing freedivers to equalize without using their hands. This becomes highly effective for disciplines like dynamic apnea, where hands are needed to be free.

Purpose: Nose clips keep water from the nose and enable a freediver to equalize with free hands. This can improve efficiency and reduce drag in a discipline requiring streamlined movements.

Uses: These are standard issues in the pool disciplines and are very useful for hands-free equalization in deep dives. Some freedivers also use them in conjunction with fluid goggles.

Fluid goggles

Fluid goggles are for advanced freedivers who reach a pretty severe depth. Instead of air, they contain a saline solution, removing mask equalization from the dive altogether.

Use: Fluid goggles allow a freediver to see underwater without expending air to equalize the mask, an essential consideration on deep dives.

How They Work: The solution inside fluid goggles is the same salinity as the eye. Thus, a freediver will see underwater clearly. Advanced freedivers of in-depth disciplines typically use them.

Dive Computers

To serve the intent, a freedive-oriented dive computer must be available to track depth, time, and other significant parameters. Consequential feedback helps freedivers determine their performance and look after security.

- **Purpose:** A dive computer keeps track of dive duration, maximum depth, and ascent rate, thus providing correct information for freedivers. This achieves both safety and training purposes.
- **Features:** Freediving computers are small and lightweight with easy-to-read screens that report depth, time, and surface intervals. Other models allow setting depth alarms and ascent rates to avoid rising too fast.

Neck Weights

Neck weights are used in pool disciplines like dynamic apnea to achieve neutral buoyancy without a weight belt.

- **Purpose:** Neck weights enable freedivers to achieve neutral buoyancy while maintaining an aquatic, streamlined position in the pool. By spreading the weight around the neck, freedivers can easily hold depth during horizontal swims.
- **Design:** Neck weights are typically adjustable, enabling freedivers to fine-tune the weight they want to settle in the water to match their buoyancy needs. They are designed to comfortably sit around the neck without restricting the ability to move freely.

Equalization (EQ) Tools

Special equalization tools help the freediver train and perfect his equalization skills, as well as a whole set of techniques for safely diving at some depth.

Purpose: The function of an EQ tool is to train for specific equalization techniques, specifically

The Importance of Physical and Mental Preparedness in Freediving

Unlike most other sports, Freediving heavily depends on the intrinsic abilities and resistance of the freediver himself. Deep underwater exploration imposes extreme physical and mental conditions on the freediver, who must work while sustaining a single breath. There is no external apparatus to support or enhance their performance; hence, physical conditioning and mental preparedness are fundamental safety, Endurance, and success issues. The efficiency of Freediving is such that the physical and mental demands are intertwined, where each enhances the efficiency of the other and, therefore, creates synergy, enabling freedivers to push their limits in the underwater world safely.

The former is physical preparation, building a freediver's body to manage physiological challenges such as pressure at great depths and the economization of oxygen. The latter, or mental component, concerns alertness and poise, enabling freedivers to remain relaxed, responsive, and resilient under high pressure. Now, look closer at physical and psychological preparedness constituents and how these elements allow freedivers to achieve new depths and push beyond personal limits.

1. Physical Preparation for Freediving

Physical preparation for freediving differs from a typical conditioning program, which any other sport would require. Freedivers work on strength, Endurance, flexibility, and breath control, training their cardiovascular system to perform better in probable oxygen deficiency conditions. A well-prepared body enables the freediver to resist the conditions of breath-holding and energy expenditure and perform all other essential functions, such as equalization and physiological changes necessary for sustaining pressure at greater depths.

Breath Control and Lung Capacity: Holding one's breath is crucial in freediving. Breath-hold training, or what is generally referred to as apnea training, forms the foundation of this element of training. By improving their lung capacity, freedivers can intake more air within a single breath, allowing them to take extended dives due to larger oxygen stores.

- **Breath Control Techniques:** Freedivers employ many breath control techniques, including diaphragmatic breathing, stretching the intercostals, and packing the lungs. Diaphragmatic breathing is an exercise where a freediver takes deep, slow breaths right from the diaphragm to fill up completely; in return, the oxygen ingestion improves. Lung packing is mainly issued for advanced freedivers, wherein a freediver breathes deeply into the lungs, and after that, it follows the "packing" of air by small compressing gulps. This technique can help advanced freedivers expand their lung volume, but it requires training and should be carried out with a lot of care.
- **CO_2 and O_2 Tolerance:** Besides building up the lung capacity, freedivers work to build up a tolerance for high levels of carbon dioxide (CO_2) and low levels of oxygen (O_2). The use of controlled breath-hold training combined with interval exercises, also known as CO_2 and O_2 tables, makes the human body adapt to low oxygen conditions. By increasing the tolerance to CO_2, a freediver can stay relaxed during high carbon dioxide levels in their bodies and avoid the discomfort caused by the "urge to breathe" because those sensors are reduced.

Cardiovascular Fitness: A developed cardiovascular system for a freediver would include support for low heart rate, circulation efficiency, and oxygen economization. The heart is developed through regular aerobic exercise such as running, swimming, cycling, and cross-training, which allows it to push blood quickly and sustain a low resting pulse.

- **Low Heart Rate Benefits:** A reduced heart rate is helpful as it reduces oxygen consumption, allowing freedivers to fully utilize the stored oxygen to support a longer breath-holding time. To conserve oxygen, a mammalian dive would naturally

slow its heart rate reflex, a natural physiological response to the face's immersion.
Improved cardiovascular fitness allows the body to maintain a lower heart rate and profit from this dive reflex.
- **Place of Anaerobic Training:** It also includes anaerobic training, which involves a high level of intensity but short spurts of exercises to build up the time spent operating with very little oxygen. Examples include interval sprints, which can simulate the demands on oxygen supply during freediving. Anaerobic training develops the body's efficiency in using oxygen and dealing with lactic acid buildup, which are both critical in the rigors of diving.

Flexibility and Core Strength: Flexibility, especially in the chest, diaphragm, and legs, is one key to efficiency while moving and equalization. The increased range of motion requires that freedivers stretch the intercostal muscles between the ribs so that the lungs can fully expand and adapt to depth pressure changes.
- **Chest and Diaphragm Flexibility:** Chest and diaphragm stretching exercises-yoga, cobra, or upward dog, for example, as a facilitative function by enabling freedivers to expand their lung capacity and control the feeling of compression as they go down to greater depths. The flexibility of the diaphragm also aids in equalization because it can give the freediver better control over air movement in the lungs.
- **Core Strength:** Core strength is associated with stability, streamlined movement, and an efficient propulsion system. It helps strengthen the muscles in the torso and stabilizes the position during the dive. It minimizes drag and conserves energy, allowing smoother, more controlled dives.

Muscular Endurance: Freediving requires peculiar muscular endurance. It requires more low-intensity, long-duration contractions than explosive power. With such training, a freediver can sustain controlled movements over an extended period with less rapid utilization of oxygen stores.
- **Leg and Finning Muscles:** The leg muscles, consisting primarily of the quadriceps, hamstrings, and calves, are also

highly involved during the dive because they drive this action for finning, which takes him down and upward. Most freedivers usually perform long-distance swimming or resistance band exercises to develop muscular leg endurance.
- **Controlled, Efficient Movements:** All movements in freediving. Freedivers stay focused; every kick and pull should be efficient, not make the body use more energy. This smooth, controlled motion minimizes the use of oxygen, so freedivers can dive deeper or stay longer.

Equalization Techniques: Equalizing air pressure in the ears and sinuses during a dive prevents discomfort or injuries such as barotrauma. This skill and flexibility may be obtained in the eustachian tubes, diaphragm, and jaw.
- **Equalization Techniques:** There are two standard equalization methods: the Valsalva and Frenzel maneuvers, which involve shutting the nostrils and using air pressure to unblock the Eustachian tubes. The more experience one gains, the more air can be mobilized, such as in a technique known as the "mouthful," in which air is stored in the mouth to equalize the ears at even greater depths. Training is critical since poor equalization could result in serious injury, significantly impacting diving performance.

2. Mental Preparedness in Freediving

Physical fitness may provide the foundation, but mental preparedness allows the freediver to have those abilities. Since physical stress and anxiety rapidly deplete oxygen stores and adversely affect the dive, Freediving requires a freediver to relax and focus. Freediving fosters calmness and builds the resilience and focus to manage discomfort, the urge to breathe, and difficult underwater conditions.

Relaxation and Stress Management: Many freedivers induce relaxation before and during the dive. When a person is under stress, the body elicits the "fight-or-flight" response, which quickens the heart rate and heightens oxygen consumption to lower breath-hold time. Meditation, visualization, and other respiratory techniques manage stress so freedivers maintain a relaxed state, conserving precious oxygen to prolong the dive.

- **Meditation and Mindfulness:** Meditation is an essential tool in freediving. It allows one to freely enter one's mind and dwell on the present moment. Through mindfulness, freedivers increase their body, breathing, and emotional awareness, which facilitates staying relaxed and managing situations efficiently underwater. Regular meditation practice has been observed to reduce resting heart rate and concentration, both of which are beneficial for freediving.
- **Breathing A Freediving Exercises:** Breathing awareness training enables a freediver to control the rhythm of respiration and reach a deep state of relaxation. This could lead to the freediver remaining relaxed, during which the mammalian dive response slows down the heart rate by centering on each breath, inhalation, and exhalation.

Focus and Concentration: Freediving requires immense concentration, particularly in the depth disciplines, when equalization, body positioning, and finning techniques must be dealt with simultaneously. Suppose anything distracts or lapses the freediver's focus. The freediver needs to be inefficient movements, better equalization, or dangerous situations.

- **Visualization:** freedivers generally perform visualization practices to mentally rehearse every part of the dive, from the surface preparation and descent to the ascent and final breaths. This allows them to visualize the steps involved in a dive and prepare themselves for eventual setbacks, thereby reducing anxiety. A freediver's confidence by visualizing a successful dive reinforces positive outcomes and builds a person with remarkable mental resilience when things don't go as planned.
- **Progressive Relaxation Exercises:** Competitive freedivers also tend to do progressive relaxation exercises, attempting to relax their body parts, from the face and neck down to the

toes. This cleanses muscle tension and improves physiological and mental comfort. A relaxed body consumes minimal oxygen and minimizes overall stress, allowing for sharper dives.

Embracing Discomfort: The myriad sensations associated with the sport of freediving, such as freediving as carbon dioxide builds up, are naturally uncomfortable. Through mental resilience training, the freediver will learn to accept such sensations without acting impulsively.

- **CO_2 Tolerance Training:** The freediver exposes the body to higher carbon dioxide levels than the average without yielding to the urge to breathe. Repeated exercises, such as breath-holding or gradually lengthening CO_2 table intervals, condition the body and mind to bear the discomfort, enhancing the freediver's capability to remain composed while the levels of CO_2 rise.
- **Mental Discipline in Breath-Hold:** Holding one's breath underwater can render an individual vulnerable and stressful, especially for competitive individuals. With self-talk, relaxation techniques, and visualization, the freediver will shift from fear to acceptance by shifting their focus away from the need to breathe and onto the objective of the dive.

Basics of Safety and Risk Management in Freediving:

Freediving is a rewarding and tranquil sport. However, specific risks emanate from the very nature of breath-hold diving and the unique demands this places on the body. Unlike scuba diving, one has no external breathing apparatus to support life in freediving. One must rely on physical conditioning, mental preparedness, and adherence to safety practices. Among them is a hazardous, even life-threatening condition against which freediving safety may protect: loss of motor control, blackouts, and decompression sickness.

Safety for a freediver occurs through the balance of such risks with varied safety practices existing for the sport-from training with a buddy to understanding the physiology of the human body and performing rescue. Knowledge, training, and adherence to safe diving principles are responsible ways of taking care of the dangers in freediving. The following work discusses some basic safety and risk management elements in freediving, including core concepts and practices that every freediver should know and follow.

1. The Buddy System: Freediving with a Partner

The buddy system is the basis of safe freediving practice. Generally speaking, diving with a duly prepared partner is always safer, as this will provide an essential layer of safety if one of the freedivers has a problem. Nobody should ever dive alone because a buddy is crucial in observing, supporting, or rescuing another in need.

Buddy Roles and Responsibilities: A buddy is expected to closely observe the freediver during the entire process, from preparation to descent and recovery after ascent to the surface. Ideally, buddies should be slightly above and on the side to have a clear view and be ready to assist if needed. A well-trained buddy identifies early signs of distress and takes quick measures to prevent a minor development.

- **Primary/Secondary Roles:** It is often convenient and helpful for a buddy team to establish primary and secondary roles for each dive. For example, while one freediver prepares to enter the water, that freediver can be assigned as the primary safety observer until the other freediver is back in the water after the dive.
- **Distance and Visibility:** A buddy should stay near but not on top of the buddy while maintaining the comfort of responding instantaneously to an immediate need. The buddy should be able to reach out and touch at all times, especially during an ascent when a shallow water blackout is most threatening. Communication regarding the depth and time planned for

the dive and specific needs, such as current situations, will better prepare the buddy for the dive.

Planning and Communication Before Any Session of Freediving: The targets on depth, expected time, and apprehensions regarding physical limitation, if any, must be given and taken between the respective freedivers. Pre-planning on hand signals and non-verbal gestures provides the means to communicate underwater effectively.

- **Emergency Cues and Hand Signals:** Develop standard hand or visual signals that anyone can give to others to indicate something is wrong. Examples include going up to the surface with an upward-pointing motion or making a flexed arm with a clenched fist and a raised thumb for "I'm ready for rescue." Besides these, communication should also cover other hand signs such as "OK" or "need assistance" to avoid ambiguities.
- **Dive Planning and Safety Drills:** Each buddy team should practice reviewing the dive plan, safety procedures, and any rescue drills. Such practice prepares a freediver's mind to show him what to do if something goes wrong. Even practiced on land, the so-called safety drills will help reinforce the rescue techniques and develop a shared understanding of the emergency protocol.

Surface Supervision and Post-Dive Monitoring: Supervising on the surface is as necessary as underwater. After a freediver surfaces, his buddy must be able to keep him in close view, especially in the case of disorders such as LMC or blackout that can develop during a time delay.

- **Buddy Breathing Observation-Post-Dive:** Buddies should observe each other's recovery breathing and general status before attempting a new dive. If they notice signs of fatigue, confusion, or shaking, the person wants more recovery time. There are risks associated with diving too quickly following a challenging breath hold.
- **Recovery Breathing Observation:** Proper recovery breathing must be observed to establish whether the freediver is

normalizing his oxygen levels and returning to normality. Waiting until complete recovery before another dive reduces the risks of hypoxia and thus becomes essential to preventing cumulative fatigue.

2. Managing Loss of Motor Control and Blackout

Two severe risks in the sport are loss of motor control and blackout, primarily because divers cannot obtain oxygen or equalize pressure on their way down. Knowledge of these conditions, their signs, and appropriate response techniques are necessary for safe freediving.

LMC: Sometimes referred to as "samba, this is a situation wherein the supply of oxygen is so low that the brain cannot control motor functions. Symptoms are involuntary muscle twitches or unsteadiness, sometimes partial loss of muscle control during surfacing. It indicates that a freediver has already exceeded their limit and is near to experiencing a much worse oxygen deficiency level.

- **LMC Symptoms** include trembling or shaking hands, face, or body, a glassy or distant stare, and losing control over movement. Freedivers, for example, cannot keep their mouths above the water's surface, sometimes creating an aspiration threat.
- **LMC Immediate Response:** If a buddy notices the symptoms of LMC in their partner, he must support and assist in keeping the freediver's head above water and guide him to carry out recovery breathing slowly. The freediver must only dive again once fully recovered because additional breath holds can increase the chance of a blackout.

Blackout: The sudden loss of consciousness due to hypoxia, i.e., deficient oxygen levels. It is most common during the ascent phase of the dive when the oxygen pressure drops dramatically with the decrease in depth, but it can happen at any time.

- **Types of Blackouts:** Two major types of UTIs are significant in freediving: deep-water and shallow-water blackouts. In deeper depths, shallow-water blackouts occur due to rapid oxygen consumption. Deep-water blackouts can arise anytime while nearing the surface when the lungs re-expand, causing a sudden drop in oxygen tension. Of these two, shallow-water blackouts are particularly dangerous mainly because they usually happen near the end of the dive, when the freediver is most tired and often ill-equipped to act.

- **Blackout Recognition:** These are confused, disoriented, or an apparent slowing or cessation of movement during ascent. A freediver who blacks out may appear limp, stop moving, or become unresponsive and need assistance IMMEDIATELY.
- **Blackout Response:** In a blackout, the freediver's buddy should immediately support his head out of the water, clear his airway if necessary, and ensure that he resumes breathing spontaneously. Some high-resolution breaths might occasionally be given if the freediver does not resume spontaneous breathing. It is vital to remain calm and keep the freediver's airway out of the water until full consciousness is regained.

3. Correct Recovery Breathing and Surface Interval Management

In that vein, recovery breathing during the ascent will also respect surface intervals. This process is intended to re-equate oxygen levels, avoid fatigue, and lessen blackout risks. This can include most of what is considered safe and sound freediving practice; hence, it is also a vital skill to be mastered by all freedivers.

Recovery Breathing is the immediate breathing process after a breath hold. It replenishes the quantity of oxygen in the blood within a very short time and assists in removing extra CO_2 from the body. For a freediver, recovery breathing is a regular pattern that prevents the sudden drop in oxygen levels that might lead to shallow water blackout or LMC.

- **Recovery Breathing Technique:** Recovery breathing consists of quick, shallow inspirations through the mouth and regulated slow exhalation. The method is usually known as a "hook breath," which allows maximum intake while

avoiding hyperventilation, which may raise carbon dioxide levels to an unsafe degree.
- **Mindful Breathing Practice:** Recovery breathing on land should become automatic for the freediver. This is an essential skill during the immediate post-dive period, considered further as a grounding mechanism and a skill that relaxes the person while setting them in preparation for the next breath hold.

Observed surface intervals: The surface interval is a promising avenue for the freediver's body to replace the body's oxygen, ultimately realize heart rate, and relax muscles before going to the next dive. Minimum rest will not leave freedivers with anything other than cumulative risk due to hypoxia, low stamina, and alertness.
- **Surface Interval Rule of Thumb:** One general rule of thumb standard among freedivers is to dive once they have stayed above the water for at least double the time spent there. If using the one-minute scenario again, one would have to wait until at least two minutes have passed since he reached the surface. This can be changed according to experience and the overall physical fitness of a freediver, just like with depth, for example.
- **Recognize the Signs of Poor Recovery:** If the freediver feels dizzy, tired, or mentally groggy, he should not continue with the dive. These signs mean the body has not recovered yet and needs more rest to continue safely.

4. Freediving Risk Reduction Strategies

The secret to successful risk management in freediving is knowing one's limits, proper gradual training, and using techniques that minimize the potential for physical or mental exhaustion. To this end, conservative diving practices and a generally slow rate of progress on the part of the freediver will ensure excellent safety.

Progressive and Confidence-Building: The proper concept of freediving is progressive. In this concept, freedivers gradually increase depth, dive duration, and other targets, but not with giant jumps to avoid exposed depth. The gradual dives build confidence while minimizing the possibility of panic or mistakes.

- **Mental Depth Limits:** The freediver should establish a personal depth limit based on experience, physical conditioning, and mental comfort. The freediver must realize that progress takes time, and respecting the limits sets boundaries to protect against hazardous overexertion.
- **CO_2 and O_2 Tolerance Training:** The comfort and acclimatization of physiological changes occurring during extended breath-hold duration will be achieved through CO_2 and O_2 tolerance training. The ability of freedivers to handle the produced carbon dioxide build-up is developed through CO_2 Tolerance exercises, such as CO_2 tables.

Breathing and Relaxation Techniques in Freediving

In the sport of free diving, breathing is an art. The freediver's breathing directly influences his relaxation, oxygen conservation, and, hence, his performance in a dive. No breathing devices are utilized in this form of diving; therefore, the sport entirely depends on the length and effectiveness of a freediver's breath retention. These breathing techniques ensure maximum oxygen intake to regulate the rise of carbon dioxide and keep the mind and body relaxed but focused. Thus, the "freedive breathing cycle" is a progressive method with four phases of immense importance: relaxation, full breath, breath hold, and recovery. It would provide each with their technique, described in a manner peculiar to that instructor so that they may be accessible in diving and excellent states of physical and psychic form.

The freediver's time, practice, and focus go toward mastering all freediving. Each stage reinforces the next to make the freediver complete his underwater undertaking. This paper aims to explain in depth every stage of the breathing cycle in freediving to explain techniques and strategies taken by freedivers to make such a dive as efficient, calm, and controlled as possible.

RELAXATION PHASE

The premise of freediving is to be relaxed; therefore, even before one takes his last breath, he should be in this rest-and-focused state. This stage continues physical preparation for the mind by lowering the heart rate and eliminating anxiety before diving. It reduces the body's overall consumption and helps the freediver have a smooth and steady descent.

It is mainly used to set the whole dive. When the heartbeat is shallow, one is relaxed, and oxygen consumption is at the barest minimum. Therefore, one can conduct much longer and safer dives. Anxiety, or vice versa, stress accelerates heart rates, burning up oxygen stores much quicker to create urgency, making the dive much shorter with increased chances of panic.

It needs to be carried out before and after a dive.

Physical Relaxation: During every freediving dive, tension stored in muscles moves to a natural position that feels good. Most attention must be transferred to the shoulder, neck, and facial areas because that is where most tension is built. This relaxation action will preserve oxygen and make the movements more fluid and aerodynamic.

Progressive Muscle Relaxation: A progressive muscle-relaxing exercise in which the freediver tenses and releases each muscle group in progression from the toes to the head, releasing residual tension and developing a feeling of looseness from head to toe. When the freediver is prepared for a full breath, his body should be weightless.

Relaxed Body Position: The body is kept nearly horizontal and floated at the surface in either the starfish or upright position or deeper water supported by a buoy or platform. A relaxed body lessens the need to tread water or perform other movements, elevating heart rate.

- **Relaxed Mind Techniques:** The mind must be as relaxed as the body. In that way, one will be able to listen more to the dive and remove from his mind those thoughts that disturb him and hamper his performance.
- **Diaphragmatic Breathing:** Of all methods suggested for the relaxation of a particular person, the most commonly recommended is diaphragmatic, or "belly," breathing. As the name perhaps may suggest, this form of breathing concerns deep diaphragmatic breathing and not shallow chest breathing.

Now try the following:
Place one hand on your abdomen. Inhale slowly through your nose- your belly should rise and exhale very slowly through your mouth.

Diaphragmatic breathing: at once sends the body a signal that it needs to relax, and the heart rate and oxygen consumption go down accordingly. Visualization is the most essential and influential mind-preparation technique for a successful dive. Most freedivers should easily visualize an entire dive from a relaxed sink and equalize it to the desired depth of the controlled ascent. This would help them build confidence and familiarity with the dive itself, reducing anxiety before the dive. It creates mental "muscle memory" by picturing a successful and relaxed dive in one's mind.

What that means:

State of being Mindful and Grounded: to be very present, or instead not allow the mind to wander elsewhere except to what one is doing at each given moment.

Most freedivers acquire it through subtle awareness of how their breath feels and the sound of the water. These give a calming realization that keeps them alert mentally. With every detail of the present time, nothing will take the freedivers' attention away from their performance and keep them composed.

Full Breath-Final Breath

The "final breath" is also more commonly known as the "final breath" and is considered the last one before immersion by the freediver. It is a vital breath-in that provides much-needed oxygen to maintain the dive. However, there is so much more to this than taking deep breaths; full inhalation ensures complete lung volume is achieved without hyperventilation.

Entire Breathing Purpose: A person should inhale and breathe fully to the capacity of the lungs. This stores the deep oxygen reserve that supplies the body's requirements during a dive.

However, this must be controlled, not with excessive tension or rapid heart rate elevation.

Complete breathing technique: Traditionally, the full breath is divided into filling the lower, middle, and upper parts of the lungs. This way, the freediver fills each part of the lungs without generating tension.

Diaphragmatic Breathing/Lower Lung Filling: Take a deep in-breath through the nose, allowing air into the lower lung. Do not inhibit one in the least. This drops the diaphragm, allowing maximum expansion within the lower parts of the lungs.

Rib Expansion—Middle Filling of Lungs: In a middle filling, the ribs must curve outward, or better yet, the chest should expand since the ribs go out to accommodate more.

Upper Lung Shoulder Lift: To fill the upper portion of the lungs, lift the chest and shoulders slightly. There is no jerkiness in the body for this upward action. After full inhalation, a little pause at the top is significant to prepare oneself mentally and physically for the fall.

Don't Hyperventilate: The mistake most freedivers make is getting rid of some carbon dioxide by hyperventilating, a style of rapid, shallow breathing. It might extend the period before one has to breathe, but this increases the risk of shallow water blackout and reduces the perception of tolerance of the freediver. This last inspiration, however, is to be a deep and slow, conscious process in itself, absolutely directed to the intake of oxygen, with no thought at all to be given to the removal of CO_2.

Passive Exhalation: Some freedivers do a passive exhalation before taking a breath. The "reset" here develops some kind of "reset" that clears their lungs from residual air to prepare them for maximum new air. This shall be light exhalation and not lead to complete deflation of the lungs, which could drop the oxygen level.

Breath Hold (Apnea Phase)

It is the state of breath-hold/apnea during the actual dive. In it, freedivers practice physical movement and mental stillness while maintaining reasonable control over their bodies and oxygen consumption. Training and conditioning merge into this breath-hold phase when one needs to measure up to utilize oxygen reserves, adapt to constantly changing pressure, and be relaxed even when the urge to breathe is enormous.

The goal during Breath Holding: In such a state of apnea, the goal would be to minimize oxygen consumption; one could stay longer and be much more profound without any. All that is about the capability to have total control of body movements and courses of thought at every single dive moment under serenity and efficiency.

Breath-Hold Psyche Control: The most crucial part of breath-hold psyche control is sustaining the discomfort and, therefore, the psychological effect one is experiencing. Visualization, mindfulness, and self-talk are techniques freedivers use to help them focus and not panic.

Smooth Descent Visualization: The other freedivers visualize a longer dive during the descent stage. They view themselves smoothly descending and relaxing as they fall slowly through the water and experience less friction. A little imagination about the smoothness and silkiness of the descent with less friction makes focusing on the essential tasks easy without distress.

It would be a build-up, the urge to breathe would increase, and it is where positive self-talk and self-reinforcement can be carried further. Several freedivers are found telling the mind to relax, saying again and again some words, "Stay calm," "Focus on the rhythm, or "You're doing just fine," which, in overall terms, helps improve the attitude positively. Such positive feedback makes the freediver relax in confidence rather than freak out.

Relaxed Motion and Streamlining: The diving freediver must not rush. There should be leisurely, well-controlled, and efficient motility to economize oxygen and reduce any drag that may sap energy.

Efficient Finning Technique: Judicious finning techniques are critical to the oxygen economy. Freedivers practice a slow and sweeping action; their leg movement should originate from the hips, not the knees. This kicking motion is highly streamlined and develops good propulsion with minimal end.

Smoothening Position: First, it creates less drag and only allows the minimum resistance. Many freedivers keep their arms at the sides or before themselves while superior hydrodynamics take over; a smooth and silent descent ensues. This will require a minimum amount of energy which is essential when considering longer dives to breathe management: The increase of CO_2 in that respect intensifies the urge to breathe; it is also termed "CO_2 narcosis" because it irks the body as well as the mind. Talking about this, the freedivers take the training of exercises of the toleration for CO_2 results through which they would gain an extended comfort zone through the control of the urge to breathe without any disruption to concentration.

CO_2 Tolerance Training: Earth's surface freedivers train to achieve increased tolerance for higher levels of CO_2 using CO_2 tables. This exercise might allow the freediver to increase tolerance for rising CO_2.

Deep Breathing in the Sport of Freediving: Yoga, Diaphragmatic Breathing, and Pranayama

Deep breathing techniques are the base of most supportive skills for freediving. Furthermore, from the point of view of survival, they also enable one to optimize performance throughout the dive by sustaining oxygen and mental clarity. In this respect, efficient breathing while freediving would mean coolness under pressure. Nowadays, yoga and pranayama-ancient breathing control place this under the spotlight, putting a freediver in a better position to control breathing, reduce stress, and expand total capacity. These types of training increase general physical condition, respiratory flexibility, and psychic preparation; hence, they allow a freediver to perform deeper diving more comfortably and safely.

Breathing is essential and cannot be underestimated. Three breathing exercises—yoga breathing techniques, diaphragmatic breathing, and pranayama—are part of the basic techniques each freediver should learn. The paper will review these topics at all phases of a free dive, from pre-dive relaxation to optimization of breath-hold and post-dive, and develop a unique, complete breathing toolkit for freedivers.

1. Yogic Breathing Techniques

Yogic tradition offers several techniques that, within one term, "Pranayama," combine the induction of control over breathing, relaxation, lung expansion, and mind focus. Yoga breathing concepts arise primarily from the notion that controlled breathing influences energy, mindset, and health. Thus, freedivers also employ yoga breathing to enhance their ability to focus, control anxiety, and optimize lung volume.

Purpose of Yoga Breathing in Freediving

The essence of yoga breathing is to relax one's mind and body up the lungs. This is very essential in freediving. Normal and controlled breathing can help a person relax before dives, lower the heart rate, and take in as much oxygen as possible without creating unwanted tension in the body. It also enables the yoga breathing to make the freediver aware of the breath-in himself, an essential component in dealing with mental and physical stresses associated with deep breath-hold diving.

Common Yoga Breathing Exercises among Freedivers

Each of these yogic breathing exercises will have a different benefit for the freediver, whether it be tranquilizing the mind or providing elasticity to the lungs:

In Ujjayi, respiration is prolonged and deep through the nostrils. It is partly attained by closing the posterior portion of the throat while inhaling and exhaling. The soft rhythmic sound it produces helps during the concentrative acts of the mind and slows the breath.

Respiration enters deep inside the nostrils, relaxing the pharyngeal region but with a relatively closed passage. For this, one can practice listening by making a soft hissing "ah" sound that one can hear. Similarly, exhalation is to be impeded so that an utterly rounded, slow, and tranquil passage of breath becomes possible. Instead, one gets continuity in the sound-humidity of Ujjayi's breathing, as the resonance of the waves may even be soothing to hear.

Freediving generally has several benefits. Before the dive, it puts an individual in a relaxed and centered state. In this rhythmical pattern, the heartbeat is slow, and oxygen is regulated. Hence, any freediver enters a trance and escapes from anxious feelings before diving. Wholesome breathing is practice and habituation that increases elasticity in the lungs.

That is Sanskrit for 'purification of the nadis,' wherein Nadi Shodhana. It is a balancing of both sides of the brain, cooling of the nervous system, and calming of the mind. Thus, the particular breath taken alternately from one nostril and then out from the other can equal freedivers' oxygen inputs in their brains and reduce mental tension before entering a dive.

Sit comfortably; technically, fold the right nostril with the thumb of your right hand. Inhale very, very slowly through your left nostril. Release the closed right nostril and shut the left nostril with the release of air using the ring finger. Immediately after exhalation starts, exhale fresh air through the right nostril, closing and exhaling through the left nostril. Repeat with another pattern.

This includes meditation, which works on keeping the mind of the freediver balanced and reducing anxiety. Therefore, freedivers can focus their minds before entering the water, which orients their mental state. This is a critical factor for managing psychological tension because of this sport. Through this technique, the blood is efficiently oxygenated to prepare the body for the efficient utilization of oxygen.

The Sanskrit word Bhramari roughly means 'bee breath'; loose because it describes the soft humming one does upon exhalation. By nature, the sound produced is usually soothing. The vibrational action of the humming releases tension from the nervous system by calming and decreasing anxiety, among other forms of mental distractions.

Technique: Sit comfortably, inhale deeply through your nostrils, release your breath at the back of your throat, and allow a low humming sound to send it out of your body. Let the vibration hum inside your head and chest cavity. Be aware of this sound and its vibration, allowing it to take your attention inside your body.

This would relax and sedate the mind so that it can focus, reducing anxiety before the actual dive. Controlling a breathing pattern allows the freediver to center his mind and reach a state of rest and control before getting into the water.

The breathing in diaphragmatic breathing, or "belly breathing," is marked by intensely regulated breaths that apply practically during the performance to enable practical application for allowing their lungs to become fully dilated and take in more oxygen when the heartbeat is slow. Generally, it has proved to be especially useful during the predive relaxation phase of the dive and during the common practice of building up breath control.

Diaphragmatic Breathing-Freediving Purpose

While it makes deeper and fuller breathing more possible through the diaphragmatic filling of the lungs, in case one has a fully functional diaphragm, the oxygen supply to the body is thus optimally realized to a limit that could be achieved. Further, it helps activate the body's parasympathetic nervous system, which generally relaxes the person and slows his heartbeat. More oversized intakes of oxygen are consequently permitted, and the body can be in a more relaxed physical state than shallow chest breaths.

Diaphragmatic Breathing Technique

Diaphragmatic breathing can be performed out or in the water with a flotation device. It is the controlled, slow inhaling and exhaling of the breath with the diaphragm:

1. Relaxed Position: Sit or lie down; assume an easy position that feels right. Place one hand on your chest and one on your diaphragm so this motion can feel and reassure you that you are not breathing through the chest.

2. Deep Nose Breathing Inhaling through the nose should be slow at the start so that the bottom part of the lungs can fill up. On every exhalation, the diaphragm goes down, and the tummy rises upwards because that is where the deepest part of the lungs expands.

3. Extended Exhalation: Exhaling through the mouth must be slow and soft so that air leaves the lungs without unnecessary tension.

4. Repeat the Cycle: Allow yourself to repeat this, focusing forward on the inhale and on the exhale to create a typical, even breathing pattern. Your diaphragm will strengthen in time, and you should have no problems holding full breaths without strain.

Applications of Diaphragmatic Breathing in Freediving

There are one or two areas in which diaphragmatic breathing assists the freediver:

Diaphragmatic breathing, performed before diving, also slows the heartbeat, thereby reducing the rate of oxygen consumption. Again, as in the footnote, the breath's depth and slowness are equated with depth and quieting the mind.

Final Breath: Most freedivers use diaphragmatic breathing to accommodate their final breath before entering the water. This allows them to position themselves with more air in their lungs, increasing their oxygen stores to support longer dives.

Benefits of Diaphragmatic Breathing within the Sport of Freediving

- **Larger Lung Capacity:** During diaphragmatic breathing, the lungs are appropriately set to expand to total capacity; hence, one can inhale the maximum amount of air per breath and, consequently, build up one's oxygen reserve.
- **Slowing of Heart Rate:** The very beginning of diaphragmatic breathing starts working on the parasympathetic nervous system. It, in turn, begins to reduce the heart rate by conserving oxygen toward the breath-hold.
- **Relaxation and Concentration:** Diaphragmatic breathing relieves the mind and body, and hence, it is easier to practice when one gets nervous before a dive, etc.

3. Pranayama Breathing Techniques

Pranayama is the technique of controlling breathing, simple awareness of the breath, and elasticity of the lungs to such a developed degree that the mind can be concentrated. Pranayama exercises are conducted to master the flow of breath, improve oxygen retention, and grow the threshold of tolerance to increased CO_2 levels-which is vitally important in this sport.

Pranayama's Purpose in the Concept of Freediving

It is expected to improve oxygen efficiency while reducing the build-up of CO_2 by developingmental and physical resistance within the freedivers through different specialised pranayama techniques for freedivers. Generally, breathing regulation, development of lung capacity, increased tolerance to discomfort, and mental clarity are all achievable through pranayama practice.

Thus, they create the perfect foundation to prepare freedivers to manage breath-holding with serenity and efficiency.

Pranayama Techniques for freedivers

Kapalabhati: The word in Sanskrit means 'shining skull'. It's an invigorating breathing practice comprising active rapid exhalation and passive inhalation. As the lungs' volume increases, the diaphragm becomes robust and more tolerant of a high intake of CO_2.

Deep inspiration through the nose initiates it. Several quick, shallow expirations follow in jerks. As the conic diaphragm propels the respiration out, the lungs are passively filled. The diaphragm undergoes repeated, rapid contractions.

It would include the following: • Kapalabhati As for a freediver, it will make the lungs solid and resilient to his benefit. CO_2 tolerance for the freediver is improved. Again, it is so valuable for training dogma contractions, and this helps the freediver to do breathing control during apnea e, even Bhastrikarika-this has been variously described as a form of "bellows breath" with deep and rhythmic inspiration and e. Itationisn performed at an accelerated rate compared with Kapal.

CO_2 Tolerance, Hypoxia, and Hypercapnia Training in Freediving: A Deep Dive

Freediving pushes the human body and mind to the limits. Not only does a freediver have to perfect their physical movements, but physiological reactions to extreme circumstances underwater must also be mastered. The rising level of CO_2 and the falling level of O_2 are common factors freedivers must cope with while maintaining their mental calmness in a gradually stressful situation. Efficient training in CO_2 tolerance, hypoxia, and hypercapnia allows the freediver to prolong breath-hold time, stay tranquil in stress conditions, and cope with those feelings of discomfort that naturally arise. By learning to manage such physiological stressors, the freediver can dive into safer conditions with much greater endurance and clarity of mind.

This informative guide explores each training area in depth, discussing the importance of each component, specific training techniques, and progressive methods that will allow the freediver to build endurance, mental resilience, and control.

1. CO_2 Tolerance Training

CO_2 tolerance training in free diving allows them to get accustomed to the uncomfortable feelings arising from high levels of CO_2 during breath-hold. When CO_2 builds up in the bloodstream, it reduces blood pH and creates an acidic environment. This action stimulates the urge to breathe. The primary goal for freedivers is to learn how to bear this feeling without panicking to reach a longer dive and improve underwater performance.

Understanding CO_2 in Freediving

Through a breath-hold, the level of CO_2 in the blood would build up while the body uses up its energy stores. This increase of CO_2 is interpreted by the brain as the signal for air starvation, hence making it send the proper signals to take in air, balancing the process. While this response is essential for safety, it tends to limit freedivers' performance because they cannot manage their urges effectively. It is done by conditioning the body to tolerate a higher level of CO_2, where the freediver, over time, trains the brain to accept air hunger for a longer time and stay longer in a dive with a gain in control.

1. **CO_2 Tables:** This is controlled, patterned breath-holding that maintains a consistent breath-hold time while gradually decreasing the rest intervals between each hold. While it does this, with each repetition, CO_2 builds up and further stresses the body to adapt to discomfort.

How to Do It:
- Establish a time for holding your breath within which you feel comfortable, say 1 minute.
- Immediately following the first breath-hold, rest for 2 minutes.
- Progressively reduce rest by 15 seconds for each successive hold while maintaining the same breath-hold time.
- Continue to reduce rest intervals until these intervals become hard, let's say a minimum of 30 seconds.

Benefits: CO_2 tables progressively condition the body and mind to tolerate increasing levels of CO_2 by reducing rest time. Over time, this tolerance will develop mental resilience, allowing the body and mind to accept more extended periods without premature surfacing.

2. **Exhale Static Apnea:** This is a breathing technique in which, after one has exhaled completely, he holds his breath as if in a high CO_2/low O_2 environment. By starting the breath hold with reduced lung volume, CO_2 levels rise more rapidly, making this a very intense, effective CO_2 tolerance drill.

How to Do It:
- Sit or lie down, exhale fully, holding your breath in this "empty" state.
- The focus is to relax while CO_2 levels build up, even when uncomfortable.
- Have repeated bouts with rest intervals in between, but gradually extend the time as your tolerance increases.

Benefits: Static exhalation apnea stimulates CO_2 adaptation, toughens the diaphragm, and helps the diver get accustomed to rising CO_2. It allows divers to tolerate discomfort better over time.

3. Breath-hold walks: This exercise combines two factors that increase CO_2: breath-holding and light physical activity. Since both involve increased muscle activity, they are suitable for building dynamic CO_2 tolerance.

How to Do It:
- Breathe in deeply, hold it, and begin to walk at a slow, unhurried pace. With the accumulation of CO_2, focus on feeling relaxed and walking until an overwhelming urge to breathe asserts itself; after that, you stop and exhale. Allow full recovery and repeat the exercise, gradually increasing the distance covered each time.
- **Benefits:** Breath-hold walks help divers develop a greater tolerance for CO_2 during physical effort. Thus, they imitate the actual conditions of freediving and teach them to stay tranquil and attentive when CO_2 levels increase.

4. Gradual Exposure to CO_2 with Pranayama: Several pranayama or yogic ways of breath control have been elaborated; these allow for an increase in CO_2 under controlled tolerance conditions.
- **Kapalabhati:** Inhale deeply and then allow rapid, powerful exhalations while the inhale is passive. Repeat for a predetermined time.
- **Bhastrika:** Breathe deeply in and out as fast as possible while establishing a rhythm.
- **Benefits:** This will build CO_2 tolerance and intensely train the diaphragm and all respiratory muscles, improving breathing control and endurance.

2. Hypoxia Training

Hypoxia, or low oxygen levels, is one of the most critical concerns in free diving whenever one holds his breath for too long or descends to suspiciously deep depths. By reducing cognitive function, hypoxia causes disorientation and can even lead to blacking out. Hypoxia training is essential to safely adapt divers to low O_2 conditions, build awareness of hypoxic symptoms, and extend times holding their breath.

Understanding Hypoxia in Free Diving

Hypoxia occurs when oxygen levels fall, reducing O_2 availability to critical organs, especially the brain. Blackout risk is high during freediving, mainly during ascents when oxygen levels drop abruptly. Training in hypoxia management will safely enable divers to push limits by making them more resilient to low conditions of O_2 and teaching early signs of hypoxia recognition.

Techniques for Hypoxia Training

Hypoxia training methods stress that low O_2 should be gradual so the diver can adapt safely. Following are some practical exercises to build tolerance to hypoxia:

1. O_2 Tables: Like the CO_2 tables, O_2 tables are conducted by gradually increasing the breath-holding time while maintaining fixed rest intervals to condition the body to adapt to low oxygen.

How to Do It:
- Start with a manageable breath-hold duration, such as 1 minute.
- Active recovery for 2 minutes between each breath-hold.
- Increase each subsequent breath-hold by 15–20 seconds; rest simultaneously.
- Continue to increase the duration of the breath-hold until it becomes problematic.

Benefits: O_2 tables help the body acclimate to low oxygen levels over time. This helps to tolerate hypoxia better, and divers can safely manage more extended breath holds.

2. Progressive Apnea Drills: This process involves holding several successive breaths. Start with small breath holds, each one a little bit longer, and tolerance for trim levoxygen levels will be achieved over time. Avoid discomfort to the body.

How to Do It:
- Begin with a light breath-hold and build up to longer and longer breath-holds.

- After every hold, make sure you recover fully.

Benefits: The person doing these drills learns to better their limits, becomes more hypoxia tolerant, and becomes more aware of the first signs.

3. Exhale Diving, or FRC, involves holding the breath on an exhale when the lungs' volume is low. This causes hypoxia faster, which is beneficial for simulating deeper dive scenarios.

How to Do It:

Completely exhale and hold your breath, but never tense up.

Allow the onset of relaxation and recognize the hypoxia signals for oxygen levels to fall.

Benefits: Exhale diving allows the body to acclimate to low oxygen conditions, enhancing lung functionality and increasing the mind's focusing ability.

4. Extended Breath Hold with Mental Focus: Prolonged breath holds combined with mental load-task counting or visualization help divers build resilience by maintaining focus during hypoxia and becoming aware of early symptoms.

How it's Done:
- Establish the target breath-hold time and inspire mental activities, such as counting or visualizing a successful dive.
- Progress until the first signs of hypoxia surface, then rest.

Benefits: It forms tolerance to hypoxia and mental awareness and control so that the diver can be better prepared for states of low oxygenation with calmness.

3. Hypercapnia Management

High CO_2, or hypercapnia, precipitates symptoms that include discomfort, anxiety, and air hunger, which can produce a need to surface prematurely. Training is essential for managing hypercapnia. It teaches the diver to remain relaxed during an increasing CO_2 level, thus allowing for longer bottom times and greater control of the breath-hold response.

Understanding Hypercapnia in Freediving

Hypercapnia is a build-up of CO_2 during a breath hold that creates sensations of air hunger or the "need to breathe." It is uncomfortable but not particularly dangerous so long as it is well-managed. Training for hypercapnia will teach the diver to become tolerant of high CO_2 and to remain calm and composed while the need to breathe vigorously increases.

Techniques for Hypercapnia Management

Hypercapnia training teaches relaxation and mental control against a rising CO_2. Some of the fundamental techniques include:

1. Controlled Breath-Hold Practice: One holds breath while focusing on relaxation to allow divers to experience and control hypercapnia safely.

How to Do It:
- Start with a comfortable breath-hold and relax with the on-rising of the CO_2.
- Learn to relax the diaphragm and not tense up the body in response to increased discomfort.
- Regular practice so that you get used to the feelings of hypercapnia.

Benefits: Controlled breath-hold practice trains the diver to act with high levels of CO_2 without panicking, thus increasing dive bottom time and a diver's tolerance.

2. Box Breathing: Also known as square breathing, this technique involves inhaling, holding the breath, exhaling, and holding in equal measures to develop a plodding, cadenced breathing rhythm.

How It's Done:
- Inhale to the count of four, hold to the count of four, exhale to the count of four, and hold off for four.
- Do this multiple times, maintaining a smooth cadence.

Benefits: Box breathing regulates CO_2 tolerance, relaxes, and builds breath control to support hypercapnia management in the water.

3. CO_2 Tolerance Games (Dynamic CO_2 Management): By adding light activities to breath-hold (slow walking and stretching), divers will build up CO_2 levels in a playful, competitive environment that will encourage dynamic CO_2 adaptation.

How to Do It:
- Hold your breath doing light exercises like walking or yoga stretches.
- Keep a tab on duration and gradually push the limits.

Benefits: CO_2 tolerance games strengthen your mental barrier and give you more control over breathing urges, which helps a diver get used to high CO_2 levels dynamically.

In conclusion, Mastering CO_2 tolerance, resistance to hypoxia, and the ability to manage hypercapnia safely means that freediving will be safer, more endurable, and more enjoyable. These training techniques condition the body and mind to prolong breath-hold times safely with calm, composed control. Regular practice can teach divers how to manage the onset of discomfort associated with breath-hold diving so that greater depths and lengths may be attained while confidently exploring the underwater world with complete mindfulness.

Immersion Physiology: Human Body Adaptation to Water

Freediving is a sport based on an incredible human body adaptation using innate physiological responses developed over thousands of years in an aquatic environment. This particular combination of adaptations allows the diver to conserve oxygen, protect the vital organs, and maintain physical functionality underwater. These are part of the mammalian dive reflex-involuntary physiological responses that enable the body to function more economically under pressure and to prolong such a non-breathing state. A question would be whether gaining these adaptations helps a freediver in training to improve performance given safety towards expanding human capability.

This sudden immersion of the body in cold water, especially with an abrupt dunking of the face into cold water, evokes a cascade of physiological responses aimed at minimal use of oxygen, reduced metabolic costs, and, most importantly, of the body's central functions. These other than one-acquired responses become instinctive reactions of mammals, including humans, and reflect the deep linkage we share in evolution with an underwater world.

The Physiology of the Mammalian Dive Reflex: A Basis of Freediving

The stimulus for response in mammals' diving reflex is immersion underwater. It is an autonomic reflex; submerging the face under water triggers various physiological reactions directed at oxygen conservation. While it is much more extreme in aquatic mammals, like seals and whales, this also occurs in humans and comes into play with frying sport-type activities.

1. Critical Components of the Dive Reflex

- **Bradycardia or Slowed Heart Rate:** One of the dive reflex's most immediate and patent responses is bradycardia or a slowing heart rate.
  This response was stimulated to minimize oxygen consumption by lowering the work required from the heart. Already exercised freedivers may experience a drop in heart rate by as much as 50% or more during dives, resulting in savings in oxygen utilization by the cardiovascular system. Such a slowing of the heart rate allows the body to prolong the time for breathing, an essential factor in longer and more profound.
- **Peripheral vasoconstriction** means that peripheral blood vessels constrict simultaneously with the beginning of the bradycardia of the blood vessels in the extremities. Blood is shifted from limbs to major organs like the heart, brain, and lungs. When oxygen levels generally start falling, the body holds onto oxygen for the most vital functions by constricting the blood supply to areas not conducive to survival.
- **Blood Shift:** Blood shift is unique when the human body is subjected to high-intensity pressure at depth.

This physiological adaptation allows the blood plasma to seep into the compressed spaces of the lungs due to pressure. This way, the human body will prevent the lungs from collapsing under such extreme pressure. This process maintains the integrity of the lung tissue and preserves lung function, thus enabling the divers to reach greater depths safely. The blood shift makes the thoracic cavity stable and nonsusceptible to any damage due to compression at high pressures. ---

2. Oxygen Conservation and Utilisation: Maximising Efficiency

For example, the body's general aim in response to a breath-hold dive is to economize on oxygen and use it better. This is achieved through the tumbling effect of reactions, whereby oxygen distribution is prioritized for organs that need it most and utilized in the best possible manner.

Reduced Oxygen Consumption

It does this through a reflexive shutdown upon diving, wherein metabolic rates are depressed-particularly in muscles not actively participating in the dive. This shutdown is a means whereby energy and oxygen reserves are conserved, thus extending the stay of the diver underwater in one breath. The body becomes more economical in expending energy by routing oxygen to vital locations while limiting consumption in non-essential places.

Delayed Onset of Lactic Acid Accumulation

This is due to the increased dependency on anaerobic metabolism, which results in an inability to deliver oxygen to the limbs and peripheral muscles, resulting in lactic acid accumulation.

Because adaptations by the mammalian dive reflex prevent this, the lactic acid accumulation begins so much later that it enables the freediver to extend his dive time without earlier signs of muscle fatigue or discomfort. In effect, these two factors come to the blood shift, and bradycardia extends the length of time the body can function without oxygen, therefore extending breath-hold capacity. Spleen Contraction: A Natural Boost of Oxygen

The spleen functions as a natural reservoir for oxygen-carrying erythrocytes.

Spleen contraction, such as water immersion, releases more erythrocytes into the circulation. The transient rise in oxygen levels due to the increase in erythrocyte number makes them a good breath-hold diver and can tolerate deep-diving stresses better. Some estimates have calculated that as much as 10% of the volume of the spleen is available to be released for red blood cells during the dive, and it would make an important contribution to the endurance of the diver. ---

3. Cardiovascular Adaptations: Supporting the Dive

Thus, the cardiovascular system changes during immersion to support oxygen conservation and maintain perfusion to the vital organs.

Bradycardia: An Important Response

Bradycardia, or slowing heart rate during submersion, is one of the diving reflex's most outstanding and essential components.

It then becomes modified based on the training conditions and the diver's status. For example, bradycardia is more pronounced in an accomplished freediver, significantly reducing heart rate and prolonging dives by economizing on oxygen. Since the heart rate would be slower, less oxygen would be needed to induce circulation; hence, the body would be more efficient in sustaining a single breath.

Increased Blood Pressure and Vasoconstriction

Even though the heart rate may slow down during a dive, blood pressure may briefly increase during peripheral vasoconstriction.

This elevation of blood pressure ensures that blood shunts from the extremities to the core well and that the vital organs receive an adequate oxygen supply. Vasoconstriction in the limbs and skin diverts the blood to its most needed locations so that the brain and heart get enough oxygen during an overall decline.

Blood Shift and Lung Protection

This blood shift is essential for cardiovascular function and protecting the lungs from collapsing under pressure.

Thus, when divers enter the water at greater depths, the lungs are compressed due to increased pressure; if there were no mechanism for such a blood shift, the lungs could be damaged or collapsed. To compensate for this, the body balances the inner pressure with blood plasma transferred into the thoracic cavity to maintain the structure and function of the lung. This adaptation is significant in dives requiring great depth and considerable pressure.

4. Training and Harnessing Physiological Adaptations

Out of utmost respect for safety, training can elicit and sharpen various physiological responses or adaptations the human body may undertake to improve its performance in free diving. Therefore, specific training practices can optimally develop and refine physiological responses.

Breath-Hold Training - Ways to Enhance CO_2 and O_2 Management

Such static and dynamic apnea training helps divers build CO_2 tolerance and O_2 efficiency. In other words, the diver holding his breath longer and longer conditions his body to resist increasing levels of carbon dioxide or lower levels of oxygen. This factor reinforces a natural dive response on the one hand, builds mental resilience on the other, and focuses on the other.

Methods of Relaxation Management to Improve Dive Reflex

The complete turn-on of the dive reflex and lowering of the heart rate are realized when a state of relaxation is maintained. Meditation, deep breathing exercises, and progressive muscle relaxation improve divers' ability to be more docile and attentive during dives. Stress and anxiety increase heart rate and oxygen consumption; hence, mastering such techniques in relaxation will be highly beneficial for the maximum utilization of the dive reflex.

Progressive Depth Training for Blood Shift Adaptation

The human body can be subjected to deeper dives; with time, the pressure changes, and the body gets accustomed to blood shifts. The other way is that divers prepare their bodies to tolerate such rigors by training safely. As depth increases gradually, the blood shift and lung protection responses could be improved, thus giving them more surety as they go deep into the water.

It is interesting to see how the human body adapts to being immersed in water, but in principle, the question is whether we desire better freediving performances and safety.

These adaptations have an effect, enabling divers to save oxygen, preserve heart function, and even protect their lungs from deep-water pressure. Those who train to heighten these adaptations will know with every breath taken that they can stay longer, safely dive more profoundly, and go further more easily. Critical points for the diver:

Improve dive reflex: Through breath-holding exercises, one can train the body to show the diving reflex right when the face touches cold water. This would extend dives and make them much safer.

The placid mental state profoundly relaxes the mechanics of diving; heart rates are reduced significantly, optimizing oxygen consumption. Therefore, methods of inducing relaxation must be added to the roster of regular training programs for divers to ensure maximum benefits from such methodology.

Depth Exposure: Progressive training with gradually increased depth exposure will eventually get the body used to pressure and blood shift demands, protecting the lungs and ensuring overall dive safety.

Conclusion

The adaptations of the human body in water make freediving possible and significant.

Other responses, such as the mammalian dive reflex, have made humans apt at deeper waters and longer immersions with excellent efficiency and safety. Gaining appropriate knowledge and training in these responses, the freediver should be in a position to press his bodily and mental limits toward deeper and longer dives with more control and composure. These adaptations are a way to exhibit the immense potentiality of the body that it develops, bearing several stresses to adapt and connect us with immense aquatic life, hence realizing the latent undertaking hidden inside each of us.

MDR, Blood Shift, and Bradycardia: The building blocks of physiology in competitive freediving

Freediving is a weird sport. It directly borrows from natural physiological responses to an underwater environment. Mostly, it descends from deep at the bottom of our evolutionary history. It involves some reasonably extreme physiological changes known as the mammalian diving response designed to optimize oxygen conservation with the aim of survivability during submergence. Bradycardia is the slowing heart rate, while peripheral vasoconstriction involves the constriction of blood vessels in either the limbs or the core areas of the body. This redistribution of blood, otherwise known as blood shift, would keep the lungs' volume during depth. Each one of these mechanisms is correct at the very core of MDR. All these processes underpin both the fragility and the resilience of the human body but prove helpful knowledge in empowering the freediver for training informed with safety and generally better performance.

1. Mammalian Dive Response: An Evolutionary Survival Mechanism

This is an evolutionary reflex common to all mammals, including dolphins, whales, seals, and humans. The sophisticated reflex response to physiological stimuli, either by contact of the face with water or icy water or merely by initiating breath holding, maintains delivery to the brain and heart while simultaneously reducing oxygen consumption in other tissues. This may enable mammals to stay submerged longer than one would have thought had no ventilatory movement occurred.

How MDR is initiated

The Following is how MDR is initiated:

Immersion of the face into water: Facial immersions in water activate thermoreceptors around the nostrils and mouth; this informs the brain to react to the dive. The effect is more pronounced when the water is cold during cold weather conditions.

Without actual submersion, the inability to exhale out of water would have activated those parts of the MDR. This forms part of the breath-hold training amongst free divers, considering what the conditions of a dive would demand.

The Essential Components of the MDR

1. Bradycardia: The early stages of MDR include perhaps the most critical response: the heart rate response is one of significant slowing, medically termed as bradycardia. This can be as large as a 50% drop or more from rest to conserve oxygen in advanced freedivers. This reduces metabolic demands for oxygen and allows the diver to stay longer underwater before he is overcome with the urge to breathe.

2. Peripheral Vasoconstriction is the narrowing of blood vessels. When blood levels fall, peripheral vasoconstriction oxygenates all the organs by redistributing blood from the skin, arms, and legs to the brain, heart, and lungs.

3. Blood Shift: Under bottom pressure, the body compresses, and the lungs collapse. This, through the blood shift mechanism, causes plasma from the blood to enter the lungs' capillaries and fill the space left by air, which collapses and hence maintains the shape of the lung. Therefore, blood shift is one of the primary adaptations to deep diving, and curiously, it is only specific to diving mammals and highly trained human-free divers.

2. Bradycardia: Heart Response to Submersion

The most salient feature of the mammalian diving reflex is reduced heart rate or bradycardia. Since then, it has been considered one of the most robust methods by which the body economizes on oxygen during submersion. The slowing heart rate is mediated through the autonomous action of the parasympathetic nervous system.

Physiological Mechanism of Bradycardia

Vagus Nerve: The vagus nerve is one of the primary mediators in response to bradycardia of the hand. Immersion of the face causes the utilization of neurons at the receptors on the face, thereby releasing the sending of such signals through the vagus nerve to the brain for interpretation. Through mediation by the brain, the rate at which the heart beats slows down. This may be within a few seconds of a person's head being submerged in the water.

Oxygen Conserving: Bradycardia's slower heart rate decreases the oxygen supplied to the body. This, in turn, is believed to increase the amount of oxygen delivered to the vital survival tissues, the brain, and the heart, allowing the freediver to extend his breath-holding time even longer.

Conditions Influencing Bradycardia

This evolves into an even more powerful bradycardic effect with cold water. The colder the water, the stronger the response; training in water temperatures is essential to any freediver's training to make this reflex as robust as possible.

The general intensity of the bradycardia effect in free diving would be much more vigorous due to the gradual strengthening of the inborn physiological response through training of repeated breath-holding-water immersion under control.

Operative of Longer Dives: The heartbeats go slow. This is directly related to the increase in dive time, which results from the reduction of the rate of oxygen use within the circulatory system.

Better Economy of Oxygen: Since the heart uses less oxygen, the brain gets the same amount to keep all life activities centered and concentrated on the keen mental and physical dive.

Adapting to Training Level: Bradycardia or the slowing down of the heart rate could be induced in trainees through repetitive breath hold and static apnea training, and the freedivers may become adept enough that this on-switch mechanism is easily turned on.

3. Blood Shift: Protecting the Lungs from Pressure

Among the adaptations necessary to enable the diver to bear up against exceptional pressure at depth, the blood shift is performed. Thus, in a dive, the deeper one goes, the greater the pressure to squeeze air out of the lungs and decrease its volume. If there had been an adaptational mechanism against that, it would have needed to collapse the lungs, called a squeeze. It does this to avoid it through the process of blood shift, which counterbalances the loss of the volume of air by compressing blood into the pulmonary capillaries for the integrity of the lungs to be held.

How Blood Shift Works

The blood compensates for the increased pressure since the depth compresses the thoracic cavity, increasing the pressure inside. In compensation, it shifts to the periphery, where the compression forces it into the lung's capillaries to affect the structural framework, thereby stabilizing it.

Protection of the Alveoli: The alveoli are tiny sacs intrinsic to the lungs. Gas exchange is susceptible to high pressure. A shift in blood flow keeps these structures open yet functional despite compression so that they will not collapse while maintaining, at least in some capacity, the opportunity for gas exchange.

Inversion occurs during gradual ascension: pressure falls, blood reaches the circulation, and the volume of the lungs becomes normal. Reversible lesion: It keeps the lung's function within the accepted safety limits during the dive cycle.

Training and Adaptation for Blood Shift
- **Progressive Depth Training** is the phenomenon whereby the depth of diving increases progressively over a certain period. The diver's body may get used to this shift in blood pressure, conditioning itself against pressure due to greater depth. This process assures better and complete efficiency of the entire blood shift response mechanism.
- **Stretching Exercises:** Yoga and stretching exercises of specific muscles improve flexibility in the thoracic cavity and, significantly, the diaphragm. Flexibility can support the mechanisms of blood shift in various pressure change cases.
- **Hydration-blood volume:** A good hydration level increases the volume of the blood since it's needed that adequate blood

supplies plasma for the blood to support shifting when that may be required.

4. Peripheral Vasoconstriction: Prioritizing Vital Organs

This is the mechanism the body initiates to ensure a blood supply during diving, especially where the need is most felt. Blood supply comes from the extremities and non-vital areas, where the vessels constrict to maintain oxygenation to the brain, heart, and lungs.

Mechanism of Peripheral Vasoconstriction
- **Immersion-Triggered:** Besides bradycardia, peripheral vasoconstriction is another well-known immersion-triggered reflex. This reflex acts in response to the face's submergence in the water. Prioritizing the use of oxygen is just as important as all the other characteristics of MDR.
- **Blood Redistribution:** It allows the constriction of the blood vessels in the extremities to distribute blood to the central parts of the body. That way, oxygen delivery is maintained to the tissues of the vital organs whose needs are not reduced by the reduced quantity of molecules in the blood.

Benefits of Apnea
- **Improved Economy of Oxygen Utilization:** Reduced blood flow through the muscles and tissues not vital during dives reduces oxygen consumption, enabling a diver to extend breathing time.
- **Thermoregulation:** During dives in cold water, peripheral vasoconstriction reduces the rate of heat loss, allowing for longer diving time and, consequently, core body temperature.

5. Development and Training of the Mammalian Dive Response

That would include a few ways the mammalian dive response can train a freediver and how those training methods can be further improved; this section shall deal with some ways divers strengthen such adaptations.

Cold Water Training
- **Face Immersion:** Repeated face immersion in cold water can activate MDR much more quickly, perhaps more profoundly. This can be comfortably practiced in the comfort of a swimming pool and, as such, diving in cold water.
- **Ful,l-body Immersion:** Even colder water full-body immersions have augmented the body's general dive response and bradycardia.

Static and Dynamic Apnea Training
- **Static Apnea:** Soon, the diver will be invited to relax in a fixed position while holding his breath. He will learn successively how to focus, turn on, and maintain MDR. During this practice, the heartbeat will be kept as low as possible to observe sensations related to bradycardia and peripheral vasoconstriction.
- **Dynamic Apnea:** Swimming with a held breath is used for dynamic apnea training, which trains the body to conserve and balance oxygen and CO_2 levels in motion. This, too, forms part of static apnea training, which develops general breath control and endurance in the diver.

Progressive Deep Dives

Progressively: Because the dive area is increased gradually, the time will shortly catch up with enough blood shift and adjustment of pressure changes. Such training progressions

Some Key Adaptations to Freediving in Water: Vision, Heat, and Buoyancy Controls

It is much more than holding one's breath and focusing. The crux is that all those shades mentioned above, visions, and heat-control buoyancy indicate a good, safe, and enjoyable aquatic experience. Each of the above colors is associated with many natural bodily functions. Each one has an intelligence within it and can add to the ability of the diving individual. Each color pertains to multiple ways that divers locomote, view, and maintain their safety underwater.

avenue Ditto

1. Vision in Water: Adaptation to an Aquatic Environment

These are great and brilliant things to view in the water; however, they will create some definite issues related to human vision's capability. Due to the nature of water, light behaves quite differently than air, and divers may see objects, colors, and distances quite differently.

How Light Refraction Creates Visual Distortion
- **Refraction of images, magnification:** Since it was a transition from medium to medium, refraction explained why light would bend around an object to distort it and make it appear 25-33% closer and more extensive than it was. This would thereby impact a person's depth perception and relation with space.
- **Corrective Measures:** The Freedivers change their expectations and visible cues every time they take a valuation of distances or negotiate various terrains underwater, and they can affect the prevention by introducing an air pocket in front of the eyes as corrective measures to the results of refraction. In this respect, the air pocket allows light into a medium that the eye can interpret correctly to offer a much more precise and sharper view. Again, the mask distorts this, but FoV is often limited and requires adaptation to a narrower field of regard.

Poor Visibility and Adaptation Strategies
- **Water Clarity Factors:** Visibility is affected by the amount of particulate matter, plankton, and sediment in the water. In clear, tropical waters, visibility is often color-coded. The normally murkier or more nutrient-rich waters in colder regions may allow only inferior visibility and create an almost claustrophobic environment for a diving operator.
- **Low-Light Training:** Such training in varying light conditions would familiarize divers with low and high-visibility conditions. Diving at low lighting conditions, either because of greater depth or high particulate content, encourages a

diver to be focused not on their eyesight but rather on other sensations, thus developing space orientation. A diver, hence, builds confidence in maintaining orientation in conditions that are either too difficult or impossible to control.

Color Perception Underwater

Color Absorption: Its weird absorption of water is such that, with the depth the divers are operating at, there is a change in the visible light spectrum. First, the red light of about 5-10 meters gets instantly absorbed as it hits the shallow depths since it has the longest wavelength, as orange and yellow get absorbed as the diver goes down further. It is at about 30 meters that colors other than shades of blue and green get filtered out. Therefore, the monotone would make shades of the two colors in the underwater world.

Safety and Navigation: Colour loss affects the degree to which equipment and markings are visible. High-contrast and fluorescent-coloured gear is commonly used at sites where safety is questioned. These colors last longer, allowing divers to view essential things like lines, buoys, and other cautionary signals further down in the water.

Visual Focus and Adjustments

Accommodation of Eye: The latter may be due to the differential density of air and water, as the human eye cannot accommodate the changed focus required underwater. Masks with lenses allow an air space that may maintain clarity of vision, though not necessarily as straightforward as that obtained in the air.

Training for Visibility: Repeated dives into waters of different natures—explicit or murky—teach the freediver to adapt immediately to the eventuality of a loss of visibility. He will learn practically how to grasp every little visual hint at changes in the environment in light of particles' movements, for instance, not to lose orientation and to employ all his skills underwater.

2. Heat Regulation: The Science of Thermoregulation in Water

Body temperature is one of the most critical variables for freediving, mainly as longer or multiple dives are performed. As a medium, water conducts heat from the body up to 25 times quicker than air. This can easily lead to hypothermia if divers do not take precautionary steps.

Why Heat Loss Is Faster in Water
- **Density and conductivity:** Water is denser than air and more thermally conductive, so it draws heat from the body much more efficiently. Even at water temperatures that may feel comfortable after some time in the water, the body rapidly loses heat, which is critical to muscle function, reflexes, and overall performance.
- **Core Temperature Maintenance:** The core temperature must be kept within one's comfort zone for high performance and safety. A drop in core body temperature reduces coordination capabilities, reflexes slacken, and cognitive functions are compromised when there is a chance of cold water shock or hypothermia.

The Body's Natural Thermoregulatory Responses
- **Peripheral Vasoconstriction:** The most common example of peripheral vasoconstriction is immersion in cold water, which decreases the rate of blood circulation through the skin and extremities to retain more heat inside the core organs. This state of adaptation protects vital functions but quickly leads to sensations of numbness or reduced dexterity in fingers and toes.
- **Shivering:** The human body has an involuntary response to shivering and can generate heat through muscle activity. This mechanism is effective but also potent. It raises the oxygen consumption rate, which is unsuitable for freedivers who need to conserve the precious supply of oxygen while prolonging breath hold.

Protective Means and Equipment
- **Wetsuits:** Neoprene wetsuits are an excellent commodity in providing thermal insulation. During this process, thin layers

of water between the suit and skin get trapped; these warm up with the body's heat, almost like an insulating barrier. The thickness of the wetsuit would vary depending on the water temperature and the duration of the dives. Common ones include the following:
- **3mm suits:** These suits should be worn in warm water conditions where a minimum of insulation is required.
- **5mm to 7mm suits:** These will be useful in cold waters and keep people warm and protected.
- **Hood, gloves, and booties:** These will cover the head, hands, and feet accordingly so that no more heat is lost and keep those body parts insulated. Usually, much more heat is lost through the head. Hence, a fitted hood is essential since sometimes some dives take longer than expected by a significant margin.
- **Dry Suits:** These are worn over a diver in icy water, and a layer of air insulation keeps the diver's body completely dry. Due to their increased buoyancy and bulk, dry suits are rare in free diving, though they may be used in some specialized dives.

Pre-Dive and Post-Dive Strategies
- **Pre-Dive Warm-Up:** Warm up before the dive to prepare the body for the water conditions and reduce initial shock before entry. The warm-up includes light exercises and dynamic stretches that increase blood flow and raise the body's general temperature.
- **Post-Dive Recovery:** It is essential to have your body heating up as fast as possible right after the dive so as not to allow further heat loss. Use towels, dry robes, or thermal blankets to get your core temperature back quickly quickly quickly. Besides, drink warm fluids.

3. Buoyancy Control: How to Achieve Neutrality and Efficiency

Buoyancy is the most basic yet crucial skill a free diver should know. It defines how a diver travels through the water; energy will be wasted or conserved, further reflecting the possibility of performing with better oxygen consumption. This lets the divers make even smoother and more efficient dives and ascents.

Buoyancy and the Principles involved

Archimedes' principle states that any object partly or fully immersed in any fluid is buoyed upward by a force equal to the weight of the fluid, which one object displaces. Thus, diver density, the quantity of air in his lungs, and the type of equipment used finally create a difference in buoyancy.

Positive, Neutral, and Negative Buoyancy:
- **Positive Buoyancy:** When a diver floats effortlessly at the surface due to air in his lungs or buoyant equipment.
- **Neutral Buoyancy:** This is where a diver neither rises nor falls and is said to be in an ideal state, economizing on energy and oxygen at that depth.
- **Negative Buoyancy** allows the diver to sink without effort and can only be achieved beneath a neutral buoyancy point. It enables the diver to initiate free fall, which can then be used to save energy during a dive.

Buoyancy Control Techniques
- **Lung Volume Management:** Buoyancy is determined by the air volume in the lungs. A full breath equals plus buoyancy, and objects breathing out result in negative buoyancy. In this case, a diver can regulate buoyancy to neutral simply by changing the volume of his lungs at differing depths.
- **Weighting Systems:** Such systems exist, and they are designed to supply divers with weight belts and neck weights to counteract the buoyancy force exerted by their bodies and wetsuits. That way, the neutral buoyancy at 10-15 meters deep is reached during descents and ascents. Appropriate weighting is essential: too much weight makes a person struggle upwards, and when the weight is too low, there may be problems with going down.

- **Free-Fall Technique:** This would make it fall freely without kicking into the free-descent technique; neutral buoyancy would do that. Completely relaxed, the diver must allow this to happen; gravity pulls him down, economizing energy and oxygen consumption. Free-fall capability realizes efficient descent through a streamlined body position with complete relaxation.

The almost not-moving descent teaches neutral buoyancy and fine-tuning pressure during training.
- **Lung Volume Management:** Buoyancy is determined by the air volume in the lungs. A full breath equals plus buoyancy, and objects breathing out result in negative buoyancy. In this case, a diver can regulate buoyancy to neutral simply by changing the volume of his lungs at differing depths.
- **Weighting Systems:** Such systems exist, and they are designed to supply divers with weight belts and neck weights to counteract the buoyancy force exerted by their bodies and wetsuits. That way, the neutral buoyancy at 10-15 meters deep is reached during descents and ascents. Appropriate weighting is essential: too much weight makes a person struggle upwards, and when the weight is too low, there may be problems with going down.
- **Free-Fall Technique:** This would make it fall freely without kicking into the free-descent technique; neutral buoyancy would do that. Completely relaxed, the diver must allow this to happen; gravity pulls him down, economizing energy and oxygen consumption. Free-fall capability realizes efficient descent through a streamlined body position with complete relaxation.

Respiratory Mechanics and Cardiovascular Responses of the Body in Conditions of Freediving

Freediving is amongst the most extreme challenges that could be thrown at the human body. This requires tremendous physical strength and, in the same breath, huge command over sophisticated physiological mechanisms. Two of the major constituents in the realm of free diving are respiratory mechanics and cardiovascular responses. The above descriptions deal with the efficiency of the diver's oxygen consumption rate at which CO_2 would start to rise in the body and adapt to the unparalleled stresses associated with deep water pressure. To safely explore those limits, however, a freediver needs information about how those systems work and interact under conditions peculiar to breath-hold diving.

1. Breathing Mechanics: Principle of Breath-Hold Mastery

Though breathing mechanics are simple, they involve a highly integrated interaction of the muscles, air-pressure gradients, and lung structures. Thus, the freediver must perfect the breathing mechanics to ensure optimal oxygen intake and more prolonged, efficient dives.

Anatomy and Physiology of Breathing
- **Diaphragm and intercostal muscles**: The huge dome-shaped diaphragm muscles contribute to respiration. During inspiration, they contract and move down, expanding the thoracic cage and building up negative pressures, drawing air into the lungs. Intercostals between the ribs raise the ribs, lifting the rib cage further and expanding the volume of the lungs.
- **Lung Structure**: Lung anatomy includes millions of tiny air sacs-alveoli-where this described exchange of oxygen and CO_2 occurs. The more the air volume reaches the lungs, the greater the amount of oxygen that can be captured into the blood. Bearing that in mind, freedivers will try to increase the effect by employing unique breathing methods.
- **Pressure Gradient**: Even in the normal process of respiration, the gradient pressure acts between the two environments, namely the lungs and the external environment. During inspiration, it is always a fact that the air pressure inside the lungs decreases compared to the outside pressure, letting the

air move inside. It pushes out air once its internal pressure exceeds it, and it deflates during the relaxation of the diaphragm and intercostal muscles. It is upon exhalation.

Advanced Techniques of Breathing in for Freediving
- **Diaphragmatic Breathing:** Divers breathe in by moving their diaphragm to take slow, deep breaths to fill their lungs. This pattern of breathing is very efficient in absorbing oxygen. It relaxes the diver, slows the heart rate, and usually works very well during a breath hold, considering that the parasympathetic nervous system works as an entire system.
- **Full Lung Inflation/Pack:** This is an advanced technique employed by professional, free divers to secure a record, which takes their lungs beyond their limits. This effect helps "pack" minute sips of air in the mouth because of total inspiratory volume and oral and throat muscle action. It is through the stretching of lung tissue to hold more air. However, this is to be done vigilantly so that overdistension of the tissue should not occur, whereby imminent lung lesions may ensue.
- **FRC Diving / Diving:** While diving, exhalation, partial or complete, can simulate the condition of deeper dives. Under that condition, the human body can adapt to more significant pressure and reduced oxygen reserves in a submerged human. The diving within FRC shall build up a tolerance for a high level of CO_2 in the blood, ing, resulting in hypoxia, which rapidly conditions it to handle depth.

1. Lung Adaptation and Compression at Depth

Boyle's Law and Lung Volume: Boyle's LAW and Boyle's Law relate the Law to gas pressure on that gas. The greater the pressure, such as during the diver's descent, the greater the compressive force on air within the lungs. This is because the pressure at 10 meters below the water surface makes the lungs feel half the volume from the volume at the surface. This effect increases with the greater area of dive more profound, where the challenge for the human body lies in functioning at minimum lung capacity.

Residual Volume (RV) is the air volume that remains in the lungs after expiration. This volume is excellent and considerable, allowing the lungs to not collapse due to pressure. Training the body to handle dives within a lung volume nearing an RV will enable one to avoid barotrauma and create an avenue for safe deep diving.

Blood Shift Mechanism: The blood shift mechanism is the most miraculous adaptation the human body can achieve. As the pressure compresses the lung, plasma moves out of the blood into the lung's capillaries and fills the space created to maintain the integrity of the lungs without letting the lung collapse. This adaptational Response becomes a response when divers reach beyond 30 meters in depth; hence, it is an essential aspect of the resounding Response.

2. Efficiency and Safety in Cardiovascular Responses

Free diving, for example, involves a set of fundamental cardiovascular system processes that ration the oxygen supply by limiting blood circulation. These processes form part of the evolutionary adaptation known as the mammalian or diving reflex. Through this reflex, mammals have generally allowed their bodies to limit oxygen supplies to only the vital organs.

Bradycardia: Slowed Heart Rate
- **Definition and Function:** Bradycardia-definition and action: slowing the rate of face immersion underwater and at the onset of breath-hold conserved oxygen since metabolic requirements have been reduced and the heart's demand for oxygen has become low enough to serve the lessened metabolic requirements. In the trained breath-hold diver, for example, bradycardia can reduce heart rate by up to 50 percent, thus allowing more efficient use of oxygen stores.
- **Vagus Nerve Activation:** One of the most determining factors would have to be the vagus nerve. Cold water in contact with the face will further increase this effect by communicating the need to slow the heart rate to the nervous system. This

reflexive incidence of bradycardia may occur more strongly in divers who are more profound or more adept at this activity.
- **Oxygen Conservation Benefits:** As heart rate slows, so does oxygen consumption; this enables divers to stay in the water longer, delaying hypoxia or low oxygen levels.

Peripheral Vasoconstriction: Re-directing Blood Flow
- **Mechanism**: That would be peripheral vasoconstriction, the constriction of the blood vessels of the limbs and other non-vital organs to divert blood to vital organs like the brain, heart, and lungs. While that is being conducted, one fundamental mechanism might help conserve breath-hold oxygen to support vital organ function.
- **Adaptive Significance**: This frees the diver's bottom time because oxygen is supplied to the body's most needed parts. Through practice, this physiological response shows that divers are at their best during dives and use oxygen well. Response.

The Spleen and Oxygen Boost.
- **Spleen Contraction**: The spleen also serves as a reservoir for oxygenated RBCs; during dives, it contracts to increase the number of circulating RBCs and, hence, the blood's oxygen-carrying capacity. Thus, iturns an unpermanent quantum rise in available oxygen.
- **These benefits**: After repeated exposure to apnea, the spleen hardens to fight the condition by supplying increased oxygen. This action complements the body's built-in mechanisms for increasing endurance underwater.

Adjustments to Blood Pressure

Maintaining Circulation: Despite bradycardia during a dive, blood pressure does not lower because it rises due to vasoconstriction. This helps maintain good circulation to the brain and heart and allows the proper amount of oxygenated blood flow to be delivered to these organs.

Balanced Response: Although blood pressure supports circulation, the corpse's cardiovascular systems are trained for Response. The Response is safe and progressive training; the body adapts to such responses without strain.

3. Techniques of Training for Improved Respiratory and Cardiovascular Efficiency

Therefore, target training would help the freediver cope better with breathing mechanics and cardiovascular responses. Exercise will also improve lung capacity, build tolerance to CO_2, and optimize the natural dive reflex.

Breathing Techniques for Lung Optimization

CO_2 Tolerance Training: The training involves several breath holds for fixed lengths. One lets one's breath out and holds it out for fixed lengths of time, with rest times between each hold that are gradually reduced. Thus, the body gets used to handling more and more CO_2 little by little and quickly suppresses the urge to breathe. Hence, one can hold his breath longer.

Tables of O_2: The tables of O_2 are designed so that fixing the resting periods increases the times for breath holding. This training form accustoms the body to hypoxia and increases low oxygen condition tolerance.

Diaphragm and Rib Cage Flexibility Training: Again, yoga exercises—with deep inhalation methods combined with stretches—will help open up the diaphragm and intercostal muscles' elasticity. Cobra, bridge, and upward dog open the chest cavity for deeper and more proficient breathing.

Cardiovascular Conditioning for Free Diving

Static Apnea Water Training: The human body can use bradycardia to save oxygen. At that specific moment, your training will have needed to provide the head with ways to relax when the levels of CO_2 are on the rise; all this reinforces psychological and physical resistance.

Dynamic Apnea Training: Dynamic apnea is underwater swimming without breathing in pool diving conditions. It also prepares the body for physical effort during the dive. This time, dynamic apnea adds some movements to breath-holding and trains your cardiovascular system to cope well with oxygen and CO_2 during physical activities.

Cold water adaptation means that after constant stimulation by cold water, the more effective dive reflex will increase bradycardia and the strength of vasoconstriction. Such training in cold water will also help divers dive in more excellent conditions, as the more pronounced dive response allows one to extend and improve his breath-holding time.

It will include visualization exercises, where the divers enact the dive in all minute details in their minds, like successful descents, relaxed free-falls, and controlled ascent. This visualization technique comforts the person by reducing anxiety and furthers the physiological Response to stressful situations.

Mindfulness and Meditation: Introducing mindfulness response training helps divers stay composed, focused, and alert. Deep meditation before entering the water during a dive relaxes the individual by slowing the heartbeat and improving the Bradycardia response.

InteRespiratory Mechanics and Cardiovascular Responses of the Body in Conditions of Freediving

Freediving is amongst the most extreme challenges that could be thrown at the human body. This requires tremendous physical strength and, in the same breath, huge command over sophisticated physiological mechanisms. Two of the major constituents in the realm of free diving are respiratory mechanics and cardiovascular responses. The above descriptions deal with the efficiency of the diver's oxygen consumption rate at which CO_2 would start to rise in the body and adapt to the unparalleled stresses associated with deep water pressure. To safely explore those limits, however, a freediver needs information about how those systems work and interact under conditions peculiar to breath-hold diving.

1. Breathing Mechanics: Principle of Breath-Hold Mastery

Though breathing mechanics are simple, they involve a highly integrated interaction of the muscles, air-pressure gradients, and lung structures.

Thus, the freediver needs to perfect the breathing mechanics so that oxygen intake is optimum and longer and more efficient dives are realized.

Anatomy and Physiology of Breathing
- **Diaphragm and intercostal muscles:** The huge dome-shaped diaphragm muscles contribute to respiration. During inspiration, they contract and move down; thus, the thoracic cage expands, and negative pressures build up in the thoracic cavity, drawing air into the lungs. Intercostals between the ribs raise the ribs, lifting the rib cage and further expanding the lungs' volume.
- **Lung Structure:** The human lung anatomy includes millions of tiny air sacs-alveoli-where this described exchange of oxygen and CO_2 occurs. The more air volume reaches the lungs, the greater the amount of oxygen that can be captured in the blood. Freedivers, therefore, try to increase this effect by employing unique breathing methods.
- **Pressure Gradient:** Even in the normal process of respiration, the gradient pressure acts between the lungs and the external environment. During inspiration, the air pressure inside the lungs continuously decreases compared to the outside pressure, allowing air to move inside. Once the internal pressure exceeds it, the lungs push out air, deflating during the relaxation of the diaphragm and intercostal muscles upon exhalation.

Advanced Breathing Techniques in Freediving
- **Diaphragmatic Breathing:** Divers breathe in by moving their diaphragm, taking slow and deep breaths to fill their lungs.

This pattern of breathing is very efficient as far as taking in oxygen is concerned. It also relaxes the diver, slows the heart rate, and usually works very well during a breath hold, considering that the parasympathetic nervous system works as an entire system.
- **Full Lung Inflation/Pack** is a more specialized technique used by professional, free divers to record the extent of their lungs beyond their limits. This effect helps "packute sips of air in the mouth because of total inspiratory volume and oral and throat muscle action.It is through the stretching of lung tissue to hold more air. However, this is to be carried out vigilantly so that overdistension of the tissue should not occur, whereby imminent lung lesions may ensue.
- **Exhale Diving (FRC Dive):** During diving, exhalation may simulate the condition of deeper dives either partially or fully. Under that condition, the human body can adapt to more significant pressure and reduced oxygen reserves a submerged human undergoes. The diving within FRC shall build up a tolerance for high levels of CO_2 in the blood, resulting in hypoxia that rapidly conditions it to handle depth.

Lung Adaptation and Compression at Depth
- **Boyle's Law and Lung Volume:** Boyle's LAW AND Boyle's Law relate the volume of a gas to the pressure on that gas. The greater the pressure, such as during the diver's descent, the greater the compressive force on air within the lungs. This is because the pressure at 10 meters below the water surface makes the lungs feel half the volume from the volume at the surface. This effect increases with the greater area of dive more profound, where the challenge for the human body lies in functioning at minimum lung capacity.
- **Residual Volume (RV):** This is the air volume remaining in the lungs following a maximal expiration. The quantity and volume are large and significant, allowing the lungs not to collapse due to pressure. Training the body on how it handles

dives within a lung volume nearing an RV will enable one to avoid barotrauma and create an avenue for safe deep diving.
- Blood Shift Mechanism is the most miraculous adaptation the human body can achieve. As pressure compresses the lung, plasma moves out of the blood into the lung's capillaries, filling up the space created to maintain the integrity of the lungs without letting the lung collapse. This adaptational Response allows divers to reach beyond 30 meters in depth, an essential Response feature.

2. Responseency and Safety in Cardiovascular Responses

For instance, it has been said that with free diving, a set of natural processes involving the cardiovascular system comes into play, rationing the oxygen supply by limiting blood circulation. These processes are part of evolutionary adaptation called the mammalian or diving reflex. Through the Response, mammals generally allowed their bodies to limit oxygen supplies to only the vital organs.

Bradycardia: Slowed Heart Rate
- **Bradycardia-definition and action:** slowing the heart rate with face immersion underwater and at the onset of breath-hold conserved oxygen since metabolic requirements have been reduced and the heart's demand for oxygen has become low enough to serve the lessened metabolic requirements. In the trained breath-hold diver, for example, bradycardia can reduce heart rate by up to 50 percent, thus allowing more efficient use of oxygen stores.
- **Vagus Nerve Activation:** One of the most determining factors would have to be the vagus nerve. Cold water in contact with the face will further increase this effect by communicating the need to slow the heart rate to the nervous system. This reflexive incidence of bradycardia may occur more strongly in divers who are more profound or more adept at this activity.

- **Oxygen Conservation Benefits:** As heart rate slows, so does oxygen consumption; this enables divers to stay in the water longer, delaying hypoxia or low oxygen levels.

Peripheral Vasoconstriction: Re-directing Blood Flow
- **Mechanism:** That would be peripheral vasoconstriction, the constriction of the blood vessels of the limbs and other non-vital organs to divert blood to vital organs like the brain, heart, and lungs. While this is being conducted, one crucial mechanism might help conserve breath-hold oxygen to support vital organ function.
- **Adaptive Significance:** This frees the diver's bottom time because oxygen is supplied to those parts of the body that need it most. Through practice, these physiologic responses become responsive, and divers are at their best during dives and use their oxygen supply well. Response.

The Spleen and Oxygen Boost.
- **Spleen Contraction:** The spleen acts like a reservoir for oxygenated red blood cells. During dives, it contracts to increase the number of circulating RBCs and, hence, the blood's oxygen-carrying capacity. Thus, it returns a temporary quantum rise in available oxygen.
- **These advantages:** After repeated exposure to apnea, the spleen hardens to fight the condition by supplying increased oxygen. It continues to act with the body's built-in mechanisms to increase endResponsenderwater.

Adjustments to Blood Pressure
- **Maintaining Circulation:** This is because, despite bradycardia during a dive, blood pressure does not decrease since it rises due to vasoconstriction. This helps keep good circulation going to the brain and heart, allowing the proper amount of oxygenated blood flow to be maintained for delivery to these organs.
- **Balanced Response:** Although response blood pressure supports circulation, the corpse's cardiovascular systems are

trained for response changes, such as safe and progressive training, and the body learns to adapt to such responses without strain.

3. Techniques of Training for Improved Respiratory and Cardiovascular Efficiency

Therefore, target training would help the freediver cope better with breathing mechanics and cardiovascular responses. It would also improve lung capacity, build tolerance to CO_2, and optimize the natural dive reflex.

Breathing Techniques for Lung Optimization

CO_2 **Tolerance Training:** The training involves several breath holds for Response Lengths. One lets his breath out and holds it out for fixed lengths, gradually reducing rest times between each hold. Thus, the body gradually gets used to it, absorbing more CO_2 and quickly suppressing the urge to breathe, allowing one to hold his breath longer.

Tables of O_2: The tables of O_2 are designed so that if the resting periods are fixed, the time for breath holding increases. This training accustoms the body to hypoxia and increases tolerance for low oxygen conditions.

Diaphragm and Rib Cage Flexibility Training: Again, yoga exercises—with deep inhalation methods combined with stretches—will help open up the diaphragm and intercostal muscles' elasticity. Cobra, bridge, and upward dog open the chest cavity for deeper and more proficient breathing.

Cardiovascular Conditioning for Free Diving
- **Static Apnea Water Training:** The human body can turn on a bradycardia process to save oxygen. At that particular moment, your training will have had to provide the head with ways to relax when the levels of CO_2 are increasing; this is important for reinforcing both psychological and physical resistance.

- **Dynamic Apnea Training:** Dynamic apnea is a type of underwater swimming without breathing in the pool conditions of diving, but also in preparation for the body's physical effort during the dive. This time, dynamic apnea involves adding some movements to breath-holding and training the cardiovascular system to cope well with oxygen and CO_2 during physical activities.
- **Cold water adaptation** means that after constant stimulation by cold water, the more effective dive reflex will increase bradycardia and the strength of vasoconstriction.

Such training in cold water will further adapt divers to dive in more excellent conditions, too, since for the more pronounced dive response, one can extend his breath breath-hold and over his breath-holding time visualization exercises, whereby the divers enact the dive in minute detail in their minds, such as successful descents, relaxed free-falls, and controlled ascent.

Visualization comforts the person by reducing anxiety and furthers the physiological response to stressful situations.

Mindfulness and Meditation: Introducing mindfulness durinResponsese facilitates' remaining composed, focused, and alert. Deep meditation before entering the water and during a dive relaxes the individual by slowing the heartbeat and improving the bradycardia response.

4. Interconnectedness of Breath and Cardiovascular Responses

These are tight, interrelated mechanics of breathing and cardiovascular responses to the experience of freediving: developing a system that maximizes oxygen use, increasing levels of CO_2-and safely adapting to changes in pressure.

Lung Compression and Connectedness of Breath and Cardiovascular Responses**

These are tight, interrelated mechanics of breathing and cardiovascular responses from the experience of freediving that develop a system for making the most of oxygen, increasing CO_2 and responding safely to changes in pressure.

4. Physiology of Breathing and Cardiovascular Responses in the Condition of Freediving

Freediving can be one of the most potent tests elicited in the human body.

The feat requires nothing but great physical strength combined with perfect and intricate control over complicated physiological mechanisms.

On the other hand, the mechanics of breathing and cardiovascular response to the body are significant prerequisites for being a good freediver.

Equations like this become useful when summation is required, such as determining how much oxygen a diver retains and how much CO_2 is produced and absorbed in the body during dives.

Knowledge of this mechanism of breathing through depth helps the free diver avoid taking undue risks while stretching one's limits in extreme conditions while holding one's breath during diving.

Scuba diving and breath-hold diving are elementary skills. However, due to respiratory mechanics, common opinion has combined them, although techniques may differ.

This intuitively is not so complicated when one envisages the whole breathing process as highly integrated: the reaction of muscles, the pressure difference in the air, and the structural form of the lungs.

The best breathing can condition the freediver to take in more oxygen and manage the CO_2 so that the diver can stay underwater longer with less effort.

This dome-shaped diaphragm is the major inspiratory muscle.

During inspiration, it contracts; hence, it flattens down-lifting the chest cavity. Thus, it creates negative pressure inside it that sucks air into the lung. Intercostals between ribs elevate the rib cage to provide room inside the lungs.

Within the lungs, there are millions of sacs called the alveoli. These provide sites for exchanging gases within the body, where O_2 and CO_2 are exchanged.

Thus, the greater the volume of the inhaled lung, the greater the amount of oxygen to diffuse into the blood. Contrasting this, what the freediver has to increase upon by employing a few selected breathing techniques is precisely the opposite.

The atmospheric or barometric pressure gradient is from the lung to the outside atmosphere.

Therefore, a fall in pressure would mean the inspiration of air within. Inspiration is characterized by an inspiratory center in the pons, which sends a stimulus for breathing through the contraction of the diaphragm and intercostal muscles' contraction of the lungs' pressure below that of the surrounding air pressure, allowing its movement into the lungs. It is allowed to run out with simultaneous complete relaxation of the diaphragm and the intercostal muscles due to contraction of the thoracic cavity.

This incidence increases the lung's inner pressure and pushes air out.

Apnea in Advanced Sport of Freediving

Diaphragmatic breathing: The major muscle is the diaphragm, which separates the chest and abdominal cavity.

A freediver can engage this muscle by utilizing a profound control, such as inhalation, and allowing the lungs to fill with air.

Breathing that encourages increased oxygen consumption to activate the parasympathetic nervous system, which builds generalized relaxation and reduces heart rate, is crucial for effective breath hold.

Full Lung Inflation-Pack: This is one of the advanced techniques freedivers carry.

It means the process in which a lung is packed.

The other explanation is that the lungs are extended beyond the diver's natural capacity.

That means they extend the tissues of the lungs beyond a full inspiration; therefore, they carry more air with them and pack small sips of additional air due to the muscles around the mouth and throat.

The fineness of practice to be cultivated here would be not to allow over-expansion of the lungs, for gradual injury might occur.

Diving-exhalation diving (FRC Diving) is the most frequent form of diving. It involves partial or complete exhalation before diving.

The conditions of dives that have to be adapted are much more profound.

Thus, they must respond to the pressure increases with low oxygen stores.

That would only allow the body to become accustomed to large quantities of CO_2 and, hence, acquire resistance to hypoxia.

Be that as it may, such mechanisms exist to save the animal against the ravages of great depth.

1. Lung Adaptation and Compression at Depth

Boyle's Law and Lung Volume The famous Boyle's Law states that the volume of anything is inversely proportional to the pressure applied to it.

In other words, it is inversely proportional to depth--the deeper one goes, the greater the pressure, and with every meter of depth gained, the air in the lungs compresses just that little bit more.

At every ten meters of depth, the pressure doubles compared to the pressure on the surface, reducing the volume of the lungs twice.

With every dive, automatically, the body goes down deeper.

With the increase of depth, a body starts building up the capacity to work with the involvement of a smaller volume of lungs.

Residual volume, or the air that remains in the lungs even after expiration, has occurred as entirely as possible. Since stroke is a volume that keeps the lung from collapsing due to such pressure, training the body to sustain such dives—at one moment when the volume of lungs approaches RV—avoids barotrauma and hence allows for safe diving to deep levels.

The most astonishing adaptations concern a blood shift mechanism.

Compressive pressurization forces blood plasma to enter the lung capillaries and fill the compression-pushing area.

This simply allows the lungs to stay intact at depth and not collapse.

This adaptive response is critical for divers beyond 30 meters and essential to deep dive safety.

2. Cardiorespiratory Responses: Efficiency and Safety

One of the most astonishing changes in the cardiovascular system of the human body is the physiological changes associated with diving.

This kind of change is related to augmented efficiency associated with oxygen consumption and utilization of the blood.

Everything is summed up in the mammalian dive reflex, and physiological adaptation is common in all mammals, which confers the body's ability to prioritize using oxygen in the vital organs.

Bradycardia: Slowed Heart Rate

This form of bradycardia, or slowing of the heart rate associated with the onset of breath holding and face immersion in water, is considered a mechanism for conserving oxygen stores through the reduced metabolic demand of the heart.

A trained freediver may experience a 50 % reduction in heart rate, enabling them to utilize the available oxygen stores more effectively.

This override of the diving reflex allows the vagus nerve to terminate in the bradycardia at the bottom of the dive itself. In addition to this effect, facial stimulation from cold water was reported to the nervous system to slow down the heartbeat.

The deeper the diver is, along with his proficiency, the deeper his reflex for the bradycardia will be.

Oxygen Conservation Benefit: The above effect would conserve oxygen by allowing the diver to extend his time in the water, thus prolonging the first stage of hypoxia.

Peripheral Vasoconstriction: Shunting of Blood Flow

This includes blood-occluding reflexes from the extremities and non-vital organs that supply blood to the more significant parts of the body, including vital organs such as the encephalon, heart, and lungs. Indeed, this preserves oxygen in breath-hold dives since it maintains the essential process.

Adaptive Value The reflex spared oxygen for the freediver and pumped into the more needy body parts of the diver; hence, the freediver could spend more time at the bottom. Physiological is built a practice for engraving into diver providing oxygens oxygen supply for long freedives.

Spleen and Oxygen Boost
- **The spleen contraction:** The spleen is one of the organs storing RBCs. It is better defined as an oxygen storage facility. Because the spleen contracts during a dive, more RBCs circulate, resulting in a sudden but significant increase in oxygen supply.
- **Training Benefits:** Repeated exposure to breath-hold conditions strengthens the spleen's response, which is in a better position to supply supplementary oxygen if needed. This adaptation forms part of the body's built-in mechanisms for extending underwater endurance.

Blood Pressure Adjustments

Blood Circulation: All diving activities have been said to increase blood pressure through a decreased heart pulse rate, medically known as bradycardia.

The only assurance of the appropriate amount of blood and its passage continuing correctly into the brain and heart would be narrowing down the size of the blood vessels for the passing of adequate oxygenated blood into the different organs themselves."

A balanced Response, though this would raise the blood pressure, allowing the blood to pass through physiologically, should train the cardiovascular system against such a response. Safe, progressive training allows the body to adapt to such responses without stress.

3. Training Techniques for Respiratory and Cardiovascular Efficiency Improvement

Perfection in breathing mechanisms and the responses of the cardiovascular system would further fine-tune the art of the freediver. On that count, training can further hone the art of the freediver by improving lung capacity, building up tolerance for higher CO_2, and better using the natural dive reflex.

Breathing Techniques for Lung Optimization

Other forms of training try to teach a person how to build resistance to CO_2. Suppressing urges to breathe easily might help one adapt to high concentrations of CO_2 and increase the time spent holding a breath.

Apply such that the O_2 training tables are integrated. Once fixed rest periods are integrated into the O_2 tables, one can build up one's breath-hold time. This exercise acclimatizes the human body against Hypoxia, Which is an efficient method of building up tolerance against conditions of low oxygen supply.

Diaphragm and Rib Cage Mobility: Yoga relaxes many free divers, as most have bigger diaphragms working in cooperation with elastic intercostals, much like any other significant breathing technique. Cobra, Bridge, and Upward Dog open the cavity for the ribs to take more profound and functional breaths.

Cardiovascular Conditioning for Free Diving

This static apnea training program causes higher rates of bradycardia. It maintains oxygen levels in a well-controlled atmosphere. Progressively increasing CO_2 underneath the work relaxation is a core part of performing static apnea training, which is one way to improve the practitioner's psychological and physical tolerance.

Special training is also carried out, including breath-holding and swimming in the pool to stimulate the dive condition. Dynamic apnea contributes to highly conceptual breath-holding only by preparing the cardiovascular system for the economical processing of oxygen and CO_2 during physical work.

It invariably responds to its subjection to cold water by further increasing bradycardia and peripheral vasoconstriction. Cold water immersion training may be essential to any diver's acclimatization to cold water diving.

There is a time allowed to let your breath hold. Extending breath-holding hyper-response enhances the performance the diving response causes.

Visualization Drills and Relaxation Techniques

Visualization drills are dives of the mind, that is, in diving. The divers are ready, set, and prepared for a descent, relaxed freefall, and controlled ascent. Visualization lessens anxiety and primes the body's response to stress.

Mindfulness and meditation keep a diver's mind quiet, focused, and limpid. Deep meditation before diving affects heart rate due to the resultant relaxation effect, and indeed, it proves to be salutary as an input into the bradycardia response.

This will correspond to très low oxygen consumption and moderate rise in CO_2 pressure; hence, changes would have remained within safety limits w.r.t. mechanics of breathing and circulatory reResponseuring apnea diving.

Lung Compression and Circulatory Adaptations

Pulmonary Volume and Pressure: Although lung pressure increases with depth, the volumizing volume reduces circulation through the cardiovascular system and maintains oxygen supply to the critical organs. The blood shift response cooperates to allow the diver to endure the most extreme pressure without injury to the lung lesions.

Heart Rate and Oxygen Maintenance: Bradycardia is the primary balancing mechanism in the body regarding oxygen supply; it is, hence, an essential factor in maintaining oxygen levels. This slowed-down heart rate is communicated through the flattened lungs of divers by way of reduced oxygen supply to collect times for a more extended breath-holding period.

Control of CO_2 and Vasoconstriction

Tolerance to CO_2 other than by vasoconstriction: The response of the body would be to emphasize major organs having raised concentration of CO_2, and with this type of response, the respiratory drive will be e retardByBy, by specific training diver a diver ng, may acquire CO_2 tolerance so that the underwater time could pro couldoalsolson air hunger is delayed.

Priority in Oxygen Delivery: Peripheral vasoconstriction ensures that delivery prioritizes the brain and heart, keeping nearly all functions running if the general oxygen supplies go down.

Conclusion

Knowledge of the mechanics of breathing control and proper ideas about circulatory-vascular responses are the most essential things a free diver can possess. The diving response, called the returning physiological mechanism, optimizes oxygen consumption with increased CO_2 by including support pressure for deeper dives. Therefore, they would stay in the middle during the quest for better performance and safety. This presupposes that a person has to train the reflexes with awareness and progressive practice in greater depth and time with confidence, for it is in the body itself, within the narrow limits of man's resistance and elasticity, that the drive's demand must be fulfilled.

Freediving Techniques and Equalization

This incredible aquatic sport, freediving, unites physical prowess, mental focus, and adaptation by the human body to survive extreme environmental conditions. It is more than the mere holding of breath; instead, it is about attaining a perfect balance between efficiency and pressure management for safe and practical exploration of the underwater world. It needs precision in body mechanics, efficient propulsion techniques, and equalized pressure while descending deeper. These will be honed through training and practice that will take the diver to another level by going deeper and keeping himself safe and in control.

This guide covers essential freediving techniques and equalization methods, focusing on efficiency, safety, and control. In addition to the critical strategies above, it emphasizes respiratory health and flexibility exercises to develop and prepare the body for potential demands.

1. The Science and Importance of Equalization in Freediving

Equalization balances pressure between the external environment and internal air spaces in the body, a process that is particularly pertinent to the ears, sinuses, and lungs. As depth increases, water pressure compresses the air spaces, and if equalization is not done correctly, the resulting discomfort or injury will impede a diver's progress.

Preventing Barotrauma: Barotrauma occurs when the body's airspace doesn't equalize the external pressure on the ears, sinuses, or lungs, causing pain or damage.

Maximizing Comfort and Focus: Successful equalization enables a diver to remain relaxed and focused, which is critical for conserving oxygen and achieving greater depth.

Enhancing Depth Capability: Deep diving, where lung compression limits available air for standard methods, requires advanced equalization techniques.

2. Techniques in Equalization: The Keys to Successful Freediving

Equalization technique mastery equates with learning and understanding different ways and techniques better for depth and experience level.

Frenzel Equalization

Brief: Frenzel is currently widely employed by intermediate to advanced freedivers. This technique is highly effective and rarely requires considerable effort, and oxygen consumption remains close to a minimum.

Working Principles

Mouth-air compressions act and route back to the Eustachian through the tongue and soft palate.

The throat is closed, and the divers achieve equalization without using the diaphragm or lungs.

Steps:

Close the nasal by pinching the nose

Close glottis to close air inside the mouth

The lower tongue works as a piston to push air into the ears to equalize their pressure.

Benefits: This type works well at deeper levels and saves oxygen.

Overview: The mouthfill is an advanced technique for deep dives where lung compression significantly reduces the availability of air for equalization. How It Works: Divers trap air in their mouths early in the dive and use that air for equalization as they go deeper. The tongue and cheeks compress the stored air, directing it into the Eustachian tubes. Steps: Take a deep breath at a shallow depth and store air in your mouth.

Seal the glottis to keep the air in your lungs separate. Use the tongue and cheek muscles to manage air release for equalization. Benefits: This technique is essential for dives beyond 30 meters, as other methods for equalizing may not work due to lung compression. Valsalva Equalization Overview: Valsalva is a simple technique meant for beginners. One exhales gently against the pinched nose to equalize the pressure. Steps: Pinch your nose and close your mouth. Lightly exhale to force air into the middle ear.

Limitations: Much less practical at greater depths owing to the amount of effort and increased oxygen consumption.

Hands-Free Equalization

Overview: In hands-free equalization, the Eustachian tubes open with throat and jaw muscles without nose pinching.

Benefits: Can equalize continuously without interrupting streamlining or movement

Best For: Advanced divers who have considerable control over soft palate and throat muscles

3. Advanced Equalization Techniques for Extreme Depths

As divers push the boundaries of depth, specialized techniques are necessary to manage the increasing pressure challenges.

Sequential Equalization

What It Is: A rhythmic approach to equalization where divers perform controlled, repeated actions to adapt to changing pressure.

How It Works:

Equalize consistently every 1–2 meters during descent to prevent pressure buildup.

Benefits: Ensures smooth and comfortable progression, especially during deep dives.

Wet Equalization

What It Is: A technique in which water in the nasal cavity or mask creates more areas for air trapping and equalization of pressures.

Best For: More Advanced No-Limits or Variable Weight disciplines when extreme depths are attained.

4. Efficient Streamlining through Body Positioning

Efficient body positioning helps minimize drag and conserve energy by consuming less oxygen while providing easy passage through water.

Duck Dive Descending into Depth

Technique :

Inhale a complete and comfortable breath.

Bend at the waist, with arms extended forward while submerging the upper body.

Forceful leg kicks to propel the body downward.

Goal: To be smooth without splash for a good dive start.

Finning Techniques

Bilateral Finning: Employed by powerful, controlled kicks from the hips. Knees should be relaxed, with toes pointed for minimal drag.

Monofin Technique: A dolphin-like motion involving the entire body in a wave pattern. This is ideal for speed and depth but requires practice for precision.

Kick-and-Glide: By switching between kicking and gliding, divers can maintain momentum with minimal energy expenditure.

Free Fall: The Passive Descent

What It Is: D divers reach a point in the water where they become negatively buoyant and can passively descend without kicking.

Technique:

Relax entirely and let gravity take your body downward.

Pay attention to staying lean to reduce drag.

Focus on being more economical with oxygen in this phase while engaging with equalization.

5. Stretching to Enhance Equalization and Lung Health

Diaphragmatic, thoracic, and neck flexibility is essential to promote equalization and optimally fill your lungs.

Diaphragm and Rib Cage Stretches

How: Increasing flexibility allows for more profound expansion and easier equalization of the lungs.

Examples

Diaphragm Stretch: Fill your lungs with air and hold it, pushing your stomach out. Now, exhale slowly.

Intercostal Stretch: With one arm over your head, bend to one side to stretch the intercostals.

Neck and TMJ Exercises

Benefits: It allows the person to have more muscle control when equalizing.

Examples:

Neck Rolls: Slowly circle the neck, releasing tension in this area.

Jaw Stretches: Open and close your jaw from side to side to loosen the muscles while equalizing.

Lung Capacity Training

CO_2 and O_2 Tables: Breath-hold training tables improve tolerance to high levels of CO_2 and low availability of O_2, hence enhancing the performance of a dive.

Blowing up Balloons: This inflates balloons and strengthens the diaphragm, increasing the lung volume.

6. Training and Mental Preparation

Equalization and body positioning take time and mental preparation to perfect.

Dry Practice

Equalization Drills: Practice Frenzel or mouthfill equalization on land to build up your neuromuscular pathways.

Visualization: Practice dive simulations, emphasizing equalization with the timing of descents.

In-Water Training

Shallow Dive Drills: Practice equalizing every 1–2 meters to refine time and coordination.

Dynamic Apnea: Practice equalizing while moving to simulate conditions in actual dives.

Relaxation and Focus

Mindfulness and Meditation: Relax and reduce stress to increase focus in dives.

Breathing Exercises: Controlled breathing before dives can help lower heart rate and oxygen consumption.

Conclusion

Mastering equalization and freediving techniques will make dives efficient, safe, and enjoyable. Techniques involve streamlined body position, effective finning, and more advanced equalization methods like the Frenzel and mouthful to negotiate greater depths confidently. Performance is enhanced through regular practice, flexibility training, and mental preparation, enabling freedivers to tap their full potential and explore the underwater world with ease and speed.

Safety Procedures and Rescue Skills: The Buddy System and Static Buddying

No other sport can provide such a view of the underwater world as freediving does. Yet, it is not without its dangers: extreme physiological stresses due to breath-hold and pressure change can develop into life-threatening situations. Knowledge of safety protocols and rescue skills will enable the freediver to train and explore confidently. The buddy system and static buddying represent cornerstones of safe freediving practice, putting a systematic and reliable risk mitigation methodology into place.

The buddy system promotes teamwork and vigilance, while static buddying provides critical support during static apnea training. This extended manual examines the principles, practices, and benefits of these essential safety protocols in their application and contribution to preventing accidents and safeguarding every freediver's well-being.

1. The Buddy System: A Lifeline for Freedivers

The buddy system is the foundation of freediving safety, with divers working in pairs or small groups to monitor each other's work, freediving from being a solitary activity into a shared experience where each diver assumes responsibility for his safety and that of his partner. Partner's Principles of Buddy System**

1. Constant Vigilance: Buddies are aware of the visual and situational aspects of the dive, from surface preparation through descent, ascent, and recovery, and they always observe the diver for signs of distress or difficulty.

2. Shared Responsibility: The buddy system thrives on mutual accountability. Both the diver and the buddy share equal responsibility for ensuring safety, requiring open communication and pre-dive planning.

3. Immediate Response: In an emergency, the buddy can immediately assist, execute rescue techniques, and seek additional aid if necessary.

Roles and Responsibilities in the Buddy System

The buddy system has well-defined roles, ensuring accountability and a smooth process related to safety.

1. Active Freediver:
- Can execute the dive with safety considerations in mind while adhering to plans and signals pre-agreed upon.
- This member informs the buddy before and after the dive about depth, time, and special needs.
- Have Confidence in the buddy watching your safety and Confidence whenever necessary.

2. Buddy (Safety Freediver):
- The safety diver monitors the active diver through the entire dive, being positioned to observe and immediately act if necessary.
- During the descent and ascent, the buddy positions themselves to intercept the diver in an emergency.
- Ensures the active diver completes recovery breathing upon surfacing and is stable before returning to their role.

Pre-Dive Planning and Communication

Pre-dive planning is part of the buddy system, where both divers ensure they are on the same page regarding safety procedures and expectations.

1. Discussion of Dive Plan:
- Depth, time limit, and purpose of the dive shall be agreed upon.
- Signals for assistance, distress, or to abbreviate the dive shall be established.

- Emergency procedures shall be reviewed along with your buddy's potential incidents.

2. Safety Check:

All gear fins, masks, and lanyards should be in good condition.

Ensure that both divers are physically and mentally healthy to perform the dive.

3. Hand Signals:

The standard hand signals for communication underwater may include, but are not limited to, "OK."

2. Static Buddying: Safety in Static Apnea Training

Static apnea is usually a form of breath-hold in a pool. Though less physically demanding than the dynamic disciplines, this discipline can produce unique symptoms after a long duration of holding one's breath, such as hypoxia and blackout. Static buddying is an exceptional development of the buddy system tailored for these risks.

Why Static Buddying is Important

1. Risk of Hypoxia and Blackout

When the breath-hold is prolonged, the blood oxygen level decreases during static apnea. This low oxygen level can paralyze all body functions, producing hypoxia and even blackouts if the body's limit is exceeded.

2. Need for Immediate Assistance:

In static apnea, there is no movement to rely upon as a distress signal. In this regard, the buddy needs to be observant and ready to act instantly if his buddy goes unconscious or reaches a state of LMC.

Role of the Static Buddy

Under the principle of Marcello's full responsibility, Budd, who monitors his condition in case rescue support is needed, has all the vision.

1. Pre-Dive Preparation:
- Discuss the estimated recovery time with the diver.
- Clearly define signals for assistance or termination of the hold.
- Establish the diver's physical and mental readiness.

2. Active Monitoring:
- The attendant stays at the water pool, maintaining continuous visual eye contact.
- Estimates time to predict when the diver may reach the near-maximum limit.
- Monitor the diver for any sign of distress, such as erratic movements, bubbles, or sudden loss of buoyancy.

3. After-Dive Recovery:

Helps the diver with recovery breathing: slow and steady exhales, then deep, controlled inhales.

Check the condition of the freediver after each session to ensure they are fully stable before continuing.

Static Apnea Rescue Techniques

In emergencies, the static buddy must move quickly and confidently to get the diver up to safety.

- **Blackout Rescue:**

1. Gently support the divediver'sediver's divediver'sacdiver'saceurface

2. If obstruction exists, such as a mask, remove it to clear the airway.

3. Give verbal reassurance such as a breath (e.g., "Breathe, you're safe").

4. If not breathing, start rescue breathing and call for medical help.

- **LMC Support:**

1. Relax the diver so the air passage is out of the water.

2. Guide them through recovery breathing until they recover to complete motor control.

3. Observe them in case of persistent symptoms and advise them to rest without activity until such time.

3. Buddy System - Benefits and Static Buddying

1. Risk Mitigation: The buddy system dramatically reduces the chances of accidents, as divers are never left to their own devices. Buddies can immediately provide assistance to prevent minor problems from becoming out of proportion.

2. More Confidence: trained buddies will monitor their safety. Confidence allows divers to focus entirely on performance and push themselves harder and more confidently.

3. Improved Learning: Buddies of confidence and observations create opportunities for mutual growth and skill development.

4. Tips to Implement Buddying Easily in the Water

1. Training Together: Regular practice of rescue techniques will keep both divers updated and ready for emergencies.

2. Building Trust: Trust forms the base of the buddy system. Both divers must be combustible, assured about each other, and take active safety measures.

3. Consistency: It instills the buddy system in every session, involving good habits and safety within the scope of freediving itself.

5. Conclusion

Buddy system, static—these safety protocols within freediving ultimately make it a shared responsibility because divers rely on each other to keep one another safe and successful. By following this protocol, freedivers can push their limits, learn about their potential, and confidently have a closer encounter with the underwater world through repetitive, confident communication. The buddy system is no longer just a question of safety; it's the backbone of every freediving adventure.

2. Identifying the Signs of Distress in Freediving: LMC and Blackouts

Freediving represents one of the most beautiful and burdensome sports, testing both human endurance and adaptation to extreme limits. On the other hand, beauty and attraction involve certain risks, which require great attention and preparation to manage them. Among the greatest dangers in freediving, some of the most serious dangers are LMC, or Loss of Motor Control, and blackouts, basically physiological responses resulting from oxygen deprivation during longer or deeper dives. Awareness of these conditions is one cornerstone of freediving safety: the sooner a condition is detected and treated appropriately, terrible consequences can be avoided and saved.

This tutorial will review the nature of LMC and blackout: their causes, signs, and key responses. Once freedivers and their buddies understand these risks and how to deal with them, their time underwater will be safer and more predictable while enjoying their sport.

1. Understanding Loss of Motor Control (LMC)

LMC, commonly referred to in freediving parlance as "d "sam" al, is a temporary loss of voluntary muscle coordination caused by a lack of adequate oxygen fed to the brain. It is not as extreme as a blackout but a definite warning that the diver is entering or has reached his physiological limit. LMC usually occurs in the last few moments of a dive, especially while ascending or immediately after surfacing.

What Happens During LMC

When the oxygen level in the blood falls below the level necessary to sustain adequate functioning, the brain sacrifices some non-critical functions, like voluntary motor control, to maintain more vital functions, like respiration. The outcome includes involuntary movements, muscle weakness, and loss of coordination.

Causes of LMC

1. Prolonged Breath-Holding: Oxygen supplies are used up, and dive times are longer, which can lead to hypoxia.

2. Rapid Ascents: During an ascent, the partial pressure of oxygen in the lungs is lowered, rapidly reducing the amount of available oxygen.

3. Hypercapnia: High levels of carbon dioxide (CO_2) increase the extent of hypoxia, thus increasing the risk of developing LMC.

4. Poor Recovery Breathing: Lack of sufficient re-oxygenation between dives can increase the risk of LMC.

Signs of LMC

Recognition of LMC symptoms by the diver or a buddy will ensure quick action to avoid complications.

1. Visible Shaking or Tremors:

Minor involuntary muscle spasms, often in the hands, arms, or head, are common symptoms of LMC.

2. Unsteady Movements:

The diver will not be able to stay in a streamlined position during the ascend or even be unsteady upon reaching the Surface.

3. Blurred Vision or Dizziness:

The brain's inability is due to a lack of oxygen or an inability to focus and feel oriented.

4. Weak or Irregular Breathing:

Shallow gasps, sometimes irregularly characterize labored or interrupted recovery breathing.

5. Partial Loss of Awareness:

The diver may be partially unconscious and only responds to verbal commands and touch very slowly or not at all.

2. Understanding Blackouts

A blackout is a total loss of consciousness due to severe hypoxia. Unlike LMC, which in most cases gives some warning, blackouts may appear without any precursors, suddenly and unannounced, in the ascent or immediately after surfacing. Because of this, they are one of the most dangerous risks during freediving and require immediate and decisive intervention.

What Happens During a Blackout

When oxygen levels become so low, the brain shuts off all non-vital functions, including a person's consciousness, to deny oxygen supply to all but the most vital organs, such as the heart. This can result in unconsciousness and possibly life-threatening complications if not dealt with promptly.

Causes of Blackouts

1. Shallow Water Blackout:
- It occurs during ascent when the partial pressure of oxygen in the lungs falls rapidly due to reduced water pressure.

2. Longer-Than-Normal Dive Duration:
- Even with the proper technique, prolonged breath-holding can reduce oxygen levels and, thus, cause hypoxia.

3. Hyperventilation:
- Overbreathing before diving by reducing the CO_2 levels in the blood postpones the urge to breathe but simultaneously increases the risk of hypoxia.

4. Insufficient Recovery Time Intervals:
- Not taking enough time between dives to replenish oxygen within the body may contribute to the likelihood of a blackout occurring.

Warning Signs for a Blackout

A quick identification of a blackout is essential to provide life-saving assistance.

1. Sudden Unresponsiveness:
The diver suddenly stops moving and becomes limp or lifeless.

2. Passive Floating or Sinking:
The body sanguinely floats upwards or sinks with no controlled movement.

3. Pale or Cyanotic Appearance:
Bluish lips or pale skin are signs of severe oxygen deprivation.

4. Absence of Breathing:
The diver does not start recovery breathing upon reaching the Surface.

5. Not Responsive to StimSurface:
The diver does not respond to verbal signals, taps, or other forms of stimulation.

3. Reacting to Distress Signals

A proper reaction to an LMC or blackout can be the difference between life and death. The buddy should remain calm, act quickly, and resort to standard rescue procedures.

For LMC

1. Assist the Diver to the Surface:
- In the case of the LMC surface, assist the diver in reaching the suSurfacehile maintaining the surface runway above the water.

2. Support Recovery Breathing:
- Instruct the diver to exhale entirely and take deep, slow, steady breaths to replace the quantity of oxygen.

3. Give Verbal Reassurance:
- Speak calmly and clearly: "You're just breathing," effectively relaxing the diver.

4. Monitor Recovery:
- Observe the diver for residual symptoms and allow the complete stabilization of the diver before proceeding.

For Blackout

1. Bring the Freediver to the Surface:
- Protect the diver's head and bring their face out of the water to avoid drowning.

2. Clear the Airway:
- Move away obstructions, including snorkels or masks, to ensure an open airway.

3. Stimulate Breathing:
- Verbal encouragement: say, such as "Breathe now," or gently blow across the face.

4. Rescue Breathing:
- If the diver does not start breathing immediately, give rescue breaths (two breaths to start, then one every 5–6 seconds).

5. Transport for Medical Care:
Even if the diver regains consciousness, a medical checkup is necessary to eliminate possible complications.

4. Prevention of LMC and Blackouts
Proper Pre-Dive Preparation
- Do not hyperventilate before a dive.
- Adequate rest and hydration to achieve peak physical condition.

Buddy System
- Dive with a similarly qualified, alert buddy who can effect a rescue.

Recovery Breathing
- Employ controlled exhalation, then inhale deeply to balance out oxygen and CO_2 in the body after each dive.

Gradual Training
- Gradually increase dive durations and depths to enable the body to adapt safely.

Know Your Limits
- The most crucial thing is always listening to your body and never forcing it beyond what feels safe, even during training or competition.

5. Conclusion
Recognizing and responding to distress signals, such as LMC or blackouts, is fundamental to safe freediving. By identifying the causes and symptoms, divers and their buddies can take immediate action to help prevent accidents and allow for safe recovery. Vigilant monitoring of proper training and adherence to prescribed safety protocols enable the freediver to enjoy the underwater world with the least risk. In other words, it is about exploring the depths of respect for the human body while keeping safety paramount.

3. Rescue Techniques for LMC and Blackouts

Freediving is a very demanding sport on both physical and mental levels. In addition to physical preparation, one must learn how to behave in specific emergencies. The two most hazardous states of emergency in freediving are LMC and blackout. In both cases, immediate intervention is necessary and should be as effective as possible; otherwise, the conditions will worsen due to rapid oxygen consumption, fast ascent, or overexertion.

This informative manual will discuss the rescue methods required for both LMC and blackouts so a diver and their buddy can quickly and appropriately respond in any life-threatening situation.

1. Understanding Loss of Motor Control (LMC)

What Is LMC

LMC, or "sambal," is a temporary loss of muscle coordination because of an absence of oxygen going to the brain. Commonly, a precursor happens in the last minutes of any dive or immediately after surfacing.

LMC Rescue Techniques

Speedy and unflustered actions assure divers' safety and recovery.

1. Assist to the Surface:

LMC is on the Surface. Passively bring the river to the Surfac, ttheSurfac, the Surface, the diver's airway, and the Surface out of the water, avoiding aspiration.

2. Stabilize the Diver:
- Generally, support the head and place the body horizontally for recovery.
- Grasp the chin or jawline to keep the airway open.

3. Encourage Recovery Breathing:
- Long, soothing verbal cues include "Exhale, then take slow, deep breaths" to get the diver started with recovery breathing.
- Recovery breathing is exhalation with slow and deep inhalations to regain oxygen.

4. Verbal Reassurance:
- Soothingly talk to them to help them compose their thoughts easily.
- Examples: "You are safe now," or "Concentrate on your breathing."

5. Monitor the Diver:
- Monitor the diver for at least 30 seconds after recovery for stability.
- If symptoms persist, rest the diver; diving is not recommended.

2. Understanding Blackouts

What Is a Blackout?

A blackout is a total loss of consciousness due to severe hypoxia. It can be sudden, without warning, especially during ascent, shallow water blackout, and immediately after surfacing. Unlike in LMC, in a blackout, the diver is completely unresponsive, and immediate action must be taken to avoid drowning or further complications.

A blackout diver rescue calls for urgency, precision, and calm execution in the name of survival.

1. Bring Diver to the Surface:
- Secure the freediver's head with one hand, keeping their face above water while using your other hand or legs to support their body.
- Maintain a firm grip to prevent their airway from submerging.

2. Clear the Airway:
- Remove any obstacles, such as snorkels or masks, that maobstructto the pathway of air.
- Look for apparent obstructions, such as water or other foreign objects.

3. Stimulate Breathing:
- Gently tap the diver's cheeks or blow softly across their face to stimulate the breathing reflex.
- Provide verbal encouragement, such as "Breathe now," to guide them back to consciousness.

4. Rescue Breathing, if Necessary:
- If, after a few seconds, a diver is unable to start breathing for them:
1. Pinch the nose shut.
2. Provide two initial breaths of resuscitation, blowing with your mouth sealed on the diver's mouth.
3. Continue the resuscitation with one breath every 5-6 seconds until he starts breathing again or until the arrival of medical personnel.

5. Call for Medical Attention:
- In case of unconsciousness only, even then, the diver, on regaining full consciousness, must be taken for a checkup at a medical facility because of possible lung barotrauma or due to injury from hypoxia.

6. Reassure and Monitor:
- Reassure the diver after gaining consciousness. Put under observation.
- Take plenty of rest from this incident and do not attempt dives so as not to build any further risks today.

3. General Best Practices for Rescues

Remain Calm and Focused
- Panic overemphasizes a situation and diminishes the positive results of rescue efforts. Stay as calm as possible to provide precise, confident assistance.

Protect the Airway
- For both LMC and blackout rescues, the most essential thing a rescuer can do is keep the diver's airway out of the water and open.

Act Quick but Safe
- While speed is essential, a rush may be dangerous and deteriorate the diver's condition.

Practice Often
- Regular training in rescue techniques will prepare the divers and their buddies to respond correctly in emergencies.

4. Prevention to Reduce the Chances of an Accident

Pre-Dive Preparation
- Avoid hyperventilation as this decreases the level of CO_2, thereby predisposing one to blackout.
- The diver must be rested, hydrated, and psychologically prepared for the dive.

Buddy System
- Dive with an appropriately trained and attentive buddy who can effect a rescue.

Recovery Breathing
- Recover breathing slowly and passively after every dive to stabilize oxygen and CO_2 levels.

Know Your Limits
Never exceed physical or mental limits, even in training.

5. The Importance of Regular Rescue Training

Rescue techniques are life-saving techniques that must be regularly practiced to become proficient. Many free diving organizations organized extra training courses and rescue into their training courses. These include:
- **Simulated Blackout Scenarios:** Real-life emergency scenario practice in controlled conditions.
- **Buddy Communication:** Distress and request for help- clear signals and protocols.

- **CPR and First Aid Training:** Basic requirements in handling more serious incidents.

6. Conclusion

Safety in freediving depends on alertness, preparation, and effective response in instances of an emergency. To this end, all freedivers and their buddies should know the signs and symptoms of both LMC and blackout; they should also be knowledgeable in applying rescue techniques that correspond to these incidences. A no-unsafe moment is having n while in the water regarding the minimum risk and acting calmly and swiftly without wasteful procedures. Continuous training, following safety, and looking after one's buddies are the cornerstones of a responsible and enriching freediving career.

4. Freediving: The Reduction of Risk, Safety Practices, and Decompression Sickness

The sport of freediving is astounding because it permits human beings to view the world underwater correctly. This sport requires massive awareness of safety protocols, physiological responses, and risk factors about oxygen management, blackout prevention, and hazard mitigation about decompression sickness, amongst many others. The proper training, knowledge, and adherence to all the established rules and measures relating to safety keep freediving safe and freedefreedivingproved guifreediving risk reduction, basic safety, and prevention of DCS in freediving have been beefefreedivinggh. This information helps freedivers remain safe and extend their diving careers.

1. Risk Reduction in Freediving

Freediving is anFreedivingcharFreedivingby physiological stresses and hostile environments. Risk reduction, therefore, focuses on minimizing possible hazards while improving the divers' preparation to cope confidently with sudden situations.

Understanding the Risks of Freediving

1. Physiological Risks
- **Hypoxia (Low Oxygen Levels):** The longer one holds one's breath, the longer he is exposed to lower oxygen levels, which may eventually cause a blackout or loss of motor control.
- **High Carbon Dioxide Levels (Hypercapnia):** The buildup of CO_2 within the body while diving could lead to anxiety, panic, and eventually, an inability to exercise pressure equalization.
- **Barotrauma:** Poor practices in descents or ascents result in injury due to the changes in pressure on the lungs, sinuses, or ears.

2. Environmental Hazards
- **Currents and Tides:** TUnderwatercurrents or tides might pull divers away from their intended course of movement.
- **Visibility Problems:** Poor water clarity can disorient divers, making navigation or communicating with a buddy complex.
- **Marine Life:** Most marine life is harmless; however, some can be dangerous if frightened or threatened.

3. Human Factors:
- **Overconfidence:** The most dangerous activity is reducing physical or mental margins.
- **Poor Breathing Techniques:** Hyperventilation or poor recovery breathing may increase the risk of blackout.
- **Disregarding safety procedures:** Neglecting a buddy system or not properly planning dives can increase the danger of an accident.

Key Strategies to Reduce the Risks

1. Gradual Training Progression:
- Increase depth and time in water only gradually, enabling the body to adapt safely.
- Never dive as if you are trying to be the best; instead, always be interested in your limits and performances.

2. Correct Breathing Techniques:
- Avoid hyperventilation before diving since this decreases CO_2 levels and prolongs the urge to breathe, increasing the risk of blackout.
- After every dive, breathing during the ascent to the surface allows oxygen and CO_2 to equalize properly.

3. PreDive Planning
- The dives should be planned about depth, time, and conditions.
- Describe the dive plan to a buddy: hand signals and emergency procedures.

4. Equipment Checks:
- All equipment is in good condition: fins, masks, and lanyards.
- There is buoyancy weighting for neutrality at 10 -15 meters for effective energy expenditure.

5. Environmental Awareness:
- Predisposition of water conditions regarding currents, temperature, and visibility
- Never dive in bad weather conditions or at an unfamiliar spot without preparation.

2. Basic Safety Procedures

Safety diving revolves around essential safety practices that all divers and freediving instructors should avoid. If one follows these rules, one can freedive safely or enjoy more confidence and control underwater.

The Buddy System

The buddy system is a crucial procedure in scuba diving. It requires never diving alone but with someone who observes their partner and helps when needed.

Roles and Responsibilities:
- **Active Diver:** Performs the dive to the planned and preagreed profile and signal.

- **Buddy (Safety Diver):** Observes the active diver performing the dive and intervenes immediately when necessary.
- **After the Dive Attention:** Wait until the driver's breathing has recovered, and then send him to another activity when he has recovered.

Operational Practices
- Constant visual contact
- Swimming, like in an ascent to rendezvous with his buddy by intercepting him if needed
- LMC or blackout rescue techniques

Recovery Breathing

Recovery breathing after every dive is essential for restocking oxygen and removing CO_2. An inability to do the recovery properly increases the chances of hypoxia or hypercapnia during successive dives.

Recovery Breathing Steps

1. Long and slow exhale to expel the CO_2.
2. Slow, deep inhalation should be done to fill your lungs, but beware of hyperventilation.
3. Do multiple cycles until you are back to your regular breathing.

Rescue and Emergency Operations

1. For LMC
- Accompany the diver to the surface while keeping his airway out of water.
- Teach recovery breathing using calming verbal cues.
- Observe the condition for continuing symptoms.

2. Blackout:
- Rush the diver to the surface and clear his airway.
- Stimulate breathing with verbal encouragement or light taps.

- If the diver is unconscious within seconds, rescue breathing should be given.
- The diver should be taken for further medical checkups.

3. Decompression Sickness in Freediving

Although developing decompression is less common, sickness can also occur during repetitive deep dives, freediving that Freedivingntervals are too short.

What Is Decompression Sickness?

DCS is a condition in which nitrogen-dissolved freediving fluid forms bubbles due to a sudden change in pressure. These bubbles may lead to joint pain and neurological complications, among other serious consequences.

Symptoms and Signs of DCS

1. Physical Symptoms:
- Joint or muscle ache is also commonly called "the bends."
- Feeling tired, weak, or stiff.

2. Neurological Symptoms:
- Lightheadedness, dizziness, confusion, or an inability to concentrate.
- Tingling sensations, numbness, or even partial paralysis in severe situations.

3. Skin Symptoms
- Itchy or mottled skin may signal problems associated with nitrogen.

Preventing Decompression Sickness

1. Adequate Surface Intervals:
- Give the body time between dives to off-gas nitrogen.
- A general rule is that one should rest at least for a period not less than twice the duration of the previous dive.

2. Controlled Ascents:
- Make a slow, even ascension to minimize nitrogen bubbles' formation and rapid expansion.
- Be sensitive around the last 10 meters because the pressure changes the most.

3. Dive Planning :
- Do not go for successive deep dives. Interspersing with shallow dives avoids excessive nitrogen absorption into the body.

4. Hydration:
- The body should always be well-hydrated to excrete the absorbed nitrogen efficiently.

Responding to DCS

Suspect DCS:
- Immediately cancel all diving.
- Allow oxygen administration to help in removing the nitrogen bubbles.
- Medical treatment provided in a hyperbaric chamber facility
- Diver observation for aggravation of symptoms and hydration

4. The Role of Education and Training

Education is the cornerstone of freediving safety, and onlonlytional, scientific, and technical education can help freedivers manage risks positively.

Freediving Courses
- freediving and certified breeding courses: risk management, rescue techniques, and decompression theory.
- Practice the usual training scenarios to become aware of yourself and prepare effectively.

Training in First Aid and CPR
- Knowledge of first aid or CPR administration may be lifesaving in an emergency.

5. Conclusion

It is an unusual combination of adventure and self-discipline, yet safety is paramount. By assuming attitudes of risk reduction, adherence to basic safety, and knowledge about decompression sickness, the freediver confidently and fully in control assumes his diving experience. Education, training, and vigilance allow the freediver to reap the benefits of freediving while making every dive as safe as thrilling.

Practical Aspects of BLS and CPR within Freediving as a Sport

Free diving is a very extreme sport, testing human limitations and connections with the underwater world. Perfect physical and psychic preparation and excellent attention to safety are required. The most critical skills that protect this sport are **Essential Life Support** and **Cardiopulmonary Resuscitation**. Availing these skills, the diver acts poised and effectively during a moment crucial for an emergency that may save one's life.

This value-added guide describes **BLS** and **CPR** in detail, explaining their importance to the free diver, how they are performed step by step, and advanced considerations about aquatic environments. The more knowledge and practice one has, the fewer risks one takes and the greater confidence one has in acting correctly in emergencies.

1. The Importance of BLS and CPR to the Freediver

Free diving is a sport that has an assortment of natural risks associated with the physiological stresses of breath-hold and depth-related pressure, not to mention the ever-changing aquatic environment. Blackouts, incidents of near drowning, or cardiac arrest can all happen in an instant, hence the need for BLS and CPR for all freedivers.

Key Reasons to Learn BLS and CPR

1. Immediate Response in LifeThreatening Situations
- Free diving emergencies can spiral out of control in seconds. The immediate action of BLS and CPR on the part of the divers stops further injury before help is on hand.

2. Buddy Diving in Safety:
- Free diving requires excellent reliance on a buddy system. Knowledge of practical life support covers the diver and his buddy.

3. Increased Confidence and Better Preparation:
- Mastering such techniques decreases panic during emergencies; thus, the diver can act calmly and accurately.

4. Required at Sites that are Remotely Located:
- Most of these sites are far from the nearest medical center. Essential Life Support stabilizes the casualty sufficiently well for them to reach advanced care.

2. Knowledge about Essential Life Support

BLS secures the patency of the airway, ensures adequate ventilation, and establishes breathing in the unconscious patient. It is indicated as the first intervention in emergencies and is critical to preventing neurological damage and other complications of anoxia.

Key Objectives of BLS
- **Restore Breathing:** ReestablishBreathingespiration to prevent hypoxia.
- **Support Circulation:** Maintain blood flow to vital organs to reduce the risk of organ failure.
- **Prevent Further Injury:** The rescuer controls the scene to protect a person from suffering an uncalled-for secondary complication of either drowning or a spinal injury.

The BLS Sequence

1. Check the Scene for Safety:
- Right before reaching the casualty, be it in the pool, lake, or ocean current, fast-moving water, and/or any floating debris pose endangerment to the rescuer and the victim.

2. Check for Responsiveness:
- Gently tap the casualty and ask, "Are you okay?" If there is no response, move on to the next one.

3. Clear the Airway:
- Lay the casualty flat on their back.
- Use the **head-tilt, chin lift technique** in opening the airway:
o Place one hand on the forehead and gently tilt the head back.
o With one hand on each side, tilt the head backward to support.

4. Look, Listen, and Feel for Breathing:
- For 5–10 seconds, see whether the casualty is breathing by:
o **Looking** for a rise and fall of the chest.
o **Listening** for air sounds past your ears from nostrils or mouth.
o **Feeling** for air on your cheeks.

5. If Not Breathing or Abnormal Breathing:
- Immediately institute direct rescue breathing to oxygenate the casualty's lungs.

6. Summon Help:
- Send any bystander available to call emergency services with the location and nature of the accident or injury.

3. Cardiopulmonary resuscitation, commonly called CPR

CPR is a lifesaving action that involves blood circulation and oxygenation through chest compressions and rescue breaths in cardiac arrest or severely hypoxic patients. It is indicated when the heart stops working or cannot pump effectively.

Steps for CPR

1. Position the Casualty:
- Lay the casualty flat on a firm surface.
- Head tilt and chin lift open the airway.

2. Begin Chest Compressions:
- Place the heel of one hand on the center of the chest well up from the sternum.
- Put your other hand on top of the first with your fingers interlocked.
- Extend your arms, but prepare to bring your shoulders over your hands.
- Compress the chest 5–6 cm (2–2.5 inches) at 100–120 compressions per minute.
- Fully release the chest to recoil between compressions and allow continued blood circulation.

3. Add Rescue Breaths:
- After each 30th compression, provide two rescue breaths:
o Pinch the nose of the victim shut,
o Breathe with your mouth sealed over theirs for about 1 second while simultaneously watching their chest rise to gauge the adequacy of ventilation.

4. Repeat Cycle:
- Continue the two breaths after every 30 compressions pattern until one of the following:
o The apparent casualty regains consciousness.
o Emergency personnel arrive on location and take charge.
o You cannot complete the dive due to physical incapacity.

4. Advanced Considerations for Freediving Emergencies

Drowning or NearDrowning
- Move the casualty into a lateral position before initiating BLS to drain water from the airway.
- Emphasize ventilation because anoxia is a significant danger when dealing with a drowning victim.

Blackouts
- Get an unconscious diver to the surface as quickly as possible while
- Mask/snorkel: this would first clear the airway and remove the obstruction.
- Utilize BLS immediately, but more about the rescue breaths since that's all he will need to recover his normal oxygenation state.

Spinal Injuries
- When there is suspicion of spinal injury, alignment of the head, neck, and spine is done throughout the process of rescue and transport.

Child and Infant CPR
- Children, ages 1–8 years:
o Compression with one hand.
o Compress the chest to about one-third of its depth.
o The breathing in resuscitation must be done with minimum force so as not to overinflate the lungs.
- Infants less than 1 year:
o Chest compressions can be done with two fingers.
o The breaths are given as soft, gentle breaths.

5. Importance of Training and Regular Practice

Constant training and hands-on practice maintain his ability to perform BLS and CPR. He will also stay updated on new protocols through regular refresher courses so he is confident in performing whatever may be required.

Recommended Training:

Take accredited courses from the following list, but not limited to the following organizations:
- Red Cross
- AIDA International
- PADI (Professional Association of Diving Instructors)
- DAN (Divers Alert Network)

Regular Training
- Practice rescue cases to get muscle memory.
- Practice on mannequins to perfect their skills in chest compressions and ventilation.

Higher Level Certifications:
- Advanced first-aid classes, including oxygen administration, to tackle complicated emergencies.

6. When to Seek Medical Attention

Even after one has successfully given BLS or CPR, there is a need for professional medical care to resolve the underlying conditions and to ensure full recovery. Seek advanced care in case:
- The victim does not respond to CPR.
- Decompression sickness: symptoms like joint pains, confusion, or other dizzy states. Severe damage to lungs or water inhalation

7. Conclusion

This water sport combines adventure with inherent risks; safety cannot be foregone. **An essential life support BLS** and **CPR** for any freediver enables him to respond to emergencies and, hopefully, save lives. The sure ways of perfecting those techniques and being alert are how to assure himself and his diving partners of safety. In short, freediving involves responsible, in-depth exploration: confidence to save a life when it comes to that.

Confined and Open Water Training: Apnea Games and Training in Confined Water

Freediving is the only sport that rushes the borders of physical, mental, and emotional endurance. This sport must be learned in controlled conditions in **confined** or controlled environments, open **water**, lakes, or deep reservoirs. Each environment offers unique advantages and challenges that contribute to the comprehensive development of a freediver. While confined water provides a controlled environment for divers to refine their technique and practice the fundamentals, open water offers real-life scenarios to adapt to depth, pressure, and unpredictability.

The most interesting variant for increasing the breath-holding capacity, mental strength, and relaxation of confined water training is making **apnea games**. These will enhance physical performance and help develop the mental clarity needed for freediving. This extended manual will broadly explain the benefits, techniques, and strategies of confined and open-water training, focusing on how apnea games can change the training paradigm.

1. The Role of Confined Water Training in Mastering Freediving

Confined water training is often the entry point for novice freedivers and a continuing process for advanced professionals. Pools and other controlled environments eliminate external risks, providing an ideal space for mastering the fundamentals.

Why Confined Water Training is Crucial

1. Safety and Control :
- Training in a predictable, hazard-free environment reduces the stressors of external factors such as currents, waves, and visibility challenges.
- Beginners can focus entirely on their breathing, technique, and mental state without concern for their surroundings.

2. Skill Refinement:
- Confined water training allows divers to perfect essential freediving techniques like equalization, streamlining, and recovery breathing.
- Practices of horizontal dynamic apnea will help divers enhance their finning techniques, streamline their bodies, and increase their lung capacity.

3. Immediate Feedback:
- Training in a pool allows instructors or buddies to provide real-time corrections, enhancing learning.
- Using video analysis in confined water helps divers visualize and correct their movements.

4. Mental Preparation:
- Confined water is a very relaxed environment where divers can develop their mental toughness and learn to manage stress and the increase in CO_2.

2. Apnea Games in Confined Water: Enhancing Performance Through Play

Apnea games are dynamic, funny ways to make training fun and effective. By incorporating competition, strategy, and fun elements, these exercises will motivate divers to push their limits while keeping them safe and concentrated.

Benefits of Apnea Games

1. Building CO_2 Tolerance:
- Games involving multiple breath-holds or restricted recovery periods help condition the body to tolerate high carbon dioxide levels, a significant element in endurance freediving.

2. Improving Mental Focus:
- Many apnea games require divers to remain composed and clearheaded under stress, emulating real-life scenarios in freediving.

3. Encouraging Teamwork:
- Most games are collaborative, building communication and trust among divers and their buddies.

4. Relaxation Techniques:
- By framing training as play, Apnea games reduce stress and help build relaxation, essential for freediving success.

Some of the Most Popular Apnea Games for Confined Water Training

1. Dynamic Relay Races:
- **How It Works:** Relay teams of divers swim underwater, taking turns and holding their breath for as long as possible.
- **Skills Developed:** Builds breath control, finning efficiency, and teamwork.

2. Underwater Retrieval Challenges:
- **How It Works:** The diver places Small objects at depth for retrieval with one breath.
- **Skills Gained:** Enhances spatial awareness, concentration, and lung capacity.

3. Longest Static Hold Competition:
- **How It Goes:** Divers try to hold their breath while remaining still in the water.

- **Skills Gained:** This enhances relaxation, CO_2 tolerance, and mental endurance.

4. Apnea Walks:
- **How It Works:** Divers hold their breath and walk along the bottom of the pool or, on land, a prepared path while focusing on relaxation and endurance.
- **Skills Developed:** Simulates an actual diving situation and builds endurance.

5. BreathHold Pyramid:
- **How It Works:** Divers breathe and increase the time they hold their breath while their recovery times remain constant with every attempt.
- **Competencies Gained:** Increases lung capacity, tolerance of CO_2, and mental control.

3. The transition from Confined Water to Open Water Training

Open-water training is the second stage of a freediver's development. It provides a platform for exploiting the skills developed in confined water in more dynamic and challenging environments. Depth, pressure, and environmental conditions challenge divers' adaptability and better prepare them for real-life situations.

Key Benefits of Open Water Training

1. Depth Progression:
- CWT, FIM, and CNF freediving disciplines can be effectively conducted only in open water.
- The ability to train at depth enables a diver to get used to the effects of lung compression, pressure change, and special equalization techniques.

2. Exposure to Natural Environments:
- Open-water diving teaches divers to adapt to variable conditions like currents, thermoclines, and visibility.
- Acquaintance with these phenomena familiarizes the freediver with various phenomena to build confidence and increase adaptability.

3. Application of Confined Water Skills:
- A range of skills developed and practiced in confined water is mastered by being transferred to open-water conditions.

4. Link with the Ocean:
- Openwater freediving elicits a connection with the ocean and living forms of the sea floor, building emotional and spiritual participation in the sport.

4. Integration of Confined and Open Water Training

Proper training should balance confined and open water to achieve all-around development of the skills.

Confined Water as Foundation
- Practice in pools to perfect static and dynamic apnea, recovery breathing, and CO_2 tolerance exercises.
- Master body mechanics like duck diving and streamlining in this phase.

Open Water for Application
- Transition to open water for deeper dives, equalization under pressure, and the ability to adapt to environmental variables.
- Add depth training and freefall techniques to develop confidence and efficiency.

Mental and Physical Conditioning
- Confined water sessions develop control and relaxation, while open water sessions develop resilience and adaptation to complex conditions.

5. Safety Considerations for Confined and Open Water Training

In Confined Water:

1. Never train alone; always with a buddy or under supervision.

2. Avoid hyperventilation before breath-hold exercises to minimize blackout risks.

3. Always notify lifeguards or other safety personnel of your activities.

In Open Water:

1. The proper equipment shall be used, including a buoy, dive line, and lanyard. 2. Environmental conditions, tides, currents, and visibility should be continually monitored.

3. Always dive with a buddy and preestablish clear safety procedures in advance.

6. Advanced Apnea Training Techniques

Further, divers enhance their skills with specialized techniques in confined water that are elated to open-water kills.

1. CO_2 and O_2 Training Tables:
- Gradually increase breath-hold times or decrease recovery to build tolerance and stamina.

2. Dynamic NoFins (DNF) Drills:
- Engage in swimming without fins underwater in the best positions for body positioning and strength in the water, in confined waters.

3. FreeFall Practice:
- Perform relaxed and streamlined freefall during open water dives to conserve energy and oxygen.

4. Visualization and Mental Rehearsal:
- Spend confined water time practicing mental focus and visualization for deeper open water dives.

7. Conclusion

Confined and open water training are the backbones of a freediver's training curriculum, each with its own set of importance complementing the other. Confined water allows for the safe learning of fundamentals, while open water provides a venue where divers can test and encounter dynamic conditions. Apnea games introduced an entertaining, fun addition to training in which there was physical and mental endurance and technical development. Mastery will be reached, confidence will be gained, and one can connect better with the underwater world by freedivers achieving a balance between these two types of training with safety protocols followed. Consistent practice combined with thoughtful progression makes the sport of freediving become less a skill as much as it is a lifetime passion.

Techniques and Safety in Open Water Diving

Open-water freediving guarantees the greatest freedom and immediacy with the underwater world. Still, the beauty and challenge of diving in natural, uncontrolled environments carry a unique risk and place peculiar demands. Mastery of **open-water freediving techniques** and adherence to **safety protocols** are necessary at all levels: training, competition, and exploratory.

It represents a guide that develops deep techniques and necessary safety precautions called for during open-water free dives to comprehensively achieve appropriate performance by minimizing risks during the entire experience with assurance out underwater.

1. Mastering Open Water Diving Techniques

Open water introduces a whole set of new variables: depth, pressure changes, currents, and visibility problems. The techniques need refinement to avoid wasting energy, maintain control, and adapt to variable conditions.

1.1 The Duck Dive: The Gateway to Depth

The **duck dive** takes the diver from the surface into a streamlined descent and is the essential start to any freedive.

Technique:

1. **Surface Position:** Lie on your stomach, filling and filling your lungs with air, then exhale partially to establish the setup position.
2. **Bend at the Waist:** Flex forward, positioning your torso vertically in the water.
3. **Leg Extension:** Lift one leg out of the water as the other starts down to create downward momentum.
4. **Arm Thrust:** Scull your arms downward, following through with a strong fin kick to continue down.
5. **Streamline Position:** Move into a horizontal or vertical position with a streamlined orientation, extending the arms above the head.

Common Errors to Avoid:
- Overexertion on the duck dive wastes oxygen.
- Shallow-angle entry into the water wastes unnecessary energy to correct the descent.

1.2 Streamlining: Minimizing Drag

The streamlined position reduces drag and allows positions to use less energy while moving, thus saving oxygen.

Key Techniques:
- **Body Alignment:** Keep your head aligned with your spine without leaning your chin upwards or downwards.
- **Core Engagement:** Engage your core muscles to maintain a straight, rigid posture.
- **Arm Position:** Extend your arms above the head in a hydrodynamically shaped position.

Benefits:
- More conservation of energy
- It is more straightforward to go down and come upwards

1.3 Finning Techniques: Power Meets Precision

Finning is responsible for moving the diver through the water downward and upward; hence, it is considered one of the most integral parts of open-water diving.

Basic Finning:
- Make a smooth, regular motion from the hips.
- Limit deep knee bends to conserve energy.

Advanced Techniques:
- **Dolphin Kick:** This movement in a dolphin's tail creates powerful propulsion. It generally applies to monofins.
- **Slow Finning:** Slower and slower fin motions allow for less use of oxygen.

Common Mistakes
- Over-kicking wastes oxygen and creates unnecessary turbulence.
- Jerky, abrupt movements instead of smooth, long strokes.

1.4 Equalization: Pressure Equalisation

Equalization is a method of equating the airspaces of the body with increased ambient pressure in the course of descent. This technique avoids discomfort, ear injury, and barotrauma.

Simple Techniques:
- **Frenzel Maneuver:** This is a commonly followed procedure in which the vocal cords are closed, and the tongue inflates the middle ear.
- **The Valsalva Maneuver** involves gently pinching the nose and blowing, which is easier for beginners but less effective at depth.

Advanced Techniques:
- **Mouthfill:** This is necessary during deep dives when air is stored in the mouth to equalize when lung volume becomes too small.
- **Sequential Equalization:** Coordinating multiple equalization methods to adapt to increasing pressure at greater depths.

Tips for Success:
- Equalize early and often before any pressure is felt.
- Equalize on land to develop muscle memory.

1.5 FreeFall: The Art of Relaxation

Freefall is a form of descent where the diver uses negative buoyancy to effortlessly sink without finning to conserve energy and oxygen.

How to Perform a FreeFall:

1. Reach neutral buoyancy at 10–15 meters.

2. Halt finning and relax all your muscles.

3. Assume an elegant position and let gravity take over.

Psychological Approaches:
- Mentally rehearse an easy, relaxed descent.
- Focus on your breath-hold and inner stillness, filtering out distractions.

2. Safety Considerations in Open Water Freediving

Safety protocols are paramount in open-water freediving because natural environments can be unpredictable. Observing these measures ensures a safe and enjoyable experience for all participants.

2.1 The Buddy System: The Core of Freediving Safety

Freediving should never be done alone. A well-trained buddy can provide monitoring, support, and rescue.

Buddy Responsibilities:
- Observe the diver from the surface and during the final ascent.
- Be ready to respond in an emergency, whether it involves a blackout or motor control failure.

Perform recovery breathing and do not change the course until the diver stabilizes.

Habits to Take into the Water:
- Establish signals for communication during a dive.
- Constantly have the active diver in view.

2.2 Plan and Brief

Good Plan = Low Risk = Fun

Dive Plan Components:
- Depth and time limits for each dive.
- Distress signals and recovery operations
- Evaluation of the conditions relating to current, tide, and visibility

2.3 Surface Procedures: Recovery Breathing

Recovery breathing is intended to replace oxygen and purge carbon dioxide. The procedure helps prevent shallow water blackouts.

Procedure:

1. Once breaking the water's surface, exhale forcibly.

2. Inhale long and slow while relaxing.

3. Continue until normal breathing is restored.

2.4 Monitoring Environmental Conditions

Open water conditions are volatile; therefore, appropriate situational awareness becomes crucial.

Factors to Monitor:
- **Currents and Tides:** Strong currents might carry the divers away from the point of origin.
- **Visibility:** Poor visibility increases disorientation.
- **Marine Life:** Knowledge of local species decreases dangerous encounters.

2.5 Emergency Preparedness

Every freediver should be informed about how to behave correctly in emergencies.

Rescue Scenarios:
- For blackout: Bring the diver to the surface, clear his airway, and stimulate breathing.
- For LMC: Assist the diver in stabilizing his breathing and monitoring his recovery.
- For decompression sickness: Seek immediate medical care and administer oxygen if available.

Training:
- Practice rescue drills regularly to build confidence and muscle memory.
- Keep up-to-date first aid and CPR.

3. Advanced Techniques for Open Water Freediving

Advanced techniques to help an experienced freediver improve performance and safety are as follows:

1. Negative Buoyancy Training:
- The training in descents with negative buoyancy increases comfort at depth.

2. Mental Conditioning:
- Visualization techniques prepare divers for deeper dives, helping them relax during such dives.

3. **Specialized Equipment Use:**
- The lanyard, buoys, and dive computer further enhanced freediving with immense safety and efficiency.

4. Conclusion

Open-water freediving incorporates athleticism, hardness of mind, and admiration for underwater nature. Mastering the techniques described herein, such as duck diving, streamlining equalization, and strict adherence to the basic safety protocols, will make every dive safe and enjoyable. Whether exploring coral reefs or training for competitive depths, preparation and respect for the environment remain key. The more refined your skills and the safer you are, the more potential open-water freediving will open up to you, with every dive an intense, life-changing experience.

Surface and Recovery Techniques in Open Water Freediving

Surface and recovery techniques are considered the foundation of freediving. Through these techniques, the diver is assured of their safety, clarity of mind, and body preparation for the next dive. These involve breathing techniques and a step-by-step procedure of maintaining oxygen and carbon dioxide levels, managing buoyancy and mental focus, and preparing the body for the stresses of underwater exploration. Mastery of such techniques allows the freediver to plunge to greater depths in longer lengths of time while returning safely to the surface, things no freediver can afford to be sans. The following detailed discussion elaborates on what a surface and recovery technique entails, why it is necessary, how best to perform them, and some tips to enhance recovery advance.

1. The Importance of Surface and Recovery Techniques

1.1 Prevention of Hypoxia and Shallow Water Blackout

Hypoxia, or a low supply of oxygen to the brain, presents one of the significant risks in freediving. SWB, a shallow water blackout, results from an abrupt loss of consciousness because of low oxygen levels during the final stages of ascent or after surfacing. Proper techniques of surface and recovery counteract these risks with the restoration of oxygen to improve mental alertness.

1.2 Restoration of Physiological Balance

Freediving disrupts the body's natural balance. Oxygen stores are depleted, carbon dioxide accumulates, and a few physiological changes occur under pressure. Breathing up and surface protocols help the body return to rest for the next dive.

1.3 Preparation for Other Dives

Recovery at the surface involves not only the postdive effects but also focuses on preparing for the next dive. Thus, it prepares the freediver physically and mentally to face further dives with utmost efficiency and minimum risk.

2. Mastering Surface Protocols

Freedivers should observe surface protocols just after surfacing. These protocols stabilize the body, oxygenate the tissues, and prevent complications.

2.1 Controlled and Gradual Surfacing

Technique:
- The ascent has to be made very girly, girly minimum during the last 10 meters, as pressure changes are quicker.
- Avoid sudden or jerky movements during ascent to conserve oxygen and maintain calmness.

Advantages:
- No sudden change in pressure leads to barotrauma or decompression sickness.
- Reduces shallow water blackout risk from acute oxygen starvation.

2.2 Clearing the Airway
- At the surface, tilt your head to one side and exhale explosively, if necessary, to blow residual water from your mouth or snorkel.
- Always keep your nose and mouth above the surface.

3. Recovery Breathing: The Heart of Surface Techniques

Recovery breathing is a conscious process of restoring oxygen and eliminating excess carbon dioxide. It is essential in maintaining body stability and avoiding any complications that may arise after dives.

3.1 The Process of Recovery Breathing

1. Exhale Fully:
- Let out all the air from the lungs immediately after the dive to eliminate the CO_2.

2. Inhale Deeply:
- Inhale slowly and deeply, allowing your lungs to fill with air.
- Allow your diaphragm to drop with every inhalation.

3. Control Exhalation:
- Slowly exhale without forcing it, keeping the pattern slow and rhythmic.

4. Repeat:
- Continue for several cycles until your breathing slows down to normal.

3.2 Psychological Benefits
- Recovery breathing normalizes oxygen levels, thus calming the mind and reducing anxiety or disorientation following a stressful dive.

3.3 Practical Tips
- Visual or mental triggers, such as counting or concentrating on the horizon, will enhance calm during recovery breathing.
- Recovery breathing needs to be practiced throughout training so that a response instinctively occurs for the diver.

4. Surface Intervals: The Key to Sustainable Diving

The surface interval refers to time spent at the surface between dives, allowing the body time to recuperate ahead of the subsequent descent.

4.1 Calculating Optimal Surface Intervals
- **General Rule:** Stay out for at least twice as long as your previous dive, resting.
  o **Example:** For a dive lasting 1 minute, the surface interval should be at least 2 minutes.
- More extended recovery periods after more profound or more star dives will prevent hypoxia or decompression sickness.

4.2 Benefits of Adequate Surface Intervals

1. Physiological Recovery:
- Provides time to eliminate the additional CO_2 and regain oxygen supplies.
- Cardiovascular activity also gets a chance to be normalized as a result.

2. Mental Recomposition:
- It helps relax and then refocus on future dive rehearsals mentally.

3. Reduces Chances of Certain Specific Dangers:
- Reduces chances of hypoxic events, blacks, or decompression injury problems.

4.3 Advanced Surface Interval Techniques
- Include light stretching or floating to enhance relaxation and muscle recovery.
- Hydrate between dives to prevent dehydration and ensure optimal performance.

5. PostDive Sensations and Recovery Strategies

Freedivers are likely to experience various physical and mental sensations right after surfacing. Adequate recovery strategies can effectively manage these sensations.

5.1 Common PostDive Sensations

1. Dizziness or Lightheadedness:
- Caused by lack of oxygen supply or changes in pressure rate.
- Addressed by focusing on controlled recovery breathing.

2. Fatigue or Muscle Tension:
- Because of the physical effort during the dive.
- Stretching, hydration, and relaxation techniques can help alleviate these symptoms.

3. Chest Discomfort:
- It may indicate a lung squeeze or mild water aspiration.
- Avoid further dives; if symptoms persist, seek medical attention.

6. Surface Recovery Safety

Safety during surface recovery cannot be overemphasized, especially in open water, where environmental factors can bring added complications.

6.1 Buddy Support
- A buddy must observe the diver closely for at least 30 seconds after surfacing. This is the critical period for shallow water blackouts.
- Verbal reassurance is given to help the diver focus on recovery, y breathing, g, and relaxation.

6.2 Environmental Awareness
- Monitor external conditions such as waves, currents, or sudden weather changes affecting surface stability.
- Flotation devices like buoys may provide additional support during recovery.

7. Advanced Surface and Recovery Strategies
More advanced freedivers can employ several advanced techniques to better their recovery and optimize performance.

7.1 Mental Visualization
- Use the surface interval to mentally rehearse the next dive, visualizing each phase with calmness and control.
- Visualize by practicing mindfulness techniques to reduce stress and enhance focus.

7.2 CO_2 Tolerance and O_2 Optimization
- Gradually decrease the recovery intervals while training to increase the threshold of high levels of CO_2.
- Practice longer exhalation during recovery breathing to increase oxygen utilization efficiency.

7.3 Hydrating and Nutritional Incorporation
- Hydrate, but not more than enough; being dehydrated would lead to poor recovery and performance.
- Ingest light energetic snacks in between dives to stock energy reserves.

8. Training Recovery Techniques

Freedivers should include surface and recovery techniques in every training to make the surface and recovery techniques second nature.

8.1 Dry Training for Recovery Breathing
- Practice land recovery breathing to learn the proper breathing technique and build muscle memory.
- Breathing exercises combined with yoga or meditation can strengthen lung capacity and relaxation techniques.

8.2 Simulated Surface Protocol
- Repeat the surface intervals in pool training for real-life scenarios and to perfect the timing.

9. Conclusion

Various methods are used in freediving's surface and recovery procedures for these purposes. These procedures prepare the body and mind for subsidies while orderly avoiding most complications regarding hypoxia, shallow water blackout, and decompression sickness. Mastering techniques, adopting advanced strategies, and strictly following safety will develop performance and build confidence. Hence, any recovered surface interval is a phase of recovery or separation.

Recovery and Rescue Skills in Confined and Open Water Settings

Recovery and rescue skills are integral to Freediving and affect the safety and well-being of the diver and buddy. Training in a controlled, confined, or unstable open-water swimming pool develops the confidence to act and react knowledgeably in an emergency.

Techniques for Recovery and Rescue in Confined and Open Waters This book focuses on preparation, practice, and awareness.

1. Importance of Recovery and Rescue Skills

1.1 Prevention of Severe Injury or Death

The dangers from freFreediving not only relate to blackout and hypoxia but also include conditions like hypercapnia and LMCs. Most of these conditions could be substantially improved if proper and timely intervention is carried out, which can make the difference between life and death.

1.2 Gain in Confidence

Knowing what to do in an emergency instills confidence and a degree of safety for the diver and the buddy.

1.3 Adaptation to Environments

Confined water is a space to train in a protected and controlled environment; open water demands depth, currents, and environmental adjustment.

2 Confined Water Recovery and Rescue

Like a pool, confined to a controlled environment to learn and master the uncovered recovery and rescue skills.

2.1 Confined Water Scenarios

Static Apnea Blackouts: An unconscious diver on breath-hold

Dynamic Apnea LMC: An LMC during underwater swim laps

2.2 Confined Water Recovery Techniques

1. Static Apnea Blackout Response
- Observe the diver for any sign of distress, such as twitching or uncontrolled movements.
- In case of blackout:
    o Gently turn the diver's face upwards to the surface.

- o Tilt their head to the back to clear their airway.
- o Verbal reassurance to breathe, "Breathe, you're ok."

2. Dynamic Apnea LMC Response:
- Count the diver's laps underwater and stay near them.
- If they give the signal for distress or suddenly surface:
  - o Positive buoyancy: Grab the chin and swim them to safety.
  - o Let them recover, breathe, and relax.

2.3 Confined Water Rescues
- Blackout or LMC can be simulated during training sessions.
- Signals and communications Practice to make it easy and smooth during emergencies.

3. Open Water Recovery and Rescue

Open water presents depth, currents, waves, and visibility. The ability to recover and rescue a diver in these conditions would need to consider such variables while offering safety to the diver.

3.1 Common Open Water Scenarios
- Blackouts During Ascent: Due to hypoxia, the diver becomes unconscious during the last few meters of ascent.
- Environmental Hazards: Currents, waves, or entanglement result in distress.
- Diver Disorientation: A diver may feel disoriented or confused in low visibility.

3.2 Recovery Techniques in Open Water

1. Surface Rescues:
- A diver blacking out or LMC at the surface:
  - o Provide urgent support to lift the victim's airway out of the water.
  - o Gently tilt their head backward to open the airway.
  - o Support recovery breathing while monitoring their air supply closely.

2. InWater Rescues:
- Inwater blackout on ascent:
  - Immediately and safely swim to the victim with your protection.
  - Reach for the victim from underneath the arms or across the chest.
  - Use aggressive, strong finning to take them to the surface.

3. Managing Currents and Waves
- Position yourself up the current of the diver to avoid any drift complications.
- Employ a buoy or a flotation device to stabilize yourself and the diver in recovery.

3.3 Apparatus for Open Water Rescues

Buoys and Dive Lines:
- Mark the position of a diver in sight and help in recoveries.

Lanyards:
- Keep the diver attached to the dive line and within reach.

4. The Buddy System in Recovery and Rescue

The buddy system is the cornerstone of freedivers' safety. A well-trained buddy ensures that every diver has immediate support during any emergency.

4.1 Buddy Responsibilities

PreDive:
- Briefing on the dive plan, depth, time, and emergency procedures.

During the Dive:
- Observe the progress of the diver and maneuver oneself for rapid response.

PostDive:
- Observe recovery breathing and do not continue until the diver has stabilized.

4.2 Effective Buddy Procedures

1. Positioning:
- Always stay slightly above the diver on the ascent to intercept any problems.

2. Communication:
- Communicate with your buddy using hand signals or gestures throughout the dive.

3. Proactive Observation:
- Always observe the diver's behavior and the ambient environment around them.

5. Training and Simulation

Constant practice will develop instinctive responses for recovery and rescue techniques in an emergency.

5.1 Simulation of Emergency Scenarios
- Instructors practice blackout and LMC in confined water.
- Gradually introduce open water with added current and wave conditions to promote adaptability.

5.2 Further Training
- Other courses in freediving cover safety and recovery.
- Take further CPR and first aid certification courses on responding to emergencies.

6. Psychological Aspects of Recovery and Rescue

Emergencies are stressful. The ability to remain calm and clear is a part of effective intervention.

6.1 Staying Calm Under Pressure
- Practice mindfulness and controlled breathing to manage stress.
- Trust your training and instincts to guide your actions.

6.2 Supporting the Diver Emotionally
- Be aware of the diver's response and reassure him calmly before, during, and after.
- Observe his mental state of condition and reassurance by

7. Conclusion

The Recovery and Rescue skills in Freediving confidently will, in both Confined Water and Open Water conFreedivingelp, the freediver acquire or master these skills necessary for minimizing the risks involved and also to be prepared against anything that may happen that contributes to a safe, positive experience for himself as also his buddies. It is an adventurous sport, yet secure and rewarding; it requires regular practice, following all the safety protocols, and continuous learning. A dive team will be prepared for and enter an underwater world with less anxiety and more confidence.

Physiology and Pathologies in Freediving

A Global Approach Related to Respiratory and Circulatory Systems

Freediving represents the most extreme sport, pushing physiology toward the most extreme limit. Human physiology requires extreme adaptation for such long breath holds and significantly related pressure gradients induced by low oxygen. However, the two most relevant systems dealing with such adaptations within the extreme ambient conditions for the diver in question are the respiratory and circulatory systems that mutually support each other against the extreme environments underwater. Just how impressive such adaptations are to mention is the possible risks and pathologies of the sport are relevant to learning to keep on learning regarding keeping divers safe but improving air performance.

This long handbook will outline the respiratory and circulatory systems, the physiological changes they undergo during a dive, and the pathologies a diver should be aware of.

1. The Respiratory System: The Oxygen Gateway to Freediving

The respiratory system of freediving includes respiration, storage, and use of oxygen and carbon diOxygenO$_2$ balance. The body uses this system to use oxygen and tolerance of CO_2 to increase breath-holding time.

1.1 Anatomy of the Respiration System

Lungs:
- Lungs are the reservoirs of Oxygengenovide, the sites of oxygen exchange where the blood can pick Oxygengen.
- They also act like an oxygen buffer when diving.

Diaphragm:
- This domeshaped muscle controls breathing, including contraction and relaxation. In free diving training, this muscle is given full priority in expanding the volume of the lungs to full size and using oxygen entry.

Trachea, Bronchi, and Alveoli :
- The pathway leading oxygen to the alveoli is oxygenated, too, for gas exchange.
- Alveoli ensure that oxygOxygens are in the bloodstrOxygennd the CO_2 goes out.

1.2 Physiological Adaptations of the Respiratory System

Compression of the Lungs:
- Because of hydrostatic pressure, the volume of the lungs decreases when diving to a quarter of its regular size at the surface level.
- The resultant pressure is stressful or harmful to a diver who is not well-trained or acclimatized.

Blood Shift Mechanism:
- This is done to shift blood from the extremities to the thoracic cavity, where it acts as a buffer to prevent the collapse of the lungs due to pressure.
- This becomes necessary during deep dives for the lungs to take on the compression strain.

Hypoxic Thresholds :
- This would mean the freediver training his body to stretch his hypoxia tolerance a little more so that he can make longer

and safer dives or even deeper dives without jeopardizing his safety.

1.3 Challenges and Risks for the Respiratory System

CO_2 Buildup:
- While the body uses Oxygen, CO_2 builds up in place Oxygengen, signaling the need to breathe.
- Too much CO_2 will result in dizziness, confusion, and blackout.

Pulmonary Barotrauma:
- Sudden pressure changes during poor equalization at descents and ascents tear the lungs.
- Further, this may lead to several disorders, including lung squeeze and alveolar rupture.

Pulmonary Edema:
- Changes in pressure can force fluid into the lungs, manifesting as labored breathing, coughing, and chest pain.

2. Circulatory System: Distribution and Conserving Oxygen

In any freediving session, the circulatory system undergoes enormous changes, shifting the availability of oxygen around the vital oxygen organs. These changes comprise oxygen-oxygenating changes in external pressure.

2.1 Anatomy of the Circulatory System

Heart:
- It pumps oxygenated blood throughout the body.
- Free diving drastically reduces heart rate to minimize the use of oxygen. This process is called bradycardia.

Blood Vessels:
- Transportation of oxygenated blood from the lungs to body tissues and deoxygenated blood back to the lungs.
- Peripheral vasoconstriction organs diverOxygengen to all vital body organs, including the brain and heart.

Spleen:
- Storage of oxygenated erythrocyte release during dives.

2.2 Physiological Adaptations of the Circulatory System

Mammalian Dive Response MDR:
- Dive reflex and protective response for the marine mammals to protect the vital organs with no consumption of O2.
- It includes:
  - **Bradycardia:** slowing the heart rates and educating the onsumpoxygeOxygengen
  - **Peripheral Vasoconstion** is supplied to the limbs, and the oxygen supply is sent only to the vital organs.
  - **OxygenShift:** The blood is shifted to the lungs so that it won't collapse due to the pressure on it.

Spleen Contraction:
- Contractions release more red blood cells into the circulation, enriching the body's general oxygen-carrying capability.
- It may increase apnea time by some seconds or up to minutes.

2.3 Circulatory Risks/Dangers

Hypoxia:
- The brain could provoke LMC or blackout because it doesn't get enough Oxygen.

Hypercapnia:
- Suddenly, increased CO_2 in large quantities will cause headaches, disturbed unrest, anxiety, and loss of concentration.

DCS:
- Although infrequent in free diving, fast ascents create a nitrogen bubble in the blood, which can cause symptoms ranging from aching joints to more serious fatigue.

3. Freediving Pathologies

Knowledge of various pathologies linked with freediving will avoid or prevent these risks.

3.1 Pulmonary Barotrauma

Cause:
- Poor equalization during the descent and ascent create differences that can cause damage to lung tissue.

Symptoms:
- Chest pain, hemoptysis, or dyspnea.

Prevention:
- Equalization techniques and gradual depth progressions.

3.2 Shallow Water Blackout

Cause:
- Hypoxia on ascent is caused by oxygen starvation, usually post-hyperventilation.

Symptoms:
- Sudden unconsciousness without warning.

Prevention:
- Never hyperventilate before diving, and always dive with a buddy.

3.3 Decompression Sickness (DCS)

Cause:
- A rapid rise results in nitrogen bubbles getting into the blood.

Symptoms:
- Joint pains, vertigo, fatigue, and partial or complete paralysis.

Prevention:
- Avoid rapid changes; stay within limits of acceptable ascent rate and avoid multiple bottom times exceeding depth limits.

3.4 Pulmonary Edema

Cause:
- The fluid buildup in the lungs is caused by increased pressure and blood shift.

Symptoms:
- Coughing, chest constriction, labored breathing.

Prevention:
- Do not dive beyond your limits; penetrate progressively in deep training.

4. Training of the Respiratory and Circulatory Systems

This will optimize a freediver's performance and safety.

4.1 RRespiration Training

Diaphragmatic Breathing:
- Strengthens the diaphragm, increasing volume.
- CO_2 Tolerance Tables:
- Increases gradually the body's tolerance of high levels of CO_2.
- O_2 Optimization Training:

This will ensure the best uptake and efficiency when using oxygen. Oxygen.

4.2 Cardiovascular Conditioning

High-Intensity Interval Training (HIIT):
- This would improve endurance and oxygenation.

Apnea Walks:
- Prolong the breath by soft exercise to provoke dynamic apnea situations.

4.3 Flexibility and Lung Health

Yoga and Pranayama:
- Chest flexibility, control of breathing.

Lung Stretching Exercises :
- Increased elasticizing elasticity increases the chances of injury due to deep dives.

5. Monitoring and Managing Risks

5.1 PreDive Preparation
- Check personal physical and mental preparedness long before diving.
- Never dive when in a fatigued, dehydrated, or stressed condition.

5.2 Dive Practices
- Dive always with a buddy who monitors your progress and is prepared to take action if an accident should happen.
- Descend deeper gradually to give the body time to equalize pressure change.

5.3 PostDive Recovery
- Look for signs and symptoms of barotrauma, decompression sickness, and hypoxia.
- Have long surface intervals between dives to allow for complete recovery.

6. Conclusion

Free diving is closely related to the human respiratory and circulatory systems. Basic knowledge of physiological adaptation and risks affecting both systems will allow the freediver to optimize his performance and establish minimal risks. Unique training, prudent preparation, and respect for safety regulations will allow him to go to any depth, extend his limits, and preserve the fragile balance in the human body.

Hypoxia and Blackout Prevention in Freediving

Freediving is an exhilarating sport that extends human limits in the aquatic environment. However, this kind of challenge and safe dives are possible only if profound knowledge is gained about two of the sport's most dangerous risks: the causes, signs, and prevention of **hypoxia** and **blackouts**.

Hypoxia occurs when the tissues and vital organs do not receive enough oxygen. Free diving generally occurs because of prolonged breath holding, hyperventilation, or other physiological problems that reduce oxygen supplies. If unaddressed, hypoxia may lead to a **blackout**, a condition in which a person becomes unconscious while underwater. It can be fatal only if the person is not brought to the surface in time.

Main Caus Hypoxia in Freediving

Recognizing some of the causes listed below will help the diver prevent hypoxia:

1. Prolonged BreathHolding:
- The longer a freediver stays submerged, the more oxygen he uses up and the closer he is to critical oxygen thresholds.

2. Hyperventilation
- Deep, rapid breathing before a dive lowers blood levels of carbon dioxide, reducing the impulse to breathe. But it also eliminates many warning signals that indicate when one is running out of oxygen, dramatically increasing the danger of a blackout.

3. Effects of Depth Pressure
- The deeper one goes, the higher the surrounding pressure, compressing the lungs and thus the oxygen within them in more significant amounts. A quick upward rise to the surface will create a sudden fall in the pressure level, resulting in a rapid fall in the oxygen level and shallow water blackout.

4. Overexertion
- Heavy exertion involved with diving, such as fighting currents or competitive speed swimming, will increase oxygen consumption.

5. Beyond the Limit
- Setting new personal records without training and having safety precautions invites dangerous consequences.

6. Poor Technique or Relaxation
- Tension and poor movement mechanics involve excessive energy use, quickly depleting the body's oxygen stores.

Recognizing the Signs of Hypoxia

For this reason, the freediver must be in tune with his body and be watchful for the early warning of shypoxia's

Physical Symptoms
- Cyanosis bluish discoloration of lips and nails.
- Tremors, shaking, or loss of motor control occasion referred to as "samba";
- Weakness, "fatigue" e, or muscle twitching.

2. Cognitive Indicators
- Confusion or not being able to pay attention to the tasks at hand;
- Tunnel vision or black spots across the field of view.

3. Behavioral Changes
- The inappropriate feeling of calm or elation underwater is a warning of an imminently dangerous hypoxic state.

Recognition of these symptoms and immediate appropriate action is the key to avoiding blackouts.

Stages of Blackout

Hypoxia can build up to a blackout, a critical condition needing immediate intervention. The stages are as follows:

1. Loss of Motor Control (LMC)
- A precursor to blackout, LMC includes such things as involuntary muscle spasms, shaking, or failure to maintain proper form.

2. Blackout
- A complete loss of consciousness due to lack of sufficient oxygen.
- Deep Water Blackout occurs at depth when the oxygen pressure in the lungs becomes inadequate to support a state of consciousness.
- Shallow Water Blackout: It also happens at the ascent. Rapidly falling surrounding pressure has increased the severity of the oxygen depletion.

Prevention Measures

Hypoxia prevention or blackout will involve proper training and awareness, taking into consideration all the necessary measures of safety:

1. Full Training
- Gradually acquire breath-holdup capacity and confidence. Unde takes formal education about freediving, teaching safety and dive techniques.

2. Avoid Hyperventilation
- Before diving, one must breathe moderately to maintain the correct level of CO_2. Hence, it is recommended that they use that internal safety mechanism.

3. Relaxation Techniques
- Save your energy: Learn to relax and use less oxygen. Proper visualization, mindfulness of the moment, and slowing of movements all contribute to the efficiency of dives.

4. Buddy System
- Never dive alone. A trained buddy should permanently be assigned to each diver and be prepared in cases of emergency intervention.

5. Recognizing the Limits
- Respect your limits and those of your surroundings. Never dive beyond the boundaries that include depth, bottom times, and conditions beyond your experience.

6. Surface Intervals
- Adequate recovery between dives allows oxygen levels to replenish and CO_2 to normalize, thus reducing the risk of subsequent hypoxia.

Importance of Surface Intervals

The recovery between dives is an essential factor:

1. General Rule
- The surface interval must be twice as long as the preceding dive. For example, a two-minute dive requires at least a four-minute surface recovery.

2. Check of Preparation
- A dive is safely initiated only when the breather is brought to a comfortable level where he is comfortable enough to have normal breathing, is clearheaded, and shows no signs of physical distress.

Onset of Blackout

Fatalities can be avoided in an attempt to act proficiently and in time against the onsets of blacks-out:

1. Rescue immediately
- Bring the unconscious diver upwards in the water so his head does not get into complications further.

2. Activate Breathing
- Blow gently across the diver's face or stimulate spontaneous breathing on unnecessary delay.

3. Post-Rescue Care
- While the diver should be allowed to reenter the water, he must be kept calm, and any delayed symptoms,d, from confusion to fatigue, must observed.

Conclusion

Oxygen and blackout are the most dangerous risks in freediving. Nevertheless, all these can be avoided by appropriate knowledge, training, vigilance about their causes, recognition of signs, observation of recovery intervals, and respect for personal limits. Safety will always outweigh ambition for any freediver if underwater adventures are exhilarating yet life-affirming.

Techniques in Ear, Sinus and Lung Protection: Barotrauma

It is a sport that demands a lot of mental focus and physical stamina with adaptation to the water. However, this dramatic change in pressure upon descent and ascent may also have repercussions associated with barotrauma since air-filled spaces exist in the ears, sinuses, and lungs. In understanding the dynamics of barotrauma, freedivers understand how to apply practical prevention techniques to minimize the risk involved and enhance the underwater experience.

What is Barotrauma?

Barotrauma is an injury sustained from unequal pressures between the outside environment and the internal air-filled spaces of the body. This occurs rapidly during depth changes in freediving because water pressure increases at depth and decreases during ascent. If equalization does not occur promptly, the developed pressure gradient could cause tissue damage or structural injuries.

Types of Barotrauma

Manifestations of barotrauma vary depending on the part of the body affected. The common types include:

1. Ear Barotraumamiddle ear and inner ear

- The most sensitive structure of pressure changes is the middle ear. Failure to equalize the pressure between the outside environment and the middle ear using the Eustachian tube connecting it to the throat could cause discomfort and injury. Barotrauma to the inner ear is rare but injurious, sometimes leading to significant hearing loss.

2. Sinus Barotrauma

- Besides, the sinus cavities in the forehead and around the nose cannot equalize pressure, leading to pain, swelling, or bleeding under extreme conditions. Blockage from congestion is usually the most frequent contributing cause.

3. Lung Barotrauma (Pulmonary Barotrauma)

- Prolonged expansive or compressive mechanisms acting upon the lungs can cause lung barotrauma. It can occur during either a descent or an ascent. During an ascent, if expanding air within a diver cannot escape properly, the alveoli—gas-filled sacs—can rupture, causing conditions as severe as collapsed lungs, pneumothorax, and arterial gas embolism.

The Mechanics of Pressure in Freediving

Water pressure increases by about 1 atmosphere (ATM) for every 10 meters of depth. On the surface, the body is subjected to 1 ATM. At 20 meters, this increases to 3 ATM, compressing air-filled spaces in the body to one-third of their original volume.

Upon ascent, the opposite occurs, and air expands with the decrease in pressure. This relationship must be understood as the basis for avoiding barotrauma.

Barotrauma of the Ear: Causes, Symptoms, and Protection

Causes
- Inability to equilibrate middle ear pressure in a particular descent
- Presence of any inflammation or congestion inside the Eustachian tube
- Any violent equalization that can eventually cause internal damage to the middle ear

Symptoms
- The painful sensation within the ears, which may cause unease or disturbances upon touching
- Noises heard complete or blockage of the ears
- Ringing in the ears (tinnitus) or hearing loss.
- Dizziness, vertigo, or disorientation; possible inner ear injury.

Protection Techniques

1. Learn and Practice Equalization Techniques
- **Valsalva Maneuver:** Pinch your nose and gently exhale to equalize.
- **Frenzel Maneuver:** Use the back of the tongue and throat muscles to equalize pressure without stressing the lungs.
- Practice these techniques on land to be assured of proficiency before diving.

2. PreDive Preparation
- Gently flex the neck and move the jaws to open the Eustachian tubes.
- Mild nasal congestion may be treated with a saline spray or decongestant.

3. Gradual Descent
- Begin equalizing at the surface and slowly descend. Waiting until pain is felt is too late and may lead to injury.

4. Avoid Diving with Illness
- These equalize the air but may block and prevent equalization in sinus infections, allergic conditions, or colds.

Sinus Barotrauma: Causes, Symptoms, and Protection

Causes
- Congestion or other anatomical abnormalities obstructing the sinuses.
- Changes in pressure happen too rapidly without the time necessary to equalize them.
- Diving during an acute sinus infection.

Symptoms
- Sharp pain or pressure in the forehead, cheeks, or around the nose.
- Nosebleeds during diving or shortly after a dive.
- Swelling, tenderness in the inus above the eyes and cheeks.

Protection Techniques

1. Maintain Sinus Health
- Regular nasal saline rinses clear the sinus passages. If congestion persists, a physician may prescribe a special treatment.

2. Control Descent and Ascent Rates
- Gradual changes in depth give the paranasal sinus cavities time for nonforced equalization of pressure differences.

3. Practice Relaxation Techniques
- Deep breathing and relaxation can help minimize facial tension.

4. Do not dive with congestion
- Diving with inflammation or blocked sinuses increases the risk of trauma. It is necessary to treat the congestion for a few minutes before trying to dive.

Lung Barotrauma: Causes, Symptoms, and Protection

Causes
- Overexpansion of the lungs during ascent.
- Closely connected with rapidly changing pressures during a deep dive brought about by external compression of the lungs.
- Poor physical conditioning of the lungs or inflexible lungs.

Symptoms
- Labored breathing or chest pain after surfacing.
- Coughing, expectorating blood, or foamy sputum.
- Fatigue, dizziness, cyanosis, bluish skin or lips discoloration.

Protection Techniques

1. Diaphragmatic Breathing Training
- Strength of lung flexibility and capacity with special breathing exercises.
- Practice static and dynamic apnea to adapt the lungs to the changes in pressure.

2. Avoid Overinflation
- Do not take deep breaths before diving, as an increased volume may cause the lungs to overexpand.

3. Controlled Ascent
- Always ascend slowly, exhaling slowly to vent expanding air. Failure to exhale during a rapid ascent can lead to injuries from overexpansion.

4. Operate Within Your Training Limits
- Do not perform dives that exceed your physiological conditioning.

General Strategies for Prevention

1. Dive with a Buddy
- Dive aAlways dive buddy trainer who is d to help in emergencies. A buddy system adds an important layer of safety.

2. Gradual Progress
- Gradually increase the depth and/or dive time not to stress your body with sudden pressure changes.

3. Hydrate and Nourish Your Body
- Be adequately hydrated because hydration keeps mucous membranes in the airways and the sinuses healthy.

4. Regular Check-Ups
- Check with the ENT regularly and a pulmonary physician to keep all the vital parts of your body related to freediving fitting.

5. Rest between dives
- Allow adequate recovery time between dives so that no buildup of pressure damage occurs.

Conclusion

Barotrauma is the most common risk in freediving, but it is wholly avoidable if preparation, technique, and self-awareness are appropriate. Knowledge of pressure mechanics, mastery of equalization techniques, good health, and avoidance of overstressing the body are ways to minimize risk to the ears, sinuses, and lungs. Safety, preparation, and mindfulness define successful freediving and ensure that every dive is exhilarating and injury-free.

Haemoptysis, Pulmonary Oedema, and Taravana: Some Freediving-Related Pathologies

Freediving pushes the human body to an extreme state, depending on mental focus, physical conditioning, and adaptation to underwater pressure. Since freediving presents these particular challenges, specific pathologies, including hemoptysis, pulmonary edema, and Taravana, raise physiological demands to breathe and cope with a rapid pressure change. This handbook will explain the series, their causes, symptoms, prevention, and treatments will be further after.

1. Haemoptysis in Freediving

Freedivingysis Haemoptysis, or the spitting of blood, is terrifying for any freediver. Generally associated with respiratory and cardiovascular problems during dives, this is brought about by excessive tension exerted on the lungs by several dives and incorrect techniques in diving.

Causes

1. Pulmonary Barotrauma
- These mainly result from rapid changes in pressure during descent or ascent, rupturing small blood vessels in the lungs. They occur primarily as a consequence of overcompression or overexpansion of the lungs.

2. Pulmonary Squeeze
- During this, water pressure at depth compresses the lungs, raising the risk of micro tears in the alveolar walls, especially in divers not accustomed to deep dives.

3. Overtraining and Fatigue
- Poor recovery between repeated dives can cause lung tissues to fail to bear the stress and breach their integrity.

4. Preexisting Medical Conditions
- Preexisting conditions, such as bronchitis, respiratory infections, or chronic inflammation of the lungs, can further weaken the lungs' resistance to injury.

Symptoms
- Blood or rust-colored sputum coughed up, most often immediately after diving.
- Chest tightness or discomfort.
- Shortness of breath, tiredness, or a dizzy feeling.

Prevention

1. Training of Gradual Depth
- Gradually increase dive depth and time, preparing the lungs against increased pressure.

2. Exercises for Lung Elasticity
- Regular stretching and breathing exercises make your lungs more flexible, thus helping them resist collapsing.

3. Correct Equalization
- The equalization techniques should not be done poorly to prevent injury to the lung tissues.

4. Avoid Overexertion.
- Give plenty of time between dives to recover, and never dive while tired or in poor physical condition.

Treatment
- Immediate Action: Stop diving immediately and rest.

- Medical Evaluation: Medical checkup to rule out severe Trasteveree underlying disease.
- Recovery: Allow the lungs to recover and be reconditioned gradually before returning to diving.

2. Pulmonary Edema in Freediving

Pulmonary edema, or fluid in the lungs, is a severe medical condition to which even the healthiest freediver might be subjected. The most common type concerning freedom divers is immersion pulmonary edema, IPE. Causes that link to freediving come down to pressure, immersion effects, and cardiovascular strain related to this sport.

Causes

1. Increased Hydrostatic Pressure
- Water pressure compresses blood vessels, which pushes fluid from the blood into the lungs' alveoli.

2. Cold Water Immersion
- Cold water causes the constriction of blood vessels, which raises central blood pressure and promotes fluid leakage.

3. Negative Pressure Breathing
- Aggressive respiration with deep descents creates negative chest pressure and forces fluid into the lungs.

4. Overhydration
- Taking on too much liquid before entering the water dilates blood volume, further aggravating conditions that lead to pulmonary edema.

Symptoms
- Dyspnea or shortness of breath during or after a dive.
- Pink, frothy sputum, expectoration due to fluid accumulation in the lungs.

- Chest tightness or discomfort.
- Weakness, dizziness, or cyanosis, in which the skin, lips, and nailbeds turn bluish due to the body not receiving enough oxygen.

Prevention

1. Controlled Breathing

Avoid excessive negative pressure breathing by practicing diaphragmatic control.

2. Gradual Acclimatization

Acclimatize your body to cold water and pressure changes by gradual exposure and warm-up dives.

3. Limited Hydration

Avoid excessive liquid intake before dives to prevent increased blood volume.

4. Monitor Physical Work

Avoid overexertion, as this increases cardiovascular stress and shifting of fluids.

Treatment

Immediate Action: Stop diving and stay in a warm, dry place.

Oxygen Therapy: Administer supplementary oxygen if available.

Medical Attention: Serious cases are generally hospitalized and treated with diuretics or other means to drain fluid out of the lungs.

3. Taravana: DecompressionLike Sickness in Freediving

Taravana is of Polynesian origin and a type of DCS or decompression sickness. This occurs when the freediver continually repeats deep dives without adequate recovery from the preceding dives. Less frequent than diving with scuba, Taravana is a well-known risk for almost all freedivers who go to extremes.

Causes

1. Nitrogen Absorption
- Repeated deep dives result in increased absorption of nitrogen into body tissues. If a diver does not have sufficient surface intervals, nitrogen can develop bubbles during ascent.

2. Rapid Ascents
- Quick ascents can promote nitrogen-related problems by narrowing the time for safe off-gassing.

3. Depth and Frequency
- In addition, diving beyond safe depth limits or making repetitive dives without allowing adequate time for recovery increases the chance.

Symptoms
- Confusion, dizziness, or disorientation.
- Nausea, exhaustion, or general weakness.
- In severe cases, unconsciousness often carries a high risk of drowning.

Prevention

1. Following Surface Intervals
- The recovery time between dives should be at least 2–3 times longer than the actual dive to allow nitrogen to dissipate.

2. Limit Depth and Dive Frequency
- Do not exceed depth limits, and avoid too many deep dives in succession.

3. Controlled Ascents
- Ascend slowly and steadily to reduce the risk of nitrogen bubble formation.

4. Adequate Hydration and Nutrition
- Balanced hydration is essential for good circulation and effective off-gas nitrogen production.

Treatment
- **Emergency Action:** Immediately cease diving and rest in a safe environment.
- **Oxygen Administration:** Symptoms can be improved by administering pure oxygen.
- **Hyperbaric Treatment:** Severe cases must be treated in the hyperbaric chamber, where the nitrogen bubbles are safely dissolved.

General Recommendations for Freediving Safety

1. Buddy System
- Always dive in with a trained partner who can monitor and assist in emergencies.

2. Regular Training and Conditioning
- Gradually build up the physical and mental resistance against the pressure and stress from the dives.

3. Stay Attuned to Your Body
- Be aware of the early warning signs, and never dive with unusual symptoms during or after a dive.

4. See Specialists
- Periodical medical checkups, especially of the respiratory and cardiovascular apparatus, are fundamental for highlighting possible risks.

5. Respect Your Limits
- It is not about how far one can push oneself in freediving; always, the priority should be safety.

Conclusion

These include hemoptysis, pulmonary edema, and Taravana, severe pathologies ensuing from freediving. Training, preparation, and adherence to safety protocols in this sport are crucial and significantly minimize the chances of these and other possible health risks. Freediving also celebrates the potential of the human body. Prioritizing safety means divers continue the sport, having exploratory fun underwater with continued confidence.

Otorhinolaryngologic Considerations and Reverse Block Management in Freediving

Freediving is a sports discipline that combines the thrill of exploring the underwater world with unique features of mental self-discipline. It thus places extreme demands on the otorhinolaryngologic system. Ears, sinuses, and respiratory pathways must resist and manage rapid and extreme changes in pressure during dives. In short, the problems divers face and the causes of this so-called reverse block, prevention, and management must be explained well. This general guide covers the ENT aspects necessary in freediving, with practical measures for maintaining health or overcoming problems like the reverse Block.

Understanding Otorhinolaryngologic Anatomy in Freediving

1. Anatomy of the Ear and Pressure Management

The human Ear is divided into three parts: the Outer, Middle, and Inner Ears:

- **Outer Ear:** The sound waves enter the ear canal and go to the eardrum.
- **Middle Ear:** The middle Ear is a chamber filled with air. The air is then injected into the throat through the Eustachian tube. During the dive, the air is in the Middle Ear.
- **Inner Ear:** The eardrum is the general area of the inner Ear. It is responsible for hearing balance and can quickly suffer from barotrauma if pressure changes are poorly regulated.

2. Sinus Anatomy and Function

The sinuses are the air-filled cavities in the skull on the forehead, cheeks, and between the eyes. They are called frontal, maxillary, ethmoid, and sphenoid. All these cavities must equalize pressure with the surrounding environment to avoid pain or injury during depth changes.

3. Eustachian Tube Role

Eustachian Eare connects the middle Ear with the nasopharynx, equilibrating pressure. Congestion or inflammation and other anatomical issues might close the tube airtight, contributing to complications of barotrauma or reeBlocklock.

Block ENT-Related Problems in Freediving

1. Barotrauma

If the equalization does not occur, the ascent or descent can lead to pressure injuries of the ears and sinuses. In extreme cases, symptoms include pain, discomfort, bleeding, or tissue damage.

2. Congestion and Blockages

Allergies, colds, or infections that cause nasal or sinus congestion block air flow and heighten the risk of complications in the ENT.

3. Reverse Block

The reverse block is a condition wherein the ascent and air trapped either in the middle Ear or the thesauruses cannot escape due to blockages in the eustachian tubes or the pathways of the sinuses.

What is Reverse Block?

A **reverse block,** or "reverse squeeze," occurs when air expands during ascent but cannot get out of the middle ear weariness due to some obstruction. The now trapped air makes for an imbalance of pressure that can be painful, with a possibility of tissue damage.

Causes of Reverse Block

1. Eustachian Tube Dysfunction
- In this case, inflammation or congestion prevents the opening of the eustachian tubes and prevents the middle Ear from equalizing its air pressure during ascent.

2. Sinus Block
- Inflammation and swelling or accumulation of mucus in the sinuses trap the air while expanding at an ascent.

3. Rebound Congestion
- Overuse of decongestants will be followed by rebound congestion. If applied, it further increases the risk of reblock with BBlockNT.

4. Fast Ascent
- Fast ascents reduce the time it takes to push air out, increasing the effect of the trapped air.

5. Allergic Reactions
- Allergies leading to nasal swelling may forbid the usual passage and equalization of air.

Symptoms of Reverse Block
- Sharp pain or feeling of pressure in the ears or sinuses upon ascent.
- A sensation of fullness or blockage in the ears.
- Dizziness or vertigo, perhaps with disorientation.
- Haring loss or muffled hearing.
- In severe cases, nosebleeds or even eardrum rupture due to pressure buildup

Preventing
Preventing a Revers Block requires propbuildupration in technique and situational awareness:

1. Pre-Dive Preparation
- **Clear Airways:** Avoid diving while suffering from nasal congestion, sinus infections, or colds. Alternatively, nasal sprays can help keep nasal passages clear.
- **Moderate Use of Decongestan:** Decongestan should be used judiciously, not habitually, to avoid rebound congestion during a dive.
- **Hydration:** Good hydration status maintains mucosal health and minimizes the possibility of blockages.

2. Proper Equalization Techniques
- **Frequent Equalization:** Early and frequent equalization during the descent builds up.
- **Passive Equalization:** During ascent, Suck, yawn, or manipulate your jaw to equalize air in your ears, as some air may have been trapped in them.
- **Forceful Maneuvers:** Vigorous manipulations are unnecessary, as they can only increase blockages or further deteriorate damaged tissues.

3. Controlled Ascent
- **Slow and Steady.** Make a slow ascent, allowing time for trapped air to be released. Suddenly ascending may raise the chances of pressure-related problems.
- **Stop If Need Be:** Should this cause discomfort, desist from it and climb down a little to relieve the pressure and proceed.

4. ENT Health Maintenance Regularly
- **Prolonged Conditions Treatment:** A specialist should consult for prolonged sinusitis, allergic rhinitis, and eustachian tube dysfunction.
- **Exercises and Stretches:** Practice breathing exercises and stretches to keep the lungs and sinuses healthy.

Reverse Block Management

If a reverse block occurs, one should not enter into a state of panic; on the contrary, corrective actions must be followed:

1. Stop Ascending
- Immediately cease the ascent to arrest further deterioration of the pressure imbalance.

2. Descend Slightly
- Go down a few meters to equilibrate the pressure in that area. This may give some relief and may open up the blocked passages.

3. Perform Gentle Maneuvers
- Exhale, yawn, or wiggle your jaw to promote airflow.
- Forceful Valsalva tends to accentuate the problem rather than diminish it.

4. Relax and Stay Slow
- Stress accentuates the symptoms. Focusing on taking slow and regular breaths can help you relax.

5. Abort Dive
- If the problem is clear but red, symptoms persist, and the operation should be aborted. The patient must also avoid using the diving utility while seated.

Seek Medical Care
See a doctor if:
- There is continued pain or discomfort after surfacing.
- Other symptoms include vertigo, hearing loss, or nosebleeds.
- You have repeated the iceblock the iceblock forBlockBlockckLongTerBlockategiesBlockENT Health

1. Regular Check-Ups
- Regular visits to the ENT specialist ensure that problems, if any, are identified and treated timely.

2. Maintain Your Airways
- Routine nasal flushing ensures normal functions in the sinuses. Keeping the air passageway broad is to choke up from other congeal elements.

3. Breathe More Technically
- Practice Yoga or diaphragm workout to keep Airways and healthy Lungs.

4. Training
- It would be related mainly to equalizing safety and keeping in good health in ENT.

Conclusion
Otorhinolaryngologic health is a cornerstone of safe and enjoyable freediving. Conditions like reverse block can significantly impact the diving experience but are preventable with proper preparation, awareness, and technique. By understanding the anatomy and mechanics of the ENT system, practicing effective equalization,

and adhering to preventive measures, the freediver can minimize risks and maximize experience underwater. With health and safety foremost, the underwater world wonder can be responsibly explored confidently.

Freediving Training and Physical Preparation

Annual Training Programs and Periodization

Freediving encompasses physical conditioning, mental toughness, and specific techniques that must be mastered. A clearly defined annual training program with periodization is essential for maximum efficiency and safety. This program will ensure progressive training while balancing intensity and recovery, peaking at the right moments.

Elements of Freediving Training

1. BreathHolding (Apnea) Training

It enhances the body's tolerance of CO_2 and its ability to slow down the process of hypoxia.
- **Static (STA):** — training by holding a breath without movement.
- **Dynamic (DYN):** — training through holding your breath while doing swim movements or traveling in the water.

2. Strength and Conditioning

Freediving requires a combination of muscular endurance and efficiency:
- **Core Strength:** Essential for body control and stability underwater.
- **Leg Power:** Important for propulsion, particularly in finning techniques.

- **Shoulder and Back Strength:** Supports arm strokes and stabilizes movements.

3. Cardiovascular Fitness

Low-intensity aerobic exercises like swimming, cycling, or jogging increase endurance and optimize oxygen use.

4. Flexibility and Mobility

Stretching the diaphragm, intercostal muscles, and chest cavity improves lung capacity and mobility underwater.

5. Mental Training
- **Meditation and Mindfulness:** Visualization enhances relaxation, concentration, and stress management.
- **Visualization:** Increases confidence and reinforces successful dive techniques

6. Equalization and Technique
- **Master Visualization:** Regularly practicing equalization methods like Frenzel and BTV ensures efficient pressure management.
- **Equalizing pressure** is critical during descent in the middle ear and sinuses. Techniques such as the Frenzel maneuver ensure efficient pressure management, reducing the risk of barotrauma.
- **Streamlining** and propulsion techniques reduce drag and conserve energy.

Understanding Periodization in Freediving

Periodization divides the annual training period into phases, each directed toward realizing a physiological adaptation relevant to the different stages. This ensures that freedivers peak at appropriate times for competitions, deep dives, or personal records.

Phases of Periodization

1. Preparation Phase (Base Building)
- **Duration:** 2–4 months
- **Focus:** Build an aerobic base, foundational strength, and technique.
- **Training Elements:**
o Low-intensity, high-volume cardiovascular exercises.
o General strength training (e.g., squats, planks, pullups).
o Diaphragm and rib cage stretching.
o Apnea tables to build tolerance to CO_2 and hypoxia.

2. BuildUp Phase (Specific Conditioning)
- **Duration:** 3–4 months
- **Focus:** Increase disoriented strength, flexibility, and the degree of apnea.
- **Training Elements:**
- Interval training to enhance the efficiency of the cardiovascular apparatus
o Core, muscle strengthening exercises with dynamic movements in aquatics, resistance band gymnastics, hyperextension workout
o Equalization techniques and exercises linked to static and dynamic apnea.
o Advanced apnea tables to increase CO_2 and hypoxia tolerance.

3. Peak Phase (Performance)
- **Duration:** 1–2 months
- **Focus:** Maximize performance and prepare for key dives or competitions.
- **Training Elements:**
o Deep dive simulations.
o Finetuning techniques, including equalization and streamlining.
o Recovery and mental focus exercises.

4. Taper Phase (Rest and Recovery)
- **Duration:** 1–2 weeks before peak dives.
- **Focus:** Allow the body to recover while maintaining sharpness fully.
- **Training Elements:**
o Reduced volume and intensity.
o Relaxation techniques and mental Visualization.

5. Off-Season Phase (Transition)
- **Duration:** 1-2 months post-peak.
- **Focus:** Active recovery and addressing weaknesses.
- **Training Elements:**
o Light aerobic activities and general strength maintenance.
o Flexibility training and rehabilitation exercises.

Sample Annual Training Program

Month	Phase	Focus	Key Activities
January–February	Preparation	Build aerobic base and foundational strength	Long swims, light strength training, diaphragm stretching.
March–June	Build-Up	Dive-specific conditioning	HIIT sessions, CO2 and O2 apnea tables, equalization drills.
July–August	Peak	Optimize performance for dives	Deep dive simulations, fine-tune techniques, mental training.
September	Taper	Recovery and fine-tuning	Light cardio, relaxation exercises, reduced dive practice.
October	Competition	Peak performance in target events	Execute competition dives under peak conditions.
November–December	Off-Season	Recovery and reassessment	Yoga, mobility exercises, review of training logs and goals.

Key Training Techniques for Freediving

1. Apnea Tables
- **CO_2 Tables:** Improve tolerance to high CO_2 by minimizing recovery time between breathholds.
- **O_2 Tables:** Improve tolerance to hypoxia by increasing the length of breathholds using the same recovery time.

2. Diaphragm and Lung Stretching
- **Rib Cage Stretches:** Increased chest cavity flexibility allows for better, increased expansion of the lungs.
- **Diaphragmatic Breathing:** Strengthen the diaphragm and enhance oxygen exchange.

3. HighIntensity Interval Training
- Relics the stressors of freediving through high-intensity bouts followed by rest. This helps increase recovery and enhances anaerobic capacity.

4. Relaxation and Visualization
- Practice relaxation before and during Visualization to minimize oxygen consumption.
- Visualization of successful dives strengthens mental preparation.

5. Relaxation and Mental Techniques
- **Progressive Relaxation:** Focus on relaxing individual muscle groups to conserve oxygen.
- **Breath Awareness:** Practice slow, controlled breathing to lower the heart rate and prepare for apnea.

6. Equalization Drills
- Use land-based exercises like the Frenzel and reverse packing techniques to perfect equalization.

7. Cross-Training for Strength and Flexibility
- **Yoga and Pilates:** Improve flexibility, mobility, and core strength.
- **Resistance Training:** Focus on functional movements that mimic freediving actions, such as finning and streamlining.

Common Challenges and Solutions

1. Plateau in BreathHold Duration
Solution: Mix apnea tables and introduce new relaxation methods.

2. Difficulty with Equalization

Solution: Perform equalization exercises, such as the Frenzel technique, and consult an ENT doctor if you have chronic anatomy problems.

3. Overtraining or Fatigue

Solution: Be more mindful of your recovery and allow yourself more rest or active recovery days.

4. Mental Stress or Anxiety

Solution: Practice mindfulness, yoga, or meditation to improve relaxation and focus.

Why Progress Monitoring is Important

Training Logs
- Record apnea times, dive depths, recovery, and heart rates to track progress.

Regular Assessments
- Test performance benchmarks every 3–4 months to identify strengths and weaknesses.

Physiological Feedback
- Monitor resting heart rate and recovery indicators to avoid overtraining

Conclusion

Freedivers interested in enhancing performance, safety, and pleasure should undergo year-round periodized training. By combining physical conditioning, apnea practice, mental training, and proper recovery, the diver can develop their skills progressively and reach peak performance. In balance with body, mind, and the underwater environment, freediving is not only about pushing the limits; it's about mastery.

Dry and WaterBased Training for Freediving

Static, Dynamic, and CrossTraining

Freediving requires excellent physical fitness, mental strength, and control over breathing. To optimize their performances and ensure safety, freedivers use dry training methods. These methods build apnea capacity, strength, flexibility, and relaxation to prepare divers for the physiological and psychological stresses of exploring the underwater world. This general guidebook considers **static**, **dynamic**, and **cross-training** elements in depth within the overall structure of a training program.

1. Dry Training for Freediving

Dry TrainiTrainingderstood means all forms of land training aimed at simulating conditions for freediving, excluding associated water risk. This is good practice for breath control, strength, and mental focus in preparation for dives.

A. Static Apnea Training

Static apnea is a breath hold while stationary. Without all the other distractions on land, the freediver can entirely focus on breath-holding techniques.

Objectives:
- Increase the time of breath hold by improving tolerance to high CO_2 levels/low oxygen levels.
- Improve the state of mental discipline and abilities in relaxation.

Training Techniques:

1. CO_2 Tolerance Tables:
- Gradually decrease the recovery times between breath-holds to make the body adapt to high levels of CO_2.
- Sample Progression: Hold for 1:30 → rest for 2:00 → hold for 1:30 → rest for 1:45 → repeat.

2. O₂ Tolerance Tables:
- Increase the length of breath holding for the same recovery time. This heightens the body's resistance to hypoxia.
- Sample Progression: Rest for 1:30 → hold for 2:00 → rest for 1:30 → hold for 2:15 → repeat.

3. Relaxation and Breathing Exercises:
- **Diaphragmatic Breathing:** One can consciously lower heart rate and oxygen consumption through deep, slow breathing.
- **Box Breathing:** Inhale for 4 seconds → hold for 4 seconds → exhale for 4 seconds → hold for 4 seconds → repeat.

B. Strength and Conditioning

Dry training also embraces strength, endurance, and flexibility exercises, which help move efficiently and use energy economically during dives.

Targeted Strength Areas:

1. Core Strength: Planks, side planks, and Russian twists increase stability and position the body in a more aerodynamic position.

2. Leg Power: Squats, lunges, and calf raises are useful for propulsion and help with efficient finning.

3. Upper Body Strength: Pullups, pushups, and exercises with resistance bands strengthen the back and shoulders to support arm strokes and good posture.

C. Flexibility and Mobility

Flexibility and Mobility increase the range of motion, reducing drag in the water and opening up a larger lung capacity.

Stretching Routines:

1. Diaphragm Stretches: One has to exhale to the end and hold to stretch the diaphragm.

2. Intercostal Stretches: Perform side bends and torso twists to expand the rib cage.

3. Shoulder and Hip Mobility: Use yoga poses such as Downward Dog and Pigeon Pose to maintain flexibility of the joints.

D. Mental Training

Training preparation and free diving are of the utmost importance since good relaxation may mean the difference between success and failure.

Meditation: It creates focus, lessens anxiety, and heightens self-awareness.

Visualization: Envision yourself with successful dives to nurture your confidence and techniques.

Progressive Muscle Relaxation: Make systematic muscle relaxations to conserve oxygen during apnea.

2. WaterBased Training for Free Diving

Aquatic Training: Diving conditions are simulated to perfect the divers' skills and adaptation to the underwater environment. Practicing breath control, efficiency of movement, and equalization techniques is essential.

A. Static Apnea in Water

Aquatic static apnea involves holding your breath and letting yourself float facedown. It resembles submerging, and the mind and body are relaxed under stress.

Objectives:
- Mental relaxation and focusing in a real diving environment.
- Increase tolerance of CO_2 buildup and hypoxia.

Training Guidelines:

1. Safety First: Always train with a buddy trained in safety protocols.

2. Gradual Progression: Start with shorter breathholds and gradually increase duration.

3. Relaxation Exercises: Relaxed breathing, body preparation for apnea.

B. Dynamic Apnea Training

Dynamic apnea involves holding your breath while moving underwater, such as swimming horizontally or practicing vertical dives. This discipline combines the aspects of controlling your breath and movement efficiency.

Goals:
- More streamlined motions to reduce drag.
- Less oxygen use while swimming or diving.

Methods:

1. Horizontal Apnea: Swimming laps underwater, smooths out, and becomes proficient in finning.

2. Vertical Apnea: Shallow water for equalization and relaxation by making controlled descents and ascents.

3. Streamlining Drills: Stay tucked to minimize drag produced while swimming through the water.

C. Equalization Practice in Water

Equalization prevents pressure change problems from arising on a given descent. Water-based practice develops this skill under actual conditions.

Essential Techniques

1. Frenzel Maneuver: Equalization is efficiently done with the tongue and throat muscles.

2. Buccal Pumping: Practice equalizing by using stored air in the mouth once lung volume at depth has decreased.

3. ShallowWater Drills: During shallow dives, practice the timing and technique of equalization.

3. CrossTraining for Freediving

Crosstraining supplements general fitness, prevention of overtraining, and correcting weaknesses aside from dry and water-based practices.

A. Cardiovascular Conditioning

Aerobic fitness increases the body's efficiency in transporting and utilizing oxygen.

Recommended Activities:

Swimming: It develops endurance and perfects finning technique.

Cycling: Enhances leg strength and cardiovascular fitness.

Jogging or Hiking: Develops aerobic capacity while controlling breathing patterns.

B. Strength and Power Development

Strength training provides functional strength for diving while preventing injury.

Key Exercises:

1. Deadlifts: The posterior chain needs to be powerful enough to keep the body vigorous.

2. Weighted Squats and Lunges: Build more muscular legs to give more power to propulsion.

3. PullUps: Build the upper body to maintain a streamlined position with powerful arm strokes.

C. Flexibility and Recovery

Flexibility and recovery training: Recover physical integrity, avoiding stiffness or possible injuries.
- **Stretching and Yoga:** Focus on dynamic stretches for mobility and static stretches for recovery.

- **Mobility and Massage:** recover muscle tension and improve circulation.

4. Adding Training to a Week of Training Day

Day	Focus	Activities
Monday	Dry Static Apnea + Strength	CO2 tables, core exercises, squats, and pull-ups.
Tuesday	Water-Based Dynamic Apnea	Horizontal laps, streamlining drills, and equalization practice.
Wednesday	Cross-Training + Flexibility	Swimming or jogging, followed by yoga or diaphragm stretching.
Thursday	Water Static Apnea + Equalization	Partner-assisted static apnea and equalization techniques.
Friday	Strength Training	Weighted squats, lunges, deadlifts, and resistance exercises.
Saturday	Long Dynamic Swim + Recovery	Long underwater swims, followed by foam rolling or massage.
Sunday	Rest or Light Yoga	Active recovery and mental relaxation.

Considerations Regarding Safety

1. Buddy System: Never train in the water alone; always train with a partner who will help in an emergency.

2. Gradual Progression: Conduct the training gradually, intensitywise, so as not to overexert.

3. Hydration and Nutrition: Well-nourishing meals will help you maintain body hydration and nutrition and endure all the training burdens.

4. Health Monitoring: If you experience constant fatigue, discomfort, or other problems, consult a medical professional.

Conclusion

A comprehensive freediving preparation approach combines dry and water training capacity and mental focus while working on water training techniques and simulating actual dive conditions. Crosstraining benefits both by generally improving fitness and flexibility. Structured and well-rounded training will achieve more in-depth duration and efficiency while minimizing risks and maximizing enjoyment in the underwater world.

Motor Coordination and Physical Fitness Techniques

Motor coordination harmonizes the nerves and muscles in the movement to be smooth, precise, and controlled in sporting performance and day-to-day functioning for general health. Physical Fitness includes strength, endurance, flexibility, and agility. Skill acquisition encompasses all of the above, which needs refining in functionality and injury rate reduction to help individuals live a better quality of life. It covers the development of coordination and physical Fitness through motor means by appropriate exercises and routines with functional methodology.

Understanding Motor Coordination

Motor coordination differentiates contractions by integrating the musculoskeletal, nervous, and sensory functions. This quality is essential for motor development in professional athletes, children, and adults who want to enhance functional movement.

Elements of Motor Coordinat on

1. Balance: This is an element of body control at different static or dynamic activities.

2. Agility: Directional changes with speed while in control.

3. Timing: Synchronization of movements about internal or external signs.

4. Hand-eye Coordination: depends upon the visual input to move rightly

5. Reaction: Time A person takes to respond to something stimuli

6. Spatial Awareness: The best definition is the person's awareness of where his body is in space and what it feels like in various places and positions.

Physical Fitness is a characteristic that allows the body to perform physical activities. Its definition embraces so many factors categorized into health—and performance-related components.

Key Components of Physical Fitness

1. Cardiorespiratory Endurance: the capacity of the heart, lungs, and blood vessels to supply oxygen in ongoing activity

2. Muscular Strength: maximum amount of force a muscle or muscles can apply

3. Muscular Endurance: how muscles maintain a continual contraction over a long period. Flexibility: range of motion of joints and muscles and muscles Composition: the relative % of body fat to lean mass

6. Strength: Power to force rapidly

7. Velocity: to be in place to accelerate

Methods of Improving Motor Coordination

Exercises with parts of the body refine motor coordination by stimulating the brain, disturbing balance, and increasing movement accuracy.

1. Equilibria training

Balance is part of motorization. It is among the most crucial stability features during dynamic and static movements.

- **Exercises:**
  - **Static Balance:** Stand on one leg for 30–60 seconds and walk on unstable surfboards like wobble boards.
  - **Bosu Ball Squats:** These are done on a Bosu ball to introduce challenging balance.
  - **Dynamic Balance:** Add heel-to-toe movement, such as walking straight or slacklining.

2. Agility drills

Agility embodies speed, control, and coordination relative to improved postural and functional movements.

- **Exercises:**
  - **Cone Drills:** Cones sare et up in patterns and weave with sprinting, side stepping, and back-pedaling.
  - **Agility:** Agility ladders can be for high knees, lateral shuffles, and in-and out hoops.
  - **Shadow Drills:** The same movements are executed with a partner to develop a reaction and the partners.

3. Hand-Eye Coordination

Handeye coordination is employed in performing an activity that involves finesse and precision.

- **Activities:**
  - **Ball Toss:** With a partner or yourself, against the wall, one leg balance.
  - **Juggling:** Perform exercises to increase concentration and coordination of motion.
  - **Play target games such as** hitting the target with equipment like darts or beanbags.

4. Reaction Training

Fast reactions improved decision-making and execution in dynamic situations.

- **Exercises:**
  - **Reaction Lights:** Get training applications or lighting systems that respond quickly against light visuals.
  - **Ball Drops:** Partner drops and catches the ball for a while on release
  - **Reflex Training Games:** The interactive tools provide rapid table tennis or tag form responses.

5. Spatial Awareness Drills

Spatial awareness gives motion to position one's body to get correct control over surroundings.

- **Drills:**
  - **Obstacle Courses:** Course structures involving stepping over, ducking under,r, and around objects.
  - **Mirror Movements:** Following a partner who initiates in one direction and then changes in another. Partner
  - **Sectional Changes:** Turns incorporating fast pivots, shuffles, and backward runs.

METHODS FOR PHYSICAL IMPROVEMENT OF HEALTH FITNESS

Among the concerned dimensions are the gain in strength and endurance. Hence, it has more components that correspond to these features.

1. Cardiovascular Training

It is also equally important during exercise to have endurance and health-related physiological capacity.

- **Exercises:**
  - **Steady-State Cardio:** Jogging, swimming, or cycling for a longer duration
  - **Interval Training:** Vigorous work followed by low-intensity exercises, such as sprints for 30 seconds, followed by a one-minute walk.
  - **Group Classes:** Diversity and motivation are the key elements in aerobics, dance, and spinning.

2. Resistance Training

Resistance Training: It helps develop mass, increases metabolism, and develops physical capacity.

- **Exercises:**
  - **Combination Exercises:** The exercises involved in larger machines are combination exercises, such as squats, deadlifts, bench presses, and rows.

- o **Bodyweight Exercises:** To improve functional strength, do super push-ups, pull-ups, and planks.
- o **Isometric Holds,** such as wall sits or static lunges, add muscular endurance.

3. Flexibild Mobility Training

The greater the mobility, the fewer the injuries. This economizes the locomotion.

- Exercise:
  - o **Dynamic Stretching:** During warm-up, the leg swings, arm circles, and spinal twists can be performed.
  - o **Static Stretching:** hamstring, quad, and shoulder stretches
  - o **Foam Rolling:** Incorporating foam rolling relaxes the muscles and helps to gain flexibility.

4. Functional Training

The exercises should also be near nature. They should consist of activity and muscular power.

- Exercise:
  - o **Slam Medicine Ball:** Explosive Power, Coordination.
  - o **Kettle-Bell Swings:** Power up the back chain and mobilize your hips.
  - o **Foam Rolling:** Farmer's Carries, Increasing Your Grip Strength and Stability.

5. Core Training

Core strength improves posture and increases balance and efficiency within your movements.

- Exercise:
  - o **Type of Plank:** side planks, reverse planks, d reaches.
  - o **Rotational Core Work:** Woodchoppers with cables or resistance bands.

o **Stability Ball Training:** Rollouts or crunches on a stability ball for added challenge.

Combination of Motor Coordination and Methods of Physical Fitness

The systematic training will combine motor coordination with the method of physical Fitness sampplow for one w is below seek.

Sample Weekly Plan

Day	Focus	Activities
Monday	Balance and Core Training	Single-leg stands, planks, and Bosu ball squats.
Tuesday	Cardiovascular Endurance	30–45 minutes of jogging, swimming, or cycling.
Wednesday	Agility and Reaction	Ladder drills, cone drills, and ball drops.
Thursday	Strength Training	Deadlifts, bench presses, and pull-ups.
Friday	Coordination and Functional Work	Medicine ball throws, obstacle courses, and juggling.
Saturday	Flexibility and Mobility	Yoga, foam rolling, and static stretches.
Sunday	Rest or Active Recovery	Light walking, stretching, or gentle swimming.

Profited by enhanced motor coordination and improved physical Fitness.

1. **Enhanced Athletic Performance:** Far better coordination, superior physical Fitness, iFitness control, effectiveness, and strength in the sport.

2. **Injury Avoidance:** Better, proportionate muscles and better stability mean a lower risk of falling and another injury.

3. **Functional Strength:** Once strength and mobility are improved, Mundane or day-to-day activities become more straightforward.

4. **BrainHealth:** In coordination exercise, both hands are involved with the body; hence, great effort is used to formulate focus, memory, and reaction capability.

5. **Long-term Health:** Regular exercise enhances cardiovascular health, bone density, and metabolic efficiency.

Conclusion

Motor coordination and Fitness are relevant for any active, fit person. Balance agility drills with cardio-vascular conditioning and resistance or strength training exercises, including all flexibility-related exercises. Gram Systems of Training Technique: A system of training techniques developing physical function supportive of mental acuity underlying longer ty, ranging from sports accomplishments to improved day-to-day capabilities and health to miserere apt, confident, resilient bodies. As it were, there is a general philosophy of correlation and witnesses.

Hypoxia and Hypercapnia Workouts, Pyramid Training for Freediving

Freediving is such a sport that pushes the human body to work efficiently in highly non-favorable physiological conditions. **Hypoxia, hypercapnia,** or high carbon dioxide levels are predominant among the most crucial factors determining performance in freediving. The training targeted at those two conditions and **pyramid training** will help improve tolerance, optimally structure breathing, and strengthen diving performance. The following manual will elaborate on hypoxia and hypercapnia, look at some practical training, and introduce pyramid training as one of the structured methods for enhancing physical and mental resistance.

Hypoxia and Hypercapnia Understanding

Hypoxia

Hypoxia is a drop in oxygen levels that impedes a person's typical physical performance and cognitive function. In freediving, this occurs more towards the end of the dive. Training allows divers to increase their dive times and safely push their limits further.

Hypercapnia

Hypercapnia is the increase of CO_2 in the blood, which is believed to stimulate breathing significantly. By building up his tolerance to CO_2, a freediver can be trained to increase his comfort zone while in apnea, thus significantly improving his performance in breath-hold diving.

1. Hypoxia Workouts

Hypoxia training forces the body to work in conditions of poor oxygenation. It enhances hypoxia resistance, delays the appearance of fatigue, and enriches, allowing for relaxation during low-oxygen phases.

Principles of Hypoxia Training

1. **Co-controlled Conditions**: Reduce risks by doing hypoxia training in safe, controlled conditions.

2. **Progressive Overload**: Gradually increase the intensity or duration to improve adaptation.

3. **Mental Relaxation**: It includes mental relaxation to decrease oxygen consumption.

Hypoxia Exercises

1. **Static Hypoxia Training:**
   - **Purpose**: Increase hypoxia tolerance during rest.
   - **How to Perform:**
   1. Do some relaxing breaths for 2–3 minutes.
   2. Hold your breath as long as possible without causing discomfort.
   3. Ret for 2 minutes, repeat for 5–8 cycles.

2. **Dynamic Hypoxia Training:**

Purpose: Practice apnea without oxygen during locomotion.

Procedure:

1. Ran underwater for 25 meters, holding your breadth.

2. Gradually increase the distance with time to 30, 35, and 50 meters over sessions.

3. Avoid jerky movements. This may consume a lot of oxygen.

3. Full Exhalation Apnea:
- **Purpose:** To simulate conditions of reduced lung volume as it would be during deep dives.
- **Protocol:**

1. Exhale to the residual volume before breath-hold.

2. Shallow swims or static hold.

3. Gradually increase the duration or length of each attempt.

4. Apnea Laps:
- **Purpose:** Combine hypoxia and endurance training.
- **Protocol:**

1. Swim 2–4 laps underwater with progressively shorter recovery intervals.

2. Start with 2-minute recoveries and decrease each cycle by 15–30 seconds.

2. Hypocapnia Workouts

Hypercapnia training focuses on the response to increased CO_2 levels, improving comfort and delaying the need to breathe during prolonged apnea.

Principles of Hypercapnia Training

1. CO_2 Adaptation: The body adapts after repeated exposure to high conditions of CO_2.

2. Short Recovery Intervals: Allowing only a short recovery time builds up the accumulation of CO_2 and brings it closer to actual dives.

3. **Controlled Stress:** Make the conditions harder over time to build tolerance but in safety.

Examples of Hypercapnic Workout

1. CO_2 Tolerance Tables:
- **Purpose:** Increase tolerance to high levels of CO_2 via formal breath-holds.
- **Protocol:**
1. Take a breath-hold for a fixed time, say 1:30.
2. Re-breathe for progressively shorter times, such as 2:00, 1:45, 1:30, etc.
3. Re-breathe 6-8 cycles, shortening hold times as appropriate about your capacity.

2. Dynamic CO_2 Training:
- **Purpose:** Enhanced CO_2 tolerance for locomotion.
- **Protocol:**
1. Aquatic swims 25 meters.
2. 15–30 seconds of recovery between each length.
3. Praggressively increases repetitions or decreases rest times.

3. Dry Hypercapnia Drills:
- **Purpose:** CO_2 Tolerance Out of the Water: It is easier and safer to build up CO_2 tolerance.
- **Protocol:**

1. Do some physical exercises like pushups, planks, or squats while holding your breath.

2. Limit the recovery periods to simulate the accumulation of CO_2.

4. Breath Ladder Training:
- **Purpose:** This form of training is to bring hypercapnia training into an aerobic workout.

- **Protocol:**
1. Take a set number of breaths, say 5, between 25-meter swims.
2. Aggressively reduce the number of breaths you are allowed.

3. Pyramid Training

Pyramid training incorporates progressive difficulty, duration, intensity, or distance up the peak and tapers down. It is an efficient method for enhancing endurance, CO_2 tolerance, and mental state.

Benefits of Pyramid Training
- There is less risk of overtraining because of the gradual approach in intensity.
- Realistic dive simulation by imitating the build-up of stress and recovery.
- Both anaerobic and aerobic capacity are improved.
- It helps in developing mental resilience by introducing challenges in a structured manner.

Pyramid Training Examples

1. BreathHold Pyramid:
- **Purpose:** To gradually increase and decrease the time of breath holding.
- **Procedure:**
1. Initially, hold for 1.00 minutes.
2. Instruct to increase it by 15 seconds step in each round as (1.15, 1.30, and 1.45).
3. At your peak - for example, at 2:00-start to work backward (1:45, 1:30, 1:15, 1:00).

2. Pyramid Distance (Dynamic Apnea):
- **Purpose:** To have a progressive increase and subsequently decrease in underwater swimming distances

- **Procedure:**
1. In the water, begin underwater swimming for 15 meters.
2. By 5 meters per lap increase, for example, 15m, 20m, 25m.
3. When peak distance is reached, begin tapering back down.

3. Repetition Pyramid:
- **Purpose:** Combine strength and CO_2 tolerance training.
- **Protocol:**
1. Do a pyramid of pushups, squats, or planks.
2. Increase repetitions each round (example 5, 10, 15, 20).
3. Work back to top in reverse: (15 → 10 → 5).

Sample Weekly Training Plan

Day	Focus	Activity
Monday	CO2 Tolerance (Dry)	CO2 tables (8 cycles), breath-hold planks, or squats with reduced recovery.
Tuesday	Dynamic Hypoxia	25m underwater swims with increasing distances or decreasing recovery time.
Wednesday	Breath-Hold Pyramid	Pyramid training with 1:00 → 2:00 → 1:00 static apnea holds.
Thursday	Exhale Apnea Training	Short swims or statics with full exhale before holding breath.
Friday	Dynamic CO2 Workouts	Laps underwater with minimal recovery (e.g., 25m swims with 15-second rest).
Saturday	Rest or Active Recovery	Yoga, stretching, and light cardio for recovery.
Sunday	Distance Pyramid	15m → 25m → 15m dynamic apnea training.

Safety Considerations

1. Buddy Training: Never train in hypoxia or hypercapnia training alone, much less in the water.

2. Being Aware of Symptoms: Learn to recognize the general discomfort and feelings associated with hypoxia and stop immediately.

3. Progress Gagradual: To avoid injury to yourself, make incremental and gradual increases.

4. Rest for Recovery: Allow the body appropriate rest and recuperation between sessions to avoid overtraining.

5. Hydrate and Nourish: Proper hydration and nutrition effectively facilitate high performance and recovery.

Conclusion

Hypoxia, hypercapnia workouts, and pyramid training are essential tools for building endurance, efficiency, and resilience in every freediver's toolbox. Periodically increasing the challenges to the body will increase tolerance against low oxygen and high levels of CO_2, enabling the diver to safely prolong breath-holding times and mentally prepare for the underwater world. Continuously applied safely and respectfully, these methods will allow freedivers to achieve new lengths and depths with controlled, sure ability.

Advanced Techniques and Training in Freediving

Dynamic Apnea Training: WarmUps, Speed, and Contractions Management

Dynamic apnea is one of the most outstanding features of advanced freediving. This dive involves horizontal and vertical motion on a single breath hold. It requires control, efficiency, and relaxation, mixing physical resistance with mental strength. Prop training in dynamic apnea increases a freediver's performance by developing awareness of physiological adversities such as contractions and the buildup of CO_2. This paper discusses advanced techniques related to dynamic apnea, including appropriate warmups, speed optimization, and contraction management for optimal performance.

1. The Role of Dynamic Apnea in Freediving

Dynamic apnea can simulate real-life situations of freediving, where a diver has to move with minimum oxygen consumption while keeping the body relaxed. In contrast with static apnea, which is performed in a state of complete rest of the body, dynamic apnea includes additional factors such as energy use, hydrodynamic resistance, and coordination.

Key Benefits
- **Improves Oxygen Efficiency:** The body can use less oxygen during sustained movements.
- **CO_2 Tolerance:** It builds up tolerance for higher levels of CO_2 without having to breathe.

- **Technique:** Perfecting technique streamlining and general movement efficiency. • Mental
- **Resilience:** It prepares divers for calm in the face of discomfort caused by contractions and rising CO_2 levels.

Dynamic apnea training forms the backbone of performance enhancement in competitive disciplines such as pu, recreation, and d, as well as depth-focused disciplines like freediving.

2. General Dynamic Apnea WarmUp

A proper warmup prepares the body and the mind for dynamic apnea. This minimizes injury, optimizes physical performance, and assures mental preparedness.

A. Dry WarmUp Techniques

1. Breathing Exercises
- Diaphragmatic Breathing: Slow, deep inhalation expands the diaphragm, allowing the body to release tension.
o For example, Inhale for 4 seconds, hold, and exhale for 8 seconds.
- This is done for 23 minutes. Box Breathing is a fine example of equal-length inhaling, holding, exhaling, and holding on for 5 seconds.

2. Stretching and Mobility
- **Diaphragm Stretches:** These are achieved by completely exhaling, holding, and leaning back to pull the diaphragm.
- **Intercostal Stretches:** Side bends extending the rib cage for increased lung capacity.
- **Hip Flexor and Shoulder Stretches:** will prepare your body for streamlined swimming with efficient finning.

B. InWater WarmUp

1. Shallow Static Holds
- Start with 2–3 short static breath-holds of 30–60 seconds, facedown in the water.

2. Short Dynamic Laps
- In a state of relaxation, swim leisurely over 10–15 meters and use exercises to relax.

3. Technique Drills
- Kick the body tightly and in line through the water to reduce drag.

4. CO_2 Adaptation WarmUp
- Take 2–3 dynamic laps with short recoveries to get your body ready for such high levels of CO_2.

3. Speed Optimization in Dynamic Apnea

Dynamic apnea needs to pace a great line between efficiency in movement and not using too much oxygen. A pace that is too fast can deplete the available oxygen; on the other hand, being too slow will build CO_2 levels that are too high for breathing and don't feel uncomfortable.

A. Finding Your Optimal Speed

1. Pacing Experiments
- Describe the velocity corresponding to greater distances by doing dynamic apnea laps at different speeds.

2. Technique of Finning
- **With Fins:** Long and smooth, controlled kicks. Avoid quick, choppy movements, raising oxygen consumption.
- **NoFins:** Strong dolphin kicks or breaststroke pullkick. The arm position is for minimal drag.

3. Heart Rate Control
- Your heart rate during and after dives should be low, reflecting good use of oxygen.

B. Speed Training Drills

1. Controlled Intervals
- Perform 25-meter dynamic sprints, then rest for 1–2 minutes. Progressively build up speed and repetitions consecutively.

2. Negative Splits
- Swim the first half of a dynamic lap at a relaxed pace and the second half faster.

3. Timed Laps
- Have a time objective over a fixed course, such as 50 meters, and pace yourself accordingly.

4. Contractions Management in Dynamic Apnea

These are the contractions of the diaphragm, which occur with rising levels of CO_2. Learning to work with contractions can increase breathing time, thus improving performance in dynamic apnea.

A. Understanding Contractions

1. Physiological Basis
- Contractions are a natural response to rising CO_2 as a response to breathing stimulus.

If treated non-panicked, they are not dangerous and should not be a source of unease or distraction.

2. Psychological Aspect
- For most divers, contractions are more of a psychological threshold. Framing them as evidence of improvement increases tolerance.

B. Ways of Overcoming Contractions

1. Relaxation
Master the mindfulness techniques to help keep calm and composed during contractions.

Visualize completing the dive; this will help reinforce positive associations with your dive.

2. Gradual Exposure

Improve tolerance through dry training: extend the hold time after contractions onset.

3. Controlled Breathing

Hyperventilation before diving suppresses CO_2 levels and delays the onset of contraction, masking a critical signal for hypoxia.

C. Contraction Training Drills

1. Static Apnea Holds
- Static breath-holds; relax by the onset of contractions. Gradually increase the length over time.

2. Dynamic Contraction Laps
- Dynamic apnea laps. Notice when the contractions start to come on. Here, make more distance with contractions coming on progressively.

3. CO_2 Tolerance Workouts
- Employ CO_2 tables with extremely short recovery times to simulate high CO_2 situations and how to manage contractions within that environment safely.

5. Advanced Dynamic Apnea Techniques

A. Streamlining and Hydrodynamics
- **Keep Alignment:** Aligning the head, torso, and legs in one line is critical to minimizing resistance or drag.
- **Limit Movements:** Only minor movements that disturb hydrodynamics and heighten oxygen consumption should be made.

B. Efficient Turns
- Practice fast and smooth turns at the pool walls for minimum loss of speed and energy expenditure.

C. Timing of Equalization
- Make equalization rhythmical with your movements, especially in VD, so as not to break the rhythm.

D. MentTraininging
- Imagine dynamic apnea training, relaxation, and interaction during mental rehearsals.

6. Sample Advanced Dynamic Apnea Training Session

Phase	Activity	Duration
Warm-Up	Diaphragmatic breathing, ribcage stretches, and short static holds	10–15 mins
Technique Drills	Streamlining drills, 15m relaxed laps, and efficient turn practice	10–15 mins
Speed Intervals	25m sprints with 1:30 recovery, gradually increasing speed	15–20 mins
Contraction Training	Dynamic laps with controlled contraction exposure, progressively increasing distance	15–20 mins
Cool Down	Light swimming, stretching, and recovery breathing	10 mins

7. Safety Considerations

1. Always Train with a Buddy
- Dynamic apnea training has some inherent risks of shallow water blackouts. Ensure there is always a person to monitor who has received such training.

2. Go Gradual
- Do not force the limit at all costs. Increase the distance, time, and ability for standing contractions gradually.

3. Watch for Warning Signs
- Immediately stop if you start feeling dizzy or tired.

4. Stay
- Proper hydration will ensure optimal performance and recovery.

Conclusion

Dynamic apnea is the fully developed freediving technique in which the diver has to push himself to overcome his inefficiency in moving with his hold of breath, contractions, and buildup. Good warmup, speed optimization, and buildup cooling contraction management can seriously impact underwater performance. Building safety measures and mental toughness would be powerful tools for achieving new milestones in freediving and developing beyond human physical and mental limitations to explore the fantastic, silent world of waters.

Static Apnea Training: Series, Psychological Blocks, and Breath Holds

Static apnea is one of the most essential disciplines in freediving. In this discipline, one must increase the time one holds one's breath while keeping the body in a single position. In addition to physical resistance, this aspect requires great psychic concentration, physical relaxation, and physiological adaptation to conditions of hypoxia and hypercapnia. Generalized static apnea training represents a series of structured psychological breakthrough techniques and advanced methods of safely holding one's breath to maximize one's performance.

1. General Overview of Static Apnea Training

Static apnea training includes holding one's breath while passively floating or lying stationary. It is performed both in and out of the water. The main goals are increasing breath-hold time, psychological strengthening, and preparing physiological systems to work harmoniously with minimum oxygen consumption.

Key Objectives

1. Oxygen Efficiency: Training the body for efficient use of oxygen in case of longer breathholds.

2. CO_2 Tolerance: To become accustomed to the irritant created by increased CO_2.

3. Relaxation of the Mind: To learn to become calm and accurate under pressure.

4. General Freediving Preparation: Preparation for apnea disciplines with depth and movement.

2. Structuring Static Apnea Training

A well-structured static apnea training program will include a warmup, a structured breath-hold series, and active recovery techniques. These contextual training aspects lead to progressive developments and heighten the practitioner's confidence.

A. WarmUp Series

A series of warmups will also prime both the body and psyche for the demands of static apnea. This reduces injury opportunities, relaxes the diver, and can be a platform for more extended breath holds.

1. Relaxation Breathing
- Diaphragmatic breathing would relax the body, lowering the heart rate.
- Example: Inhale for 4 seconds, hold, exhale for 8 seconds, and repeat for 2–3 minutes.

2. Light Apnea Holds
- Prediscontinue with 35 short static holds for 3060 seconds with relaxed recovery breaths.
- Be aware of the relaxation and the ease of breathing in and out.

3. Stretching and Mobility
- Diaphragm, rib cage, and shoulder exercises to open up your lungs' capacity and release tension.
  o **Diaphragm Stretch:** Exhale completely, hold, and lean backward.
  o **Intercostal stretch:** Bending sideward with the expansions of the rib cage, releasing neck and shoulder rolls.
  o **Neck and shoulder rolls:** loosen tensions within the body.

B. CO_2 and O_2 Tolerance Tables

In the tables of CO_2 and O_2 tolerance, structured training causes the body to experience high levels of CO_2 and a lower quantity of oxygen in its usual form.

1. CO_2 Tables
- Focus on decreasing the recovery intervals to create a tolerance for CO_2 buildup.
- Protocol:
  o Static breath holds at a fixed time, ex, 1:30
  o Recovery with decline: 2:00 → 1:45 → 1:30 → 1:15 → 1:00
  o Repeat 6-8 runs, ups and downs

2. O_2 tables
- Gradually extend equal periods of breathing to resistance against hypoxia.
- Protocol:
  o Rest: 1:30.
  o Breathhold: 1:30 → 1:45 → 2:00 → 2:15 → 2:30.
  o Repeat for 6–8 cycles.

C. Maximum BreathHolding Attempts
- Include 2 to 3 maximal breath-holding attempts in one session.
- Rest for 3–5 min between attempts, relaxation, and recovery breathing.

3. Overcoming Psychological Blocks

In contrast, psychological factors may be more critical in determining breath-breath-Goldman than physiological ones. Learning to transcend these barriers can help the diver realize his full potential in static apnea.

A. Common Psychological Barriers

1. Fear of Hypoxia: One of the more significant reasons why breath holds are terminated prematurely is a fear of hypoxia.

2. Discomfort due to Contractions: The rise in CO_2 causes the diaphragm to contract, which gives the urge to breathe.

3. Mental Fatigue: The inability to focus or resist negative thoughts compromises performance.

B. Techniques to Overcome Psychological Blocks

1. Reframing Discomfort
- Contraction is a good indication and not a warning signal.
- It also considers that the body still has sufficient oxygen at the initial contractions.

2. Relaxation and Concentration Practice
- Meditate or relax via yoga.
- Prostatic apnea progressive muscle relaxations before and during the hold relieve physical tension.

3. Visualization
- Imagine running through a static apnea session in the head and being successful.
- Visualize contractions, no distressachieve goal time.

4. Positive Self-Talk
- Repeating, for example, "I am in control and relaxed" or "I am at ease with this feeling" can banish doubts.

5. Progressive Achievement
- Progressively build up breath holds to build trust and become accustomed to the sensation of partial distress.

4. Static Apnea Breath-Hold Techniques

Relaxation on a hold optimizes oxygen consumption by relaxing into more extended states of static apnea.

A. Relaxation Phase

1. Relaxation Breathing
- Slow, controlled breathing relaxes the body and slows heart rate.
- Do not hyperventilate to avoid dangerous lowering of CO_2 levels.

2. Full Inhale
- Deep diaphragmatic inhalation: the ribcage expands toward the top of the chest.
- Do not overinflate, as this may result in tension or discomfort.

B. Execution Phase

1. Relax
- Conserve oxygen by not moving unless necessary.
- Release tension in the neck, shoulders, and jaw.

2. Mental Focus

These include visualization, counting, or mantras to help focus and reduce tension.

3. Monitor Contractions

Accept the contractions as a process and let relaxation techniques help one through them.

C. Recovery Phase

1. Exhale Slowly
- First, one must breathe slowly to avoid vertigo or discomfort.

2. Recovery Breathing
- Short, rapid breaths and longer exhalation to stabilize oxygen.

3. Reflection
- Check oneself for weaknesses.

5. Advanced Techniques to Extend BreathHold

1. Progressive Breath-Hold Series
- Times can be extended over weeks and months using relaxation and control.

2. CO_2 Workouts
- Squats, planks, or light jogging while holding your breath may increase your tolerance to CO_2.

3. Pulmonary Flexibility Training
- Rib cage and diaphragm stretching for volume increase to accommodate comfort at full inspiration.

4. Psychological Conditioning
- Build resilience through meditation, visualization,n and calmness when one feels stressed outside of training.

5. Cardiovascular Training
- Some cardio workouts include swimming, cycling, or running, which can increase the body's oxygen delivery and improve general endurance.

6. Sample Static Apnea Training Plan

Phase	Activity	Duration
Warm-Up	Diaphragmatic breathing, light stretching, short breath-holds	10–15 minutes
CO2 Table	Breath-holds with decreasing recovery intervals (6 cycles)	15–20 minutes
O2 Table	Breath-holds with increasing durations (6 cycles)	15–20 minutes
Maximum Attempts	2–3 maximum-duration breath-holds with full recovery	20 minutes
Cool Down	Recovery breathing and light stretching	5–10 minutes

7. Safety Considerations

1. Buddy System
- Always practice with a buddy who can assist in unconsciousness.

2. Avoid Hyperventilation
- Hyperventilation depletes CO_2, masks the symptoms of hypoxia, and creates the risk of blackout.

3. Ease Up
- Notice the progressive gains so as not to overexert one's self.

4. Physical and Mental Condition
- Stop exercising at the onset of lightheadedness, vertigo, or extreme fatigue.

5. Hydration and Nutrition
- Proper hydration and good nutrition are conducive to your training.

8. Mental and Physical Gains by Static Apnea Training

1. Relaxation Improved: Gives a much better sensation of relaxation and concentration.

2. CO_2 and O_2 Tolerance Increased: Generally increased breath-holding capacity.

3. Improved Performance: Set up reasonable dynamic apnea and depth dive platforms.

4. Mental Strength: Teaches the ways of persistence and control during difficult situations.

Conclusion

Static Apnea training is an advanced technique for building physical and mental resistance, enabling divers to go for the structural series, overcome psychological problems, and hold their breath. This kind of diving is, when performed habitually, with some observance of precautions, the stepping stone of static apnea to every new record beaten in this sport of free diving that links up with the body and psyche at more extraordinary lengths.

Deep Freediving Techniques: Free Fall, Lung Packing, and Equalization

Deep freediving requires physical and mental endurance. Several advanced techniques are needed to overcome pressure, oxygen conservation, and mental clarity. Among the most critical skills for success are free-to-fall, lung packing, and Equalization techniques for achie, which lower depth efficiently, energy conservation, and safety maintenance. This guide delves into the details of these practices, providing detailed insights, training tips, and safety considerations to help you raise your deep freediving bar.

1. Free-Fall: Mastering Passive Descent

Free fall is a transition phase of deep freediving in which the diver does not swim actively but lets gravity take them toward depth. This usually starts once the diver reaches negative buoyancy, which is between 15 and 30 meters for most divers, depending on body composition, lung volume, and weight setup.

Benefits of Free-Fall

1. Energy Savings: The use of oxygen is minimized because active movements such as finning are not used.

2. Mental Relaxation: Relaxed, meditative state for better focus and enjoyment during the dive. **3. Streamlining:** Hydrodynamic positioning for less resistance for the best possible efficiency during the descent.

4. Depth Adaptation: The psychological and physiological adaptation in front of deep dives and more significant pressure.

FREE-FALL TECHNIQUES

1. Optimal Weighting:
- Be neutrally buoyant at 10 meters depth to ensure a smooth transition into negative buoyancy.
- Avoid overweighting, which enhances resistance in the upward movement and decreases safety.

2. Streamlined Body Position
- The body should be aligned, with the arms above the head or relaxed along the sides.
- Light engagement of the core is needed to maintain a straight posture without tension.

3. Relaxation and Concentration
- Release all unnecessary tension in the muscles.
- You can use visualization techniques or focus on the sensation of the descent, such as the feeling of the water rushing past your body.

4. Descent Speed Management
- To refine speed, make slight adjustments in body position. For example, bringing arms closer to the body or extending them overhead can affect drag.

5. Depth Awareness
- Use a dive line or depth markers to monitor equality and make equality constant.

Free Fall Training

1. Buoyancy Drills
- Practice your neutral buoyancy point in shallow water. Progressively go to deeper water to get used to negative buoyancy.

2. Simulated Free Fall
- Descend by using light finning until negative buoyancy is reached, then shift into a passive glide.

3. Exercises for Mental Relaxation
- Practice mindfulness or meditation to develop the mental calmness needed during the free fall phase.

2. Lung Packing: Expanding Breath-Hold Capacity

Lung packing, or "glossopharyngeal insufflation," is an advanced technique allowing the freediver to increase their lung volume beyond a natural full inhalation. Extra air packed into the lungs allows the freediver to store more oxygen, have better buoyancy in shallow depths, and equalize more efficiently.

Benefits of Lung Packing

1. Extended BreathHold: Increases oxygen reserves, enabling longer dives.

2. Improved Equalization: Provides additional air for EqualiEqualizationeater depths.

3. Increased Buoyancy: The negative buoyancy of the initial descent phase is counteracted.

Risks and Considerations

1. Overpacking: Forces the lungs, diaphragm, or chest muscles too hard and may cause barotrauma.

2. **Discomfort:** Beginners may feel tight or have to work at breathing relaxed.

3. **Gradual Introduction:** Lung packing should be introduced gradually to allow the body to adapt.

Lung Packing Technique

1. Preparation

Begin by breathing diaphragmatically to expand the lungs fully.

Then, take a few deep, controlled breaths to prepare the body.

2. Packing Air
- With a full inhale, open your mouth slightly and use your tongue and throat muscles to "gulp" air into the lungs.
- Each "gulp" adds a little air. Keep going until you are comfortably full.

3. Comfort Check

Stop if you become uncomfortable, dizzy, or your chest becomes tight.

4. Pursed Lip-Breathing
- Rib cage strtcstretchesddiaphragm exercises can be done to expand lung capacity and minimize discomfort.

Lung Packing Training

1. Start Small
- Start with 3–5 packs per session and progress.

2. Add to Stretching
- Stretch the intercostals and diaphragm to prep the lungs for higher volume.

3. Incorporate into Equalization Practice
- Practice packing a lung with equalization drills and build-up time to simulate actual conditions in a dive.

3. Equalization: Managing Pressure at Depth

Equalization balances pressure in air-filled spaces, such as ears, sinuses, and masks, with the surrounding pressure as depth is gained—inability or ineffective. Equalization to barotrauma and discomfort for the diver, limiting his ability to dive deeper.

Equalization Techniques

1. Valsalva Maneuver
- Pinch your nose and gently exhale to equalize the pressure in your ears.
- It is best adapted for shallow dives or is for beginners and inefficient at depth due to increased resistance.

2. Frenzel Maneuver
- Forward the air with the tongue and throat into the Eustachian tubes while the glottis is closed.
- It is ideal for deeper dives since it requires less effort than Valsalva.

3. HandsFree Equalization (BTV)
- Contract throat and jaw muscles to open the Eustachian tubes without using your hands.
- It requires significant practice and is highly effective for advanced divers.

4. Mouth-Fill Equalization
- **What It Is:** A technique where a diver stores air in the mouth early in the dive, using it for equalization as lung volume decreases with depth.
- **How It Works:**

1. During the descent, inhale profoundly and transfer air from the lungs into the mouth before the residual volume of the lungs becomes too small to provide enough air for equalization.

2. Seal the air in your mouth by closing the glottis and keeping the tongue in a position that traps the air.
3. Push the stored air into the Eustachian tubes using the tongue, cheeks, and throat muscles to equalize.
   - **Why It's Effective:**
   o It is essential for dives beyond residual lung volume, as lung compression at depth limits the availability of air for equalization.
   o It enables deep divers to continue equalizing effectively, even at great depths.
   - **Practice:**
   o Begin practicing the mouth-fill technique in shallow water to develop muscle control.
   o Combine with Frenzel to maximize equalization efficiency.

Common Equalization Challenges

1. Sinus Congestion
- Blocked sinuses can block air from reaching the Eustachian tubes. Use saline rinses or decongestants if needed.

2. Mask Squeeze
- Equalize by blowing slightly into the mask, letting the air equalize the pressure inside so it does not cause discomfort.

3. Pressure at Depth
- As depth increases, EqualiEqualizationbe becomes equal and acceptable as air volume compresses.

Equalization Tips

1. Start Early and Often
- Begin equalizing before the descent and continue doing so frequently.

2. Head Position
- Keep the chin tucked in to align the Eustachian tubes for easier Equalisation.

3. On Land Practise
- Dry drills for Frenzel or BTV methods are conducted to build muscular memory.

4. Deep Freediving Training Techniques

A. Free Fall Training
- Practice finding your neutral buoyancy and drop into free fall.
- Relaxed through mental focus points: counting or depth markers.

B. Lung Packing Drills
- Do the lung packing exercises regularly by increasing the number of packs gradually.
- Deep breathing and stretching together can be used to increase the flexibility of your lungs.

C. Equalization Drills
- Frenzel or BTV practices during shallow dives will help to refine the skills.
- Use a dive line for controlled depth training and regular equalization intervals.

By consistently incorporating and practicing these techniques, divers can effectively manage pressure at depth, allowing for safer, more enjoyable, profound freediving experiences.

5. Sample Deep Freediving Training Session

Phase	Activity	Duration
Warm-Up	Diaphragmatic breathing, light stretching, and relaxation exercises	10–15 minutes
Free Fall Practice	Descend to neutral buoyancy and practice passive gliding	15–20 minutes
Lung Packing	Perform 5–10 packs, incorporating ribcage stretches	10 minutes
Equalization Training	Frenzel or BTV drills during shallow descents	15–20 minutes
Cool Down	Surface breathing, light swimming, and reflective stretching	10 minutes

6. Safety Considerations for Deep Freediving

1. Always Dive with a Buddy
- Make sure there is always a trained partner who can keep an eye on your safety.

2. Progress Gradually
- Increase depth, lung packing capacity, and equalization skills over time.

3. Monitor Your Body
- If you feel discomfort, pain, or a problem with equaliEqualization.

4. Hydrate and Equalization
- Good hydration and rest will help in general performance.

5. Seek Professional Guidance
- Find a certified freediving instructor who can help perfect your technique and help you stay safe.

7. Psychological Benefits of Mastering Advanced Techniques

1. Gained Confidence: Expertise in free fall, lung packing, and EqualiEqualizationlls confidence in you.

2. Enhanced Focus: Equalization Techniques help increase mindfulness and clarity of your mind.

3. Stress Management: The sport teaches one to move gracefully through pressure, underwater, or in life.

Conclusion

Deep freediving requires physical conditioning, advanced techniques, and mental discipline. To reach greater depths, divers must master free fall, lung packing, and Equalization. The structure, gradual progression, and adherence to safety protocols will allow divers to realize new potential, explore deeper underwater realms, and experience the profound serenity of the ocean.

Technical Information on Different Freediving Depth Disciplines

Freediving depth disciplines are defined by the technique, equipment, and type of movement employed to descend and ascend underwater. Each discipline challenges different aspects of the diver's physical endurance, mental focus, and mastery of specific skills. Each discipline has its technical peculiarities that are important for safe and practical training, performance, and progress. Below, an improved version of the significant depth disciplines is given, along with technical details, challenges, and training strategies.

1. Constant Weight (CWT)

Description

In this category, the freediver makes a descent and ascent by their effort with fins or a monofin but does not change their weight setup during the dive. CWT focuses on efficiency in propulsion and saving energy.

Technical Aspects

Movement:
- Effective propulsion with finning or monofin at minimum oxygen consumption.

- Continuous, regulated kicks allow for the most length with one kick cycle.

Streamlining:
- Hydrodynamic position maintenance or how to minimize drag: head, spine, and legs in perfect continuity.

Equalization:
- Mastery of Frenzel or mouthfill will be essential in always having constant pressure while going down.

Equipment:
- Monofin advanced propulsion; randifins, universal.
- Lightweight wetsuit in construction and low-friction profile.
- A nose clip or mask for efficient equalization.

Key Challenges
- Balancing physical exertion with the economy of oxygen when swimming actively.
- Significant buoyancy changes with depth- the greater the lung compression, the more critical the buoyancy change.
- Continuous, particularly on deeper dives.

Training Tips

1. Finning Practice: Practice smooth, relaxed finning in a pool or open water technique and minimize energy use.

2. Buoyancy Adjustment: Experiment with weights to achieve neutral buoyancy at about 10 meters, transitioning naturally into free fall.

3. CO_2 and O_2 Tolerance: Use dynamic apnea training to increase tolerance for rising CO_2 and low oxygen levels with longer dives.

2. Constant weight without fins (CNF)

Description

In CNF, the freediver goes down and up without fins, entirely relying on arm strokes and leg kicks for propulsion. Technique, strength, and coordination are necessary for this discipline.

Technical Aspects

Movement:
- Smooth, rhythmic coordination stroke-ordination.
- Proper recovery of arms and legs to maintain streamlining in the water.

Streamlining:
- The body should be aligned to reduce drag, even during the transition between strokes and kicks.

Equalization:
- More sophisticated techniques include mouth-filling to equalize pressure changes that happen quickly.

Equipment:
- A flexible, lightweight wetsuit that provides agility in the water.
- Equalization is hands-free with a nose clip.

Key Challenges
- It requires more physical effort due to the lack of fins.
- Coordinating as a co-ordinate of buoyancy and attention at free fall.

Training Tips

1. Dynamic No-Fin Training: Train your arm and leg coordinatco-ordinationool by practicing a rhythm.

2. Strength Training: This includes, but is not limited to, pull-ups, planks, and squats, which help develop the strength required to propel effectively.

3. Mental Conditioning: Practice mindfulness and visualization to keep yourself calm and focused under great exertion.

3. Free Immersion (FIM)

Description

In FIM, a freediver descends and ascends along a vertical dive line by pulling himself along the line without using fins or swimming motions. This event deals more with relaxation and the economy of energy.

Technical Aspects

Movement:
- Smooth, continuous motions by employing hand-over-hand pulls.

Relaxation:
- During the downward, relax to preserve oxygen.

Equalization:
- With each pull, equalize at just the right moment.

Equipment:
- Dive line - anchored correctly and not too slack or taut
- Light wetsuit to provide minimal drag

Main Hazards
- To time equalization with pulls: a challenging proposition
- Avoid too much tiredness in ascent.
- The ability to deal with the psychological pressures of a free fall while not actively swimming.

How to Train

1. Technic Technic: Do controlled and smooth pulls in a pool or shallow water.

2. Static Apnea: Learn mental relaxation to be still during passive descents.

3. Strengthening: Hand strengthening and developing upper body endurance are key to maintaining productive pulling.

4. Variable Weight (VWT)

Description

The diver goes down with the help of a weighted sled and comes up under their power, either by pulling the dive line or using fins.

VWT permits deeper dives with less physical effort on the descent.

Technical Aspects

Descent:
- Relax and align your body correctly during the descent with the sled.

Ascent:
- Use good propulsion or tractor technique for a self-powered ascent.

Equalization:
- Mastery of the most advanced equalization techniques for fast descents, like mouthfill.

Equipment:
- Weighted sled with adjustable weight.
- The dive line was pulled for reference with proper tension.
- Fins or monofin for propulsion during ascent.

Key Challenges
- To manage rapid pressure changes associated with sled-assisted descent.
- To manage a smooth transition from the sled descent to self-powered ascent.
- Maintaining focus and oxygen reserves for the ascent phase.

Training Tips

1. Equalization Drills: Practice rapid equalization techniques to prepare for fast descents.

2. Aerobic Conditioning: Build cardiovascular endurance to sustain oxygen reserves during the ascent.

3. Simulation Training: Use controlled environments to familiarize yourself with sled operation and transitions.

5. NoLimits (NLT)

Description

The weighted sled is used for the descent, while the lift bag or buoyancy device assists in the ascent. This discipline allows the greatest depths but involves the highest risks.

Technical Aspects

Descent:
- To maintain relaxation and mental focus during the sled descent.

Ascent:
- Proper lift bag or buoyancy device operation for controlled return to the surface.

Equalization:
- Advanced equalization skills, for the most part, extreme depths.

Equipment:
- Weighted sled.
- Lift bag or buoyancy device with reliable controls.

Key Challenges
- Fast changes in pressure on the way down and on the way up.
- Mastering the operation of equipment during the extreme depths.
- Controlling mental and physical challenges of the dive.

Training Tips

1. Practice Extreme Equalization: Perfect your mouthfill and Frenzel technique for rapid changes in pressure.

2. Familiarization with Equipment: Lift devices and sleds in a controlled environment can be used before greater depths are attempted.

3. Psychological Training: Mental robustness is developed through exercises in visualization and relaxation, among others.

General Safety Considerations for All Disciplines

1. Dive with a Trained Buddy: Always make sure a buddy or safety diver is present to observe and assist.

2. Gradual Progression: Increase depth and duration incrementally to avoid overexertion or injury.

3. Master Equalization: The key to avoiding barotrauma is constant and proper equalization.

4. Monitor Recovery: Allow adequate surface recovery time between dives to reduce hypoxia risks.

5. Hydration and Nutrition: Proper fluid intake and appropriate nutrition ensure peak performance in divers.

Conclusion

Each depth discipline, such as CWT, CNF, FIM, VWT, and NLT, requires a unique combination of physical endurance, technical skill, and mental discipline. Mastering these aspects allows divers to safely push their limits and explore greater depths in their quests to achieve their goals. Consistent training, gradual progression, and adherence to safety protocols ensure that freedivers can fully enjoy the profound and transformative experience of the underwater world.

Nutrition recovery to freediving: detailed nutrition recommendations and hydration strategies.

Above all, free diving is honed in physical prowess, sharp mental acuity, and adequate oxygenation. Good nutrition and hydration ensure peak energy optimization, performance, and recovery. Nutrition planning has got to feed the body. The nutritional stresses of free diving fortify and enrich health for a long. This discussion covers almost every area of nutrition and recovery, individually related to free food.

1. Nutrition in Freediving

The nutritional approach for a freediver may be based on general health-enhancing principles while considering specific answers to the demands of this sport.

- **Energetic Optimization:** creates sustained energy for short, intensive dives and long training sessions. It also assures
- **Efficient Oxygen Utilization:** all nutrients help maintain cardiovascular health, improve circulation, and reduce oxidative stress.
- **Recovery Enhancement:** Human nutritional needs include muscle repair, inflammation reduction, and muscle glycogen restoration.
- **Mental Clarity:** It enhances the focus-relaxation feature, immediately becoming the most critical parameter in freediving performance and safety.

2. Nutritional Specifics for Freedivers

A. Balance of Macronutrients

1. Carbohydrates:

Why They're Important: Carbohydrates are an essential energy source needed during anaerobic activities such as breath-hold training or dynamic apnea.

Best Sources:
- Whole grains - quinoa, oats, brown rice.
- Tuber vegetables: sweet potatoes, carrots.
- Fresh fruits: bananas, apples, berries.
- Legumes: lentils, chickpeas.

Timing:
- Complex carbohydrates, as listed, should be consumed 2–3 hrs before diving or training. This ensures that the glycogen stores are replenished.
- Simple carbohydrates can be consumed, giving a quick energy source 3060 minutes before exercise.

2. Proteins:

Why They are Important: use proteins to build, repair, and strengthen muscles.

Best Sources:
- Lean meats: chicken, turkey.
- Fatty fish: salmon, adding mackerel to enrich the quantity of Omega-3 - 3 intakes.
- Plants: tofu, tempeh, lentils
- Dairy: Greek yogurt, cottage cheese.

Timing:
- The most crucial timing of proteins is after dives or training to allow the body to recover well.

3. Fats

Why They Are Important: Healthy fats, one fuel type, provide more energy and give a healthy brain to keep clear.

Best Sources:
- Nuts and seeds: almonds, chia seeds, flaxseeds
- Avocados and olive oil.
- Fatty fish will add anti-inflammatory properties, too.

Timing:
- Healthy fats can be taken anytime during the day, but they must not be taken in considerable amounts before diving as they will make a person sleep.

B. Focus on Micro-Nutrient

1. Iron:
- It facilitates the transportation of oxygen and is, therefore, of prime importance in making RBCs; hence, dusting must replace it.
- Inclusions: red meat, spinach, fortified cereal, lentils, and dark chocolate.

2. Magnesium:
- It helps reduce muscle cramps, participates in energy metabolic pathways, and is a sleeping aid.
- **Sources:** Dark leafy greens, bananas, almonds, and sunflower seeds.

3. Potassium:
- keeps electrolytes maintained with no muscle cramping of divers during and after dives
- **Sources:** Bananas, sweet potatoes, oranges, beans

4. Omega-3 Fatty Acids :
- Anti-inflammation improves heart condition and Concentration.
- **Sources:** Concentrationrel, walnuts, chia seeds, and flaxseeds.

5. Vitamins C and E :
- It has anti-oxidative properties, hence diminishing oxidative stress from long breath-hold activities.

- **Sources:** Citric fruits, berries, kiwis, nuts, and seeds.

6. **Zinc:**
   - It helps in improving immune function and recovery processes.
   - **Sources:** Oysters, pumpkin seeds, whole grains.

C. Pre-Dive Nutrition

One should only eat light, easy food before diving because oxygen competes between activity and digestion.

Ideal Snacks Before Divings:
- Banana or apple with almond butter
- Greek yogurt with honey and berries.
- A light bowl of oatmeal with honey.

What Shouldn't Be Consumed:
- High fatty or high-fiber food would make the freediver lethargic and bloated.
- Much blood will be sent to digest the food rather than to the muscles and brain.

3. The Role of Hydration in Freediving

A. Why Hydration Matters
- Hydration allows for good blood flow, equalization, and performance.
- Poor hydration increases cramping, fatigue, and poor recovery, making equalization more difficult.

B. Hydration Guidelines

1. Daily Intake:
- Drink 2–3 liters daily, depending on activity level and climate.

2. PreDive Hydration:
- Stay hydrated throughout the day, but do not try to drink a lot before diving.

C. Electrolyte Balance
They help your body maintain fluid balance, nerve functions, and muscle contractions.

Replenishment Sources:
- Coco-water.
- Electrolyte tablets or natural powders.
- Homemade electrolytes drink water, a pinch of sea salt, honey, and lemon.

D. Substances to Avoid
- **Too much caffeine:** Though small dosages may increase Concentration, they concentrate the body.
- **Alcohol:** Generallit dehydrates the body and helps the recovery process.

4. Freedivers Recovery Techniques

A. Nutrition after Dive

1. Carbohydrate and Protein Recovery:
Take in a meal for replenishment of glycogen and building muscles simultaneously, whether as a drink or even a meal:

Examples:
- Grilled chicken or fish should go with quinoa and roasted vegetables.
- Smoothie: Banana, spinach, protein powder, almond milk in a mixer.

2. Anti-inflammation Foods
- Turmeric, ginger, green tea, and berries for anti-inflammation.

B. Recovery Hydration
- Rehydrate from lost fluids during dives or training by taking water and electrolytes.

C. Stretching and Mobility Work

1. Diaphragm and Ribcage Stretch:
- Child's pose, cat-cow, and cobra would release tension from the core in yoga.

2. Dynamic Mobility:
- In freediving, there is a long, passive stretch of the shoulders, neck, and back to relax the muscles.

D. Rest and Sleep
- Sleep 7–9 hours of quality sleep to enable your body to complete recovery.
- Nap or do mindfulness exercises like a guided meditation to fall asleep.

5. Sample Freedivers Daily Nutrition Plan

Meal	Example
Breakfast	Scrambled eggs with avocado on whole-grain toast and a side of berries.
Mid-Morning	A smoothie with banana, spinach, chia seeds, and almond milk.
Lunch	Grilled salmon, quinoa, roasted carrots, and steamed broccoli.
Afternoon Snack	Greek yogurt with honey, almonds, and fresh fruit.
Dinner	Grilled chicken, sweet potatoes, and sautéed kale with olive oil drizzle.
Pre-Dive Snack	A banana with a small handful of almonds.
Hydration	Sip water throughout the day, adding electrolytes as needed.

Conclusion

Nutrition and hydration are crucial to every training session. Healthy food will meet the sports needs of the freedivers by keeping them healthy and reinforcing them. By being aware of nutrition and recovery, a freediver reaches the best physical and mental state for optimal training, competition, or recreation. Awareness of all these ongoing cares will help the freediver reach his goal by staying healthy and keeping him in contact with the underwater world for as long as possible.

Nutritional management: physical Exercise and apnoea - a unified concept.

Training in apnea and free diving involves physiological stress, hypoxia, hypercapnia, and physical and dynamic movements. Significant nutrition intake is vital for maintaining energy and optimizing oxygen use in a controlled manner, which enhances CO_2 development and recovery. Therefore, this book will elaborate on the complications and make specific recommendations concerning nutrition, hydration, and performance optimization in physical exercise-apnea training, considering the needs of a river.

1. Nutritional Role in Exercises and Apnea Training

Nutrition is not just fuel; it is the most critical factor that directly and indirectly enhances performance in both aerobic and anaerobic activities. It increases the capacity for holding one's breath, as there is an improved utilization and reduced associated pCO_2 discomfort. Replenishment of liver glycogen, repair of damaged muscles, and decreased pCO_2 may facilitate quicker recoveries after Training.

Relaxation: Mental concentration and relaxation are favored and essential in apnea performance.

The specificity of practice can adapt to a general diet throughout one's life, which is suitable for general performance and safety in free diving.

2. Pre-Exercise and Pre-Apnea Nutrition

A. Pre-exercise nutrition objectives
- Enable the organism to obtain Enough Energy for the expenditure, especially during long breath holds.
- Blood sugar should be maintained without GI irritation to avoid stimulating appetite.
- The body should be adapted to utilize up to rid of waste product CO_2.

B. Macro-Nutrients to Highlight

1. Carbohydrates
- functions: Breaking Down Energy to energy-dense energy activities

Food sources :

Whole cereals, quinoa, oats, beans, sweet potatoes, and brown rice. Fruits like bananas, apples, and de-energy Complex Carbohydrates: Consume 2–3 hours before any exercise.

Consume simple carbohydrates for 30–60 minutes of Training for that quick energy source.

2. Proteins

Re-EnergyTo build muscles and recover for general strength.

Best Sources :
- Lean meats, fish, eggs, tofu, Greek yogurt, chicken, turkey, salmon, tuna.

Timing:
- Have small portions of protein for 1–2 hours of Training. Fats

Role: To provide sustained Energy management focus.

Best Sources:
- Avocados, nuts, almonds, walnuts, seeds, chia, flax, and olive oil.

3. Hydration
- Maintain fluid balance to support circulation and reduce the risk of dehydration.
- **Best Choices**: Water, electrolyte drinks, or coconut water.

C. Timing :
- Eat healthy fats early in the day to avoid being sluggish.
- Training. Pre-Exercise Snacks.
- Banana with almond butter.
- A light bowl of oatmeal with honey and berries
- A fruit smoothie that also comprises spinach, banana, and almond milk.

D. Foods to Avoid Before Training
- High-fat or high-fiber food results in bloatedness or indigestion
- Sharp food is too salty for it invites dehydration

3. Nutrition During Exercise and Apnea Training

A. Energy Management During Training
- Where the behavior is terrible, all physical exercises and apnea training are also enervating because they all involve extreme energy consumption of carbohydrates in the low-energy state.
- One will take small portions of the exercises for over 60 minutes. Easily digestible carbs along with energy gels or chews.
- Dates, raisins, and orange slices are some foods one may incorporate into their diet.
- **Hydration During Training:** Hydration should be taken in small portions with breaks. I add an electrolyte solution. Training is highly associated with sweating or lasts more than an hour,

B. Proper Nutrition required for the Apnea Training

Do not Over-consume Accordingly.
1. Large meals compete for oxygen to digest with the rest of your body, making breathing much less effective.
2. Oxygen-Boosting Foods: Beets, spinach, and arugula contain high amounts of nitrates, which may elevate oxygen delivery through improved nitric oxide production.
3. Promote Tolerance to CO_2 Foods high in magnesium, such as bananas and almonds, relax muscles and improve comfort during high CO_2.

4. Nutrition Post-Exercise and Post-Apnea

A. Nutritional goals post-exercise: Restore exercise stores worn out during the Exercise.
- Exercise-induced muscle damage repair encourages rebuilding.
- Rehydrate and restore the salt balance.

B. Nutrition-Macronutrients Recovery

1. Carbohydrates
- Why: Restores glycogen storage quickly and provides fuel for all recovery processes.
- The best sources are Sweet potatoes, quinoa, brown rice, oranges, fruits, and mango.

2. Proteins
- Why: The body needs amino acids for repairs to grog growths, thus chicken, fish, eggs, Greek yogurt, protein shakes, and lentils.

3. Electrolytes
- Why: Replace lost minerals for hydration and muscle function.
- Best Sources: coconut water, electrolyte drinks, bananas, and leafy greens.

4. Anti-Inflammatory Foods
- Action: Inhibit exercise breath-hold-Exercise inflammation.
- Best Sources: turmeric, ginger, berries, fatty fish, and green tea.

C. Timing of Recovery Meal
- Food and drink for recovery must be taken 30–60 minutes after the Training duration Strategies.

5. Specific Considerations for Apnea Training

A. Oxygen Efficiency and Nutrition
- Apnea training requires the body to operate efficiently under limited oxygen availability.
- Foods high in nitrates, such as beets and leafy greens, improve oxygen delivery and utilization by enhancing nitric oxide production.

B. CO_2 Tolerance and Nutrition
- Managing CO_2 buildup is critical for apnea performance.
- Magnesium-rich foods like almonds and spinach help relax muscles and reduce cramping caused by high CO_2 levels.

C. Foods That Enhance Relaxation
- To promote relaxation and mental clarity, eat foods rich in tryptophan, such as turkey, bananas, and dairy.

6. Hydration During Training and Recovery

A. Pre-Hydration
- Start hydrating early in the day and take the water to maximum level.

- Avoid overhydration. It will result in bloated discomfort during Training.

B. Hydration During Training
- During the session, take in Training electrolyte drinks.
- In longer sessions, coconut water automatically replaces electrolytes.

C. Recovery Hydration
- After Training, rehydrate with water added by electrolytes. Training hydrants are for severe dehydration after long training sessions.
- Sample Daily Nutrition Plan for Freedivers

7. Advanced Nutrition Management and Apnea

Timing	Meal/Snack
Breakfast	Scrambled eggs with avocado on whole-grain toast and a side of fresh fruit.
Mid-Morning	A smoothie with spinach, banana, chia seeds, and almond milk.
Lunch	Grilled chicken breast with quinoa, steamed broccoli, and olive oil drizzle.
Afternoon Snack	Greek yogurt topped with nuts, honey, and fresh berries.
Dinner	Baked salmon with sweet potatoes and sautéed kale.
Pre-Training	A banana with almond butter or a small bowl of oatmeal with honey.
During Training	Water or coconut water, a piece of orange or an energy chew.
Post-Training	A recovery smoothie with protein powder, spinach, and frozen mango.

Timing	Meal/Snack
Pre-Training	Oatmeal with honey and banana, or Greek yogurt with berries and a drizzle of honey.
During Training	Sip water or an electrolyte solution; a small piece of fruit (e.g., orange slice).
Post-Training	Grilled chicken with quinoa and steamed broccoli, or a protein smoothie with spinach, banana, and almond milk.
Dinner	Salmon with roasted sweet potatoes and sautéed kale, plus a green tea.
Snacks	Nuts, seeds, or a piece of dark chocolate for an energy boost.

A. Type of nutrition and oxygen efficiency
- Intake of the same quotidian food that contains nitrate. Beetroot and leafy greens are at the top of the list as the best food to improve oxygen efficiency.

Time Nutrition and Apnea
- No heavy meals at least 2 hours before the treat holding sessions to ensure digestion is complete

C. Optimize CO_2 Tolerance
- Take magnesium and potassium from bananas and nuts, respectively. Both relax the muscles, resulting in quicker recovery.

D. Eliminate Energy Sags
- Blood sugar maintenance: Snacks and meals shall be enriched with carbohydrates, protein, or fats.

8. Most Important Common Mistakes to Avoid

1. No Meals Before Dive
- Lethargic Energy Energy Water

2. Low Energy
- That would make a diver uncomfortable and make it hard to relax.

3. Forgetting the Hydration Factor.
- Where the acute fluid deficit would negatively affect endurance, equalization, and recovery

4. Late Nutrition Recovery
- After all, training muscles and glycogen stores.

Conclusion

It will be all about nutrition and proper hydration—in other words, all the performance training and physical activities. This will include nutritionally dense foods, keeping hydrated, timing, and personalized pre-training, during-activity, and post-training nutrition. These will keep a freediver's energy level high, optimize oxygen consumption, and speed recovery. Performance techniques with free potential will be introduced.

Metabolism Considerations for Freediving: A Comprehensive Guide

Freediving is a sport that requires an elaborate knowledge of body metabolism for further performance, efficiency, and Recovery processes, usually under the heading RecoRecovery. Metabolism is central to energy production, oxygen use, and CO_2 management, which are all necessary during breath-hold activities. Optimizing metabolic efficiency through a personalized diet, training, and recovery approach can unlock new performances. This extended guide will examine some metabolic considerations for freediving in greater detail and provide practical insights and strategies.

1. Metabolism and Its Function freediving

Metabolism is the sum of all the biochemical processes in the body, transforming for energy. Energy for freedivers: metabolic efficiency is further needed for

Generate Energy: This is the physical effort during dives and training.

Conserve Oxygen: means obtaining oxygen through aerobic Metabolism only in the delayed Metabolism hypoxia set.

Manag CO_2 means adapting to high levels of CO_2 with less discomfort and longer breath-holding times.

Assist Recovery: Replenish energy supplies and rebuild tissues after training sessions or freedive.

2. Freediving Energy Systems.

Throughout a single dive, the three systems are engaged, one after freediving; thus, their function in freediving could be highlighted below:

A. Aerobic Energy System
- **Primary Role:** Long-duration but low-level work uses oxygen to convert carbohydrates and fat energy.
- **Features Of Energy:**
  o Energy Highly Efficient; Dependence on Oxygen End.
  o Powers activities include relaxed finning, free fall, and long static breath hold.
  o Conserves the glycogen needed for high-intensity efforts.
- **Key Nutrients:** Carbohydrates and fats.

B. Anaerobic Glycolysis
- **Primary Role:** Provides energy rate for high-intensity activities without requiring oxygen.
- **Key Characteristics:**
  o Energy produces lactate as a waste product.
  o Fuels short sprints of high-intensity effort, like rapid finning during ascent.
- **Prime Energy Source:** Glucose.

C. Phosphagen (ATPCP) System
- **Primary Role:** Supplies immediate energy for high-intensity, short-duration efforts (10–15 seconds).
- **Key Characteristics:**
  o Powers explosive movements, such as a fast descent or initial propulsion.
  o It is quickly depleted and requires aerobic recovery to replenish.
- **Key Nutrient:** Stored ATP and creatine phosphate.

3. Physiological Adaptations in Freedivers

The freedivers develop specific adaptations that increase metabolic efficiency and enhance performance.

A. Mammalian Dive Reflex

1. Bradycardia:
   - It reduces oxygen consumption and diverts its use to vital organs.

2. Peripheral Vasoco striction:
   - Blood flow is shifted from the extremities to the core organs, sparing oxygen supply for the heart.

3. Spleen Contraction:
   - It contracts to release more red blood cells into the circulation, increasing oxygen-carrying capacity.

B. CO_2 Tolerance
- Regular training increases the body's tolerance to high levels of CO_2, which delays discomfort and allows longer breath-hold times.

C. Lactate Metabolism
- Efficient lactate clearance reduces muscle fatigue, enabling the diver to recover more quickly from anaerobic bursts.

D. Increased Fat Utilization
- With adaptation, freedivers become efficient in using fats as an energy source, thereby saving glycogen when needed.

4. Conventional Ways to Support Metabolism

A. Macronutrients Metabolism

1. Carbohydrates:
   - The primary Metabolism Energy for both aerobics and anaerobics.

- **Foods containing:** Whole grains, fruits, vegetables, and legumes
- **Timing:** Complex carbohydrates should be taken 2-3 hours before diving to replenish glycogen stored in muscles

2. **Proteins:**

Essential for muscle repair and recovery.

Sources: Lean meats, fish, eggs, tofu, and dairy

Timing: Add protein after diving and Recovery meals

3. **Fats:**

Provide long-lasting energy, particularly during aerobic phases.

Sources: Avocados, nuts, seeds, olive oil, and fatty fish.

Timing: The intake of fats should be during meals but not heavily before dives.

B. Micronutrients

1. **Iron:**
   - It enhances the delivery of oxygen by red blood cells to all parts of the body.
   - **Sources:** spinach, red meat, lentils, fortified cereals.

2. **Magnesium:**
   - It helps in energy production and reduces muscular cramping.
   - **Sources:** Nuts, seeds, leafy greens, and whole grains.

3. **Nitrates:**
   - Improve nitric oxide production, enhancing blood flow and oxygen delivery.
   - **Sources:** Beets, spinach, arugula, and celery.

4. **Antioxidants:**
   - Combat oxidative stress from long breath-holds.
   - Sources: Berries, citrus fruits, green tea, and dark chocolate.

5. Length for Ideal tab license Operation

A. The Role of Hydration
- It maintains the viscosity of the blood at its optimum level and favors better transportation and flow of oxygen.
- Maintains Metabolism and delays metabolism fatigue.

B. Recommendation Metabolism

1. **Daily Hydration:**
   - Drink 2–3 liters a day, depending on activity and weather.

2. **PreDive Hydration:**
   - Drink constantly throughout the day and not in large amounts directly before diving.

3. **Electrolytes:**
   - Electrolyte solutions or natural sources, like coconut water, can replace lost serum, potassium, and magnesium during exercise.

6. Training Methods to Improve Metabolism

A. CO_2 Tolerance Training

Use either CO_2 tables or apnea exercises with a gradually decreasing time between breath-holds to improve tolerance.

B. Aerobic Conditioning

Exercise Recovery, such as moderate-intensity swimming, cycling, or jogging, improves oxygen efficiency and fat utilization.

C. Interval Training

Brief, high-intensity exercise followed by active recovery recovery and anaerobic capacity.

D. Diaphragm and Respiratory Muscle Training

Exercises involving resistance breathing or diaphragmatic stretches will help strengthen respiratory muscles and improve oxygen utilization.

7. Post-Dive Recovery and Metabolic Replenishment

A. Key Nutrients

1. Carbohydrates: Whole grains, fruits, and starchy vegetables replace glycogen stores.

2. Proteins: Lean proteins like chicken, fish, or tofu contribute to rebuilding the muscles.

3. Anti-inflammatory food: Adding turmeric and ginger and consuming foods with Omega-3-Rich decreases oxidative stress.

B. Hydration
- Rehydrate by water intake and electrolyte solution to rebalance the body and prevent dehydration.

C. Active Recovery
- Light exercises such as yoga and swimming promote blood circulation and thus help remove lactates.

D. Rest and Sleep
- 7-9 hours of good quality sleep is a must in favor of metabolic Recovery

8. Common Mistakes to be avoided

1. **Skipping PreDive Meals:** causes less energy level that directly reduces performance

2. **Overer/ Wrong kind Eating Before Dives:** C au is dyspeptic and interferes with the utilization of O_2

3. **Ignoring Hydration:** Dehydration impairs oxygen transport and recovery.

4. **Inadequate Recovery Nutrition:** Slows glycogen replenishment and muscle repair.

9. Sample Daily Nutrition Plan for Metabolic Support

Timing	Meal
Breakfast	Oatmeal with almond butter, sliced banana, and a sprinkle of chia seeds.
Mid-Morning	A smoothie with spinach, beetroot, Greek yogurt, and berries.
Lunch	Grilled salmon with quinoa, roasted sweet potatoes, and steamed greens.
Pre-Dive Snack	A banana with a handful of nuts or a small energy bar.
Post-Dive Meal	Chicken breast, brown rice, and sautéed kale with olive oil.
Dinner	Tofu stir-fry with brown rice and mixed vegetables.

Conclusion

Metabolism is the heart of freediving performance. It defines energy production, revitalization, recovery systems, and interaction with various recovery Strauss by understanding and discovery-specific training that heightens physical performance without sacrificing long-term health. Thus, multidimensional tuition, hydration, and rehydration will prepare the freediver for his sport and take him to new personal bests in the underwater world.

Recovery Techniques and Prevention of Overtraining for Freedivers

It is a sport that requires balance in physical endurance, clarity of mind, and recovery strategies. While training improves performance and increases adaptation, poor Recovery or overtraining may bring about performance decrement, injury, and burnout. Good recovery techniques and prevention methods against overtraining will keep the freedivers at the top of their performances, minimize risks, and enable them to progress throughout their diving careers. The following guide updates how to use recovery methods and overtraining prevention strategies for freedivers.

1. Importance of Recovery in Freediving

Recovery is more than just resting; it is a critical stage of training during which the body rebuilds, adapts, and becomes stronger. Freedivin pushes the body with hypoxia (lack of oxygen), hypercapnia (high CO_2), and physical effort, which makes a recovery vital for the following reasons:
- **Muscle Repair** involves micro-tears and soreness resulting from repetitive finning or static holds.
- **Nervous System Reset:** A chance for the brain and the autonomic nervous system to "rest" from the stress of diving.
- **Adaptation:** Improving oxygen utilization, tolerance for CO_2, and general efficiency.
- **Mental Recharge:** Relief from the psychological stress of apnea and pressure while deep diving.

2. Signs and Risk of Overtraining in receiving

A. Physical Signs of Overtraining
- Prolonged or recurrent muscle soreness or stiffness lasting longer than expected recovery time.

- Reduced strength or endurance despite continuing the training.
- Injury or chronic complaints that occur with increasing frequency may involve joint pain or muscle strains.

B. Mental and Emotional Signs
- Can not concentrate during the training or diving.
- More irritable, anxious, or depressed than before.
- Has lost enthusiasm for freediving.

C. Physiological Indicators
- Increased resting heart rate or a significant drop in HRV.
- Poor sleep, such as insomnia or waking up without feeling rested.
- Increases the risk of catching colds, infections, or illnesses.

D. Risks of Overtraining

Performance Decline: Without recovery and further training, negative returns are produced.

Injury: Overuse injuries or chronic conditions, such as tendinitis.

Burnout: A loss of interest and enjoyment in freediving long-term stress.

3. Comprehensive Recovery Techniques for Freedivers

A. Post-Training Nutrition

1. Replenishing Glycogen:
- Consuming complex carbohydrates is necessary to regain energy.
- **Examples** include brown rice, sweet potatoes, quinoa, and whole grains.

2. Protein for Muscle Repair:
- Include high-quality proteins that help rebuild tissues and adapt them.
- **Examples:** Chicken, fish, eggs, lentils, or other high-protein plant-based alternatives.

3. Replenishment of Electrolyte:
- Replace the most minerals with electrolyte drinks or natural sources like coconut water, banana, and spinach.

4. Anti-Inflammatory Foods:
- Add to your diet foods that help reduce oxidative stress and inflammation.
- **Examples** include turmeric, ginger, berries, and fatty fish like salmon.

B. Hydration
- **Daily Hydration:** A minimum of 2–3 liters daily for fluid balance.
- **During Training:** Take small sips of water or electrolyte-rich drinks during prolonged sessions.
- **Post-Training:** Hydrate promptly with water or an electrolyte drink to reestablish balance.

C. Active Recovery

1. Low-Intensity Activity:
- Engaging in light activities such as swimming, yoga, or walking increases blood flow, facilitating the removal of metabolic waste.

2. Mobilize with Stretching:
- Use dynamic and static stretches to reduce stiffness and increase flexibility.
- **Target Areas:** Focus on the Diaphragm, shoulder, lower back, and hamstrings.

D. Breathwork for Recovery

Diaphragmatic Breathing:
- Relaxed respiratory muscles and enhanced oxygenation are products of slow and deep breathing.

Controlled Exhalation:
- Prolong the exhalation phase to stimulate the parasympathetic nervous system for relaxation.

E. Cold and Heat Therapy

1. Cold Therapy:
- Ice baths or cold water immersion reduce inflammation and muscle soreness.
- It finds its best application post-workout, right after high-intensity sessions.

2. Heat Therapy:
- Applying heat through saunas or hot baths relaxes the muscles and increases blood flow.
- It should not be used post-workout but on rest or active recovery days.

F. Massage and Myofascial Release

Foam Rolling:
- Use foam rollers or massage balls to release tension and increase mobility.

Professional Massage:
- Regular deep-tissue or sports massage will help endurance chronic tightness and blood flow.

G. Sleep and Rest

Quality Sleep:
- Sleep uninterrupted for 7–9 hours to ensure your body is recovered.
- Sleep routine: Development of a sleep routine involving mindfulness or reading.

Power Naps:
- Use brief naps between training sessions or refreshments - 15-30 minutes.

H. Mental Restoration

1. Mindfulness Meditation:
- Devote daily hours to mindful actions that will ease stress and enhance focused attention.
- Utilize guided meditation prepared explicitly for the freediver.

2. Visualization:
- Mentally rehearse dives for success, confident feelings, and relaxation without reaching physical fatigue.

4. Prevention of Overtraining in Freediving

A. Planned Training Cycles
- Program high-level training sessions along with low-level recovery sessions.
- Allow at least one full rest day following each period within the training phase.

B. Periodization
- Develop training phases that include planned peaks and plateaus together with Recovery:
  o **Macrocycles** last 6–12 months and include competition prepRecoveryand off-seasons.

- o **Mesocycles** are intermediate cycles lasting 4–6 weeks, focusing on specific goals such as depth or CO_2 tolerance.
- o **Microcycles** are weekly cycles that balance training intensity with recovery.

C. CrossTraining
- Use other activities that complement your sport, such as recovery swimming, cycling, or Pilates, to develop your general fitness while minimizing the stress on your diving muscles.

D. Monitoring Training Load
- Track Metrics:
- o Log training intensity, duration, and perceived effort.
- o Monitor heart rate variability using wearables as an indicator of recovery status.

E. Adapting to Fatigue
- Change or cancel sessions if there is suspicion of overtraining.
- Listen to your body and take rest when necessary.

5. Freediver Weekly Recovery Plan

6. Tools to Support Recovery and Overtraining Prevention

Day	Activity	Recovery Focus
Monday	Moderate-intensity dynamic apnea training	Post-training stretching, hydration
Tuesday	Light yoga and diaphragmatic breathing	Active recovery, flexibility enhancement
Wednesday	CO2 tolerance drills (high intensity)	Ice bath, anti-inflammatory nutrition
Thursday	Complete rest with guided meditation	Passive recovery, mental relaxation
Friday	Depth training (low intensity)	Electrolyte replenishment, light foam rolling
Saturday	Interval training with static apnea	Heat therapy, protein-rich meals
Sunday	Gentle swimming or snorkeling	Active recovery, long sleep session

1. **WearableTrackers:**
   - Monitor HRV, resting heart rate, and sleep to assess and ensure recovery.

2. **Recovery Applications:**

Use applications for training logs or recovery situations to monitor progress and mental relaxation.

3. **Breath Training Devices:**

Employ resistance-based trainers to lengthen respiratory muscles and aid Recovery.

7. Conclusion

Recovery and prevention of overtraining are crucial parts of any successful freediving program. Structured training, balanced recovery strategies, and mindfulness practice can help the freediver maintain the best performance and long-term health. Nutrition, hydration, and active recovery-mental relaxation also help the diver prevent the risks of overtraining and be more confident when exploring the underwater world. Care for Recovery is a must, but it is also one of the keys to progressing and having fun in freediving.

Connection with Marine Environments

The Role That Freedivers Play in Ecological Awareness and the Promotion of Marine Conservation

Freediving instills a deep-seated connection to the marine environment, placing individuals literally in the underwater world in its most natural, undisturbed state. This unique interaction allows freedivers to witness the beauty, fragility, and challenges facing ocean ecosystems. With this perspective, freedivers can play a vital role in promoting ecological awareness and championing marine conservation efforts. By knowing their responsibilities and opportunities, freedivers can mobilize to take action to protect and preserve the oceans for future generations.

1. Freediving as a Gateway to Marine Connection

Freediving is not only a sport but a way into the ocean's rhythm and its ecosystem's fragile balance. Such a connection nurtures:

- **Sensory Immersion:** During free dives, the silence, buoyancy, and life colors of the underwater world create an atmosphere for profound appreciation.
- **Empathy for Marine Life:** Seeing them in their natural setting engenders respect and shows that we understand their needs and challenges.
- **Personal Responsibility:** First-hand experience with environmental changes gives them a responsibility to care for and protect marine environments.

2. Ecological Awareness through Freediving

Freedivers are among the first witnesses to observe the change and plight of the marine environment in aspects such as:
- **Coral Bleaching:** Color and health changes in coral due to rising sea temperatures and acidification.
- **Marine Pollution:** Encountering plastic debris, fishing nets, and other artificial waste.
- **Biodiversity Shifts:** NoticinWaste decline in the fish population or changes in species behavior because of degraded habitat or overfishing.
- **Ocean Health Indicators:** Water clarity, algae blooms, and invasive species are tracked.

These observations provide critical insights into the health of marine ecosystems and point out areas that need urgent attention.

3. Freedivers as Ambassadors of Marine Conservation

This is where the freedivers inspire changes in marine conservation through experiences and actions. They would be able to:
- **Educating people** about the underwater world and its problems through personal accounts, pictures, and videos can create awareness.
- **Sustainable Practices:** People can be motivated to be more environmentally friendly by reducing single-use plastics or buying sustainable seafood.
- **Lead by Example:** Model responsible diving practices and environmental stewardship.

Case Studies:

1. Underwater Photography for Awareness: Divers like Cristina Mittermeier use photography to show how beautiful marine life is and how much it suffers from human actions in the ocean.

2. Social Media Campaigns: Impactful visuals and messages related to pollution and marine degradation make freedivers' voices louder on social media sites like Instagram.

4. Conservation Programs That Freedivers Are a Part Of

Freedivers can be helpful in direct marine conservation based on the following points:

A. Underwater Clean-up Campaigns

Objective: Cleaning dive sites, reefs, and beaches from plastic, fishing nets, and debris.

Impact: Protection of marine habitats from pollution and optimizing living conditions for aquatic species.

B. Coral Restoration Projects
- **Objective:** Provide hands-on contributions to scientists, transplant coral fragments, and monitor the reef post-transplant.
- **Impact:** Contributing to rebuilding degraded coral reefs and increasing biodiversity.

C. Marine Surveys and Citizen Science
- This would document research observations on marine species, water quality, or habitat conditions.
- It will be helpful for researchers and conservational groups to gather data.

D. Marine Protected Areas (MPAs) Advocacy
- **Goal:** To reestablish and manage MPAs for biodiversity protection.
- **Impact:** Critical marine ecosystems are protected, and species are saved from overfishing and habitat loss.

5. Ethics in Freediving

It does not harm the environment, and it is very commendable that freedivers are highly ethical and follow the rules for sustainable diving:

1. Respect Marine Life:
- Never touch or disturb marine animals.
- Instead, observe them from a distance to avoid stressing or disrupting their natural behaviors.

2. Protect Coral Reefs:
- Do not stand on or touch corals because they are fragile and easily damaged.
- Be fin-aware: Avoid stirring sediment or breaking reef structure.

3. Use Eco-Friendly Products:
- Making use of non-toxic chemicals in reef-friendly sunscreens.
- Using diving or snorkeling gear made from sustainable or recycled material.

4. Reduce waste:
- Reusable water bottles and waste can also help reduce plastic waste by minimizing single-use items.
- Clean up during each dive or trip.

6. The Role of Freediving in the Expression of Climate Change

Freedivers witness the results of climate change first-hand, which positions them as an influential mouthpiece for positive action in the face of such changes:

Coral Bleaching Awareness:
- Explain how heating oceans causes coral stress and loss of biodiversity.

Rising Sea Levels:
- Share knowledge of how coastal ecosystems and communities are impacted.

Species Migration:
- Record changes in marine species distributions due to shifting temperatures.

Freedivers' Contributions:
- Collaborate with organizations like **Reef Check** or **Mission Blue** to amplify their observations.
- Produce powerful media to leverage the attention of global audiences on how the ocean is experiencing climate change.

7. Freediving and Community Involvement

Freedivers can inspire others to take an interest in the care and protection of the ocean by:

Training Programs:
- Include conservation education in freediving courses to stress ecological responsibility.

Workshops and Seminars:
- Host events to share knowledge about marine ecosystems and sustainable practices.

Storytelling:
- Use personal experiences and encounters with marine life to connect with diverse audiences.

8. Examples of Successful Freediving Conservation Efforts

A. "Dive Against Debris" Campaigns
- These programs, organized by groups like Project AWARE, enable divers to monitor debris and record their findings for global databases.

B. Freediving Coral Gardeners
- Collaborations with marine scientists in restoring coral reefs through planting and monitoring activities.

C. Social Media Movements
- Create viral campaigns about underwater plastic pollution as freedivers to inspire the world to reduce waste.

D. Marine Life Monitoring
- Collaboration of freedivers with research institutions helps monitor populations of endangered species, mantas, and sharks.

9. Ecological Responsibility-the Freedivers Checklist

Action	Why It Matters
Use reef-safe sunscreen	Prevents chemicals from harming corals and marine life.
Avoid touching marine creatures	Protects fragile species and maintains their natural behaviors.
Participate in cleanups	Removes debris that threatens marine habitats and species.
Advocate for sustainable seafood	Reduces overfishing and supports healthy marine ecosystems.
Support eco-conscious dive operators	Encourages sustainable tourism practices.
Promote awareness through visuals	Inspires conservation efforts by showcasing underwater beauty and challenges.

10. Empowerment of the Future Generation

Freedivers will play a significant role in inculcating a sense among the young generation of the care and protection of marine environments:

- **Youth Education:** The workshops for schools and community groups on marine conservation.
- Accessible Freediving
- **Experiences:** Avail opportunities for young people to explore the underwater world first-hand and foster a lifelong connection to the ocean.
- **Mentorship:** Guide aspiring freedivers in combining their skills with ecological advocacy.

11. Conclusion

But arguably, what they get in its place is a genuine bond with the marine world, in which freediving can raise ecological awareness and call for its conservation. By embracing sustainable diving practices, participating in restoration activities, and promoting claims for the seas, one becomes an ocean caretaker to be reckoned with. Exploring the underwater world with each dive means protecting it for future generations.

Marine Biodiversity and Environmental Responsibility

Marine Biodiversity and Freedivers: Custodianship of Ocean Life in the vast oceans is meaningful in balancing Earth's ecological processes. Variety within species and ecosystems and genetic diversity on the high seas imply marine biodiversity. To respond to this challenge, freedivers should be able to observe more closely and thus respond. By following environmentally responsible practices, promoting conservation, and restoring, freedivers can play a protective role in marine biodiversity and foster sustainable interactions with the ocean.

1. The Importance of Marine Biodiversity

Marine biodiversity underpins Life on Earth, from affecting ecosystems and economies to human health and well-being. Some key benefits include:

A. Ecosystem Services

1. **Production of Oxygen:** More than half of the oxygen we inhale in our lifetime comes from phytoplankton and other marine plants.
2. **Carbon Sequestration:** Oceans are vast carbon sinks that buffer the effects of climate change. **Food Security:** Fisheries

and aquaculture supply vital protein sources to billions of people worldwide.
3. **Regulating the Water Cycle:** Oceans contribute to weather conditions, the water cycle, and temperature regulation.

B. Cultural and Recreational Value
- Various other ocean activities, including freediving and snorkeling, expose humans to the beauty and wonder of marine Life and engender stewardship.

C. Economic Importance
- Coastal tourism, fisheries, and marine biotechnology generate billions of dollars of revenue annually for economies worldwide, but all depend on healthy ecosystems.

2. Threats to Marine Biodiversity

Marine ecosystems face numerous challenges, most of which man has contributed to. Among those who shall be able to witness these in action are freedivers, and they will be optimally positioned to see them. These include:

A. Climate Change

1. **Rising sea temperatures** cause coral bleaching and threaten reef ecosystems, which host a quarter of all marine species.
2. **Ocean Acidification:** Weakens coral skeletons and interferes with the processes by which marine organisms build their shells.
3. **Sea-Level Rise:** results in the Loss of key coastal habitats such as mangroves and seagrass meadows.

B. Pollution Plastic Waste:

1. **Plastic Waste:** Entangles and is ingested by marine animals.

2. **Chemical Runoff:** Runoff from farms and factories leads to dead zones, where too little oxygen exists in the water to support Life.
3. **Oil Spills:** Destroy whole marine ecosystems that might take decades to recover.

C. Overfishing and Bycatch
- The lack of responsible fishing methods reduces the fish stock and kills non-target species such as turtles, dolphins, and sharks.

D. Habitat Destruction
- Coastal development, bottom trawling, and dredging destroy or disrupt vital habitats.

3. Freedivers and Their Relationship with Marine Biodiversity

The sport of free diving has an immediate, intimate exposure to marine ecosystems and engenders:
- **Sympathy and Understanding:** Seeing marine Life in its natural environment evokes greater affinity and a desire to protect it.
- **Direct Experience:** The freedivers, keener to note biodiversity and habitat changes in minute detail, acted as the first warning about the environmental decline.

Unique experiences of the free divers:
- To follow the manta ray as it glides with grace across the plankton-choked waters,
- To follow the symbiotic relations of clownfish and sea anemone
- Exploring colorful, varied Life on coral reefs or kelp forests with their ghostly beauty

4. Contribution of Freediver in Marine Conservation

Freedivers can go a long way in conserving marine resources through action, advocacy, and education.

A. Citizen Science and Monitoring

Conduct marine surveys to document:
- Fish numbers and species types.
- Coral health and bleaching incidents.
- Invasive species or pollution.

B. Environmental Advocacy

- Social Media: Utilize social networking sites, blogs, and public speaking to raise awareness about the threats to marine biodiversity and ocean health.
- Partner with other organizations to amplify your messages

C. Direct Conservation Efforts

1. **Marine Clean-ups:**
   - Conduct clean-ups in dive sites, beaches, and reefs.

2. **Rehabilitation Programs**
   - Rehabilitate coral reefs by transplanting fragments or reseeding seagrass meadows.

3. **Promotion of Marine Protected Areas**
   - Establish and manage MPAs for the protection of critical habitat and biodiversity.

5. Ecologically Responsible Freedom

By observing such guiding principles of sustainability and ethics, a freediver should have the least possible impact on the environment to wit:

A. Interacting with Marine Life:

Be Responsible

1. **Observe, Don't Touch:**
   - Never touch, chase, or feed marine Life.

2. **Respect Natural Behaviors:**
   - Keep a reasonable distance from the subjects to avoid stress and prevent them from changing their natural behavior.

B. Sustainable Gear and Products

- Freediving gear is made from environmentally friendly materials.
- Unlike common sunscreens, reef-safe sunscreens do not contain lethal chemicals such as oxybenzone, which is already prohibited.

C. Low-Impact Freediving

Maintain Neutral Buoyancy:
- Be buoyant enough never to touch either the corals or the bottom accidentally.

Minimize Sediment Disturbance:
- Be very careful with your fin movement in sensitive ecosystems.

6. The Role of Marine Protected Areas

A. Benefits of MPAs

1. **Biodiversity Conservation:**
   - Protection of habitats and species from overfishing and habitat destruction.

2. **Spillover Effect:**
   - MPAs increase their stocks to resupply surrounding areas.

3. **Tourism Opportunities:**
   - Well-managed MPAs create value for eco-aware tourists and provide sustainable incomes for local communities.

B. How Freedivers Can Support MPAs
- Support the establishment and funding of MPAs through petition or action with a community.
- MPA research and monitoring.
- Share your MPA experience with the world through stories and/or media.

7. Climate Action and Marine Biodiversity

Freedivers can take climate action to address one of the biggest drivers of loss to marine biodiversity.

A. Carbon Footprint Reduction

1. **Eco-Friendlier Travel:**
   - Public transportation or carpools to and from dive sites

2. **Energy:**
   - Invest in renewable energy projects. Reduce personal energy use.

B. Sustainable Seafood
- Purchase seafood that is well caught or harvested or plant-based lower impact options

C. Raising Awareness about Climate Impacts
- Discuss with local and global communities changes caused by climate change, such as coral bleaching or shifts in species distribution.

8. Informing and Educating Others

Freedivers can share their experiences with others to help them care about the ocean.

Community Outreach:
- Organize workshops or school visits on marine biodiversity and conservation.

Social Media Storytelling:
- Publish videos from the underwater world on Instagram, YouTube, or TikTok and add your conservation message to them.

Mentorship:
- Mentor young and upcoming freedivers on being eco-friendly freedivers and becoming responsible stewards.

9. Freediver's Checklist on How to Be an Eco-Friendly Freediver

Action	Why It Matters
Use reef-safe sunscreen	Prevents coral bleaching and protects marine life.
Avoid touching marine creatures	Protects fragile species and maintains natural behaviors.
Minimize single-use plastics	Reduces ocean pollution and the risk of ingestion or entanglement.
Participate in underwater cleanups	Removes harmful debris from marine habitats.
Support eco-friendly dive operators	Encourages sustainable tourism and diving practices.
Advocate for MPAs	Protects biodiversity and enhances ecosystem resilience.

10. Conclusion

Marine Life is crucially important for the planet's health, and freedivers have the advantage of being utterly involved in the world. This enables divers to discover the beauty of marine Life, its outfits, and the ecosystems and inspire it through a more ecologically responsible way, spreading conservation and methods of sustainability with every dive, allowing them to perpetuate their marvels for future generations.

Future of Freediving and Technological Innovations

The Growing Impact of Freediving on Ocean Sciences and Conservation

Freediving is among the oldest activities conducted by humans and is fast emerging as one of the essential ways of learning how to save the world's oceans. Since it uniquely combines tradition, direct contact with marine environments, and advanced technologies, freediving increasingly supports ocean sciences, conservation, and public awareness. As changes in technology merge with the call for prioritization of the environment, so too is the potential contribution freedivers can make concerning marine research, conservation strategies, and solving environmental problems worldwide.

1. The Dual Role of Freediving: To Explore and Conserve

Freediving is non-invasive and quiet, thus allowing the divers to:
- **Be Immersed in Marine Ecosystems:** Observe and document marine life without interrupting their natural behaviors.
- **Contribute to Conservation:** Restoration projects, ecosystem monitoring, and promoting sustainable practices are all part of this.
- **Bridge Tradition and Technology:** Ancient techniques combined with modern tools amplify its impact.

Freediving nurtures environmental stewardship and catalyzes global conservation efforts by connecting with the ocean.

2. The Contribution of Freediving to Ocean Science

Freediving provides unparalleled access to fragile and remote marine ecosystems, opening up unique opportunities for scientific research in the following ways:

A. Monitoring Marine Ecosystem
- **Studies of Biodiversity:** These freedivers chart observations of species and marine habitats, usually where traditional methods are impossible.
- **Long-term Detection of Change:** Regular freediving at the site for observations allows for monitoring changes in biodiversity, coral cover health, and water quality over time.

B. Data Collection and Citizen Science

The contributions by free divers are immense regarding the addition of scientific databases in programs like :

1. **Reef Check:** Conduct surveys for coral reefs, fish populations, and water conditions.

2. **CoralWatch:** Monitors bleaching and recovery.

3. **Ocean Conservancy Projects:** Marine debris and pollution patterns documentation.

C. Underwater Archaeology and Exploration
- Freedivers play a significant role in studying submerged cultural sites, such as ancient ships and cities, which require nondestructive, cautious access.

3. Technological Innovations in Freediving

Recent technological developments are changing the face of freediving, making this sport safer, more efficient, and increasingly important for research and conservation.

A. Advanced freediving gear

1. **Smart Dive Computers:**
   - Display real-time data on depth, time, oxygen levels, and ascent speeds.

   Safety warnings to avoid hypoxic incidents.

2. **Lightweight Wetsuits:**
   - Newer materials provide better thermal protection with reduced drag, allowing longer dives.

3. **High-Performance Fins:**
   - Carbon fiber and composite fin strong propulsion with minimal effort results in longer dives with much less fatigue.

4. **Eco-Friendly Equipment:**
   - Sustainable production alternatives using recycled neoprene, among other materials, make for a low ecological footprint from freediving gear.

B. Imaging and Documentation Tools

1. **Compact Underwater Cameras:**
   - Taking quality shots of high resolution, they shoot footage of marine life and their habitat for ocean biodiversity awareness.

2. **360-Degree Cameras:**
   - Panoramic visuals take the underwater world to broader audiences in VR experiences.

3. **Underwater Drones:**
   - Extend exploration capabilities to extreme depths or dangerous locations.

C. Digital Platforms and AI Integration

1. Data Analysis Software:

- AI-driven platforms analyze images and footage taken for species identification, biodiversity monitoring, and understanding temporal changes.

2. Virtual Reality Training:
   - VR simulators simulate the underwater environment where freedivers practice and learn various breath-holding techniques in safety.

4. Contribution of Freediving to Conservation

Freedivers are increasingly doing direct activities in the name of ocean conservation:

A. Habitat Restoration

1. **Coral Reef Restoration:**
   - Freedivers transplant coral fragments into the damaged reef and follow up on its progress.
   - They also take part in seeding new coral colonies at sites that bleached.

2. **Seagrass and Mangrove Restoration:**
   - Freedivers support replantation for seagrass meadows and mangroves for both carbon sequestration and protection of coasts.

B. Marine Debris Removal

1. **Underwater Cleanup Campaigns:**
   - Freedivers' contribution becomes crucial in cleaning debris from sensitive ecosystems, such as coral reefs or sea caves.
   - This can be a simple task that can be scaled up with other organizations, such as Project AWARE.

2. **Microplastic Research:**

- Collect water column and seafloor samples contributing to microplastic distribution and impact investigations.

C. Marine Protected Areas

1. Advocacy for MPA Establishment
- Freedivers call for the expansion of MPAs, protection of biodiversity hotspots, and time to allow marine ecosystems to recover.

2. MPA Monitoring
- Regular freediving in MPAs helps monitor their effectiveness and note changes in species' relative abundance and habitat health.

5. Freediving and Climate Action

Freedivers witness the effects of climate change firsthand, making them vital contributors to global climate action:

A. Documenting Climate Effects
- **Coral bleaching** is one of the events freedivers could monitor and visually share with others to raise awareness.
- **Species migration:** Document species entering new areas because of warming seas

B. Carbon Sequestration Support
- Freedivers support projects to protect and restore blue carbon, such as mangroves, seagrasses, and salt marshes.

C. Advocacy and Education
- Use storytelling through media to convey the urgency of taking action on behalf of climate change and its impact on the ocean.

6. Growing Influence of Freediving on Public Awareness

Freedivers are increasingly using their experiences to educate and inspire the public:

A. Visual Storytelling
- Freedivers create documentaries, photography exhibitions, and VR experiences that connect audiences to the underwater world.

B. Social Media Advocacy
- On platforms such as Instagram, YouTube, and TikTok, conservation messages reach hundreds of millions worldwide.

C. Community Outreach
- Integrating conservation education into freediving schools and organizations raises a new generation of ocean ambassadors.

7. The Future of Freediving and Ocean Science

This integration of technology and conservation will define the future of the sport on various levels, including the following:

A. Enhanced Training and Safety
- Wearable technology, along with AI and virtual reality, will make the sport of free diving incomparably safer and accessible to many more people.

B. Greater Contribution to Science
- Freedivers will cooperate with marine scientists to supply the key data to monitor biodiversity, conduct climate studies, and preserve the aquatic environment.

C. International Cooperation
- Online platforms will connect freedivers, researchers, and conservationists worldwide, enabling them to share their knowledge and take action together.

D. Wider Public Engagement
- The freedivers will catalyze more amazing environmental stewardship by connecting people with the ocean in an immersive, interactive manner.

8. List of Freedivers Contributing to a Sustainable Future

Action	Impact
Use sustainable diving gear	Reduces environmental impact and promotes eco-conscious production.
Document marine life and habitats	Provides valuable data for scientific research and public awareness.
Advocate for MPAs	Protects critical ecosystems and promotes biodiversity recovery.
Participate in restoration projects	Actively restores degraded habitats and enhances ecosystem resilience.
Share conservation messages	Inspires others to care about and protect the ocean.
Collaborate with researchers and NGOs	Strengthens conservation efforts and amplifies their reach.

9. Conclusion

It inextricably ties the future of freediving to the health of our oceans and the innovations driving how we explore and protect them. Because this is a modern generation of explorers and conservationists, freedivers hold a singular position to influence ocean science and drive action worldwide. By introducing better technology, actively participating in nature conservation, and narrating touching stories, a freediver can make a difference and ensure that the beauty and biodiversity of the underwater world are preserved for generations to come.

Advances in Freediving Equipment and Technologies: The Leap into the Future of Underwater Exploration

While freediving has powerful historical roots, it has changed dramatically in many respects with time due to technological advances that have improved safety, efficiency, and performance and broadened its role in marine conservation, scientific research, and public awareness. Technology has put freediving at the forefront of sustainable underwater exploration because while it stretches human capabilities, it can promote environmental stewardship in its evolution.

1. The Evolution of Freediving Gear

Specialized freediving equipment has made this sport safer and more accessible to people who want to explore deeper waters for longer.

A. Dive Computers: Smart Devices for Safety and Performance

1. **Features for Freediving:**
   - Track depth, dive time, ascent/descent speeds, and surface intervals.
   - Real-time safety alerts for exceeding depth or time thresholds

2. **Advanced Integration:**
   - Incorporate heart rate and oxygen saturation monitoring to optimize training and prevent hypoxia.
   - Bluetooth-enabled devices sync with apps for detailed post-dive analysis.

3. **Lightweight and Durable:**
   - Compact designs for freediving conditions, with minimum drag and maximum reliability.

B. Wetsuits: Comfort, Efficiency, and Sustainability Combined

1. **Improved Thermal Insulation:**
   - Neoprene materials of the latest generation, such as Yamamoto 45, assure great warmth and elasticity.
   - The smooth-skin outer layer reduces drag and facilitates streamlined movement in the water.

2. **Eco-Friendly Options:**
   - Plant-based or recycled materials reduce environmental impact without sacrificing performance.
   - Non-toxic adhesives and production methods are in line with sustainable diving.

3. **Custom Fit Technology:**
   - Custom-fit wetsuits enhance thermal retention, comfort, and buoyancy to maximize efficiency.

C. High-Performance Fins

1. **Material Innovations:**
   - Carbon fiber and composite materials have given fins unparalleled propulsion with minimum effort, using less oxygen.
   - Fiberglass options stay robust and flexible in various diving conditions.

2. **Custom Designs:**
   - Modular systems let divers choose blades and foot pockets according to their diving depth and technique.

D. Masks and Snorkels

1. **Low-Volume Masks:**
   - It requires less air for equalization, thus enabling deeper dives with less energy.

- Ergonomic designs increase comfort and improve the field of view.

2. **Hydrodynamic Snorkels:**
   - Streamlined shapes reduce drag when surface breathing.
   - Silicone mouthpieces increase comfort during long uses.

E. Buoyancy Systems

1. **Safety Buoys:**
   - Incorporate storage compartments, flags, and points of attachment for dive lines.
   - These are critical tools for support and visibility during surface operations in open water.

2. **Adjustable Weight Systems:**
   - This will allow the divers to achieve the best buoyancy at any depth and under all conditions, making the process far safer and quicker.

2. Training Tools and Techniques Boosted by Technology

Freedivers use top-notch equipment that enhances their training, physiological monitoring, and performance optimization.

A. Virtual Reality Training and Augmented Reality

1. **Simulation of the Aquatic Environment:**
   - VR replicates marine environmental conditions, allowing freedivers to practice equalization, relaxation, and static apnea.

2. **Dynamic Scenario:**
   - AR offers real-time feedback during pool training, which helps divers perfect their form and improve their performance.

B. Breath Training Devices

1. **Respiratory Strengthening:**
   - PowerBreathe and SpiroTiger strengthen the diaphragm and intercostal muscles, increasing lung capacity.

2. **Real-Time Feedback:**
   - Devices measure CO_2 tolerance, oxygen consumption, and heart rate to track tracking of progress.

C. Mobile Apps for Training

1. **Performance Analytics:**
   - Apps like Dive+ and FreedivePro record dives with depth and time, including surface and recovery time.
   - Visualizations of trends are generated to emphasize areas of improvement.

2. **Apnea Tables:**
   - The table-format coached CO_2 and O_2 tolerance exercises progress gradually in developing a diver's breath-holding capacity.

D. Innovations in Pool-Based Training

1. **Weighted Sleds:**
   - Mimic vertical descents in controlled environments and optimize equalization and depth adaptation.

2. **Resistance Bands:**
   - Strengthen and develop finning force and efficiency for dynamic apnea, thus extending the duration.

3. New Concepts that Make Advanced Techniques in Freediving Possible

Advancements in technology have indeed changed how freedivers can train for and perform advanced techniques:

A. Hydrodynamics
- Improved equipment design reduces drag, enabling divers to see more and use less oxygen.

B. Equalization Techniques

1. **Mouth-Fill Mastery:**
   - Specialized training devices help divers master this highly advanced equalization technique for deep dives.

2. **Pressure Monitoring Tools:**
   - Monitor middle-ear pressure during training and provide immediate feedback on how to refine techniques.

C. Optimized CO_2 and O_2 Tolerance

1. **Personalized Training Protocols:**
   - Wearables and apps create personalized apnea tables to build tolerance safely.

2. **Data-Driven Progress:**
   - Analyze physiological responses during training to fine-tune breath-hold strategies.

4. Freediving Safety Innovations

Safety is an issue in this sport, and technology has been bringing some changes that diminish the risks of practice:

A. Emergency Response Systems

1. **Automatic Safety Buoys:**
   - Recognize an unconscious diver's state of distress and can resurface.

2. **Smart Dive Lines:**
   - Constantly track depth and duration while alerting safety teams of an impending malfunction.

B. Wearable Monitors
- Monitor life functions such as heart rate variability and oxygen level during a dive to detect hypoxia in time.

5. Contribution of Freediving to Marine Science and Conservation

Freedivers are in a privileged position to contribute to environmental projects using their skills and access to marine ecosystems.

A. Underwater Imaging and Mapping

1. **High-Resolution Cameras:**
   - Take high-quality images and footage of marine biodiversity and the health of ecosystems.

2. **3D Mapping Technology:**
   - Make detailed models of coral reefs and other habitats to monitor changes.

B. Citizen Science Programs
- Through programs such as Reef Check, freedivers participate in and record data on coral health, water quality, and fish populations.

C. Plastic Pollution Research
- Freedivers help collect microplastics and remove garbage to clean up marine pollution.

6. Future of Freediving Technology

A. Artificial Intelligence (AI)

1. **Data Analysis:**
   - With the integration of AI, technology identifies species, analyzes dives data, and observes ecosystem changes.

2. **Training Optimization:**
   - AI-powered applications will create personalized training plans based on individual performance parameters.

B. Sustainable Innovation
- With carbon-neutral production processes, gear made from biodegradable materials aligns with environmental objectives.

C. Smart Wearables
- Suits and masks integrated with real-time monitoring capabilities for immediate feedback of physiological and environmental conditions.

D. Stronger Collaboration with Marine Scientists
- Freedivers will be instrumental in data gathering concerning research on climate change, biodiversity studies, and habitat restoration.

7. The Position of Freedivers in Shaping the Future

Freedivers are not simple consumers of technology but active agents of innovation and ecological awareness. In sum, their contributions include the following:

Feedback to Developers:
- Insights by seasoned freedivers inform the design of safer, more efficient gear.

Educational Outreach:
- Freedivers turn their experiences into inspiring others on conservation awareness and sustainability.

Global Advocacy:
- Through stories and social media, freedivers raise the call for protecting marine ecosystems loud and clear.

8. Conclusion

Technological innovations have completely changed the face of freediving, making this sport safer, more efficient, and ecologically friendly. From advanced dive computers to AI-powered training tools and eco-friendly equipment, innovations empower freedivers to rapidly push their limits while growing closer to the underwater world. As freediving continues to evolve, it will redefine human capabilities. It has been integral to marine conservation, research, and the protection of our oceans for generations.

Freediving Equipment and Techniques: Technological Advancements Pointing at the Future of Underwater Explorations

Freediving has long served as a testament to human resilience and the bond shared with the ocean. What began as a necessity in hunting for food has evolved into a sport, a scientific tool, and an avenue to extend marine conservation. Advanced freediving technology has completely revolutionized how divers train, explore, and work toward environmental stewardship. From advanced equipment to novel techniques, technological development will continue to shape the future of freediving in terms of safety, efficiency, and concern for the environment.

1. Evolution of Freediving Equipment: Precision and Performance

The design of freediving gear has significantly evolved, with a significant focus on performance, safety, and sustainability. Each step of innovation furthers the efficiency and precision with which a diver can function underwater.

A. Dive Computers: Real-time Monitoring for Safety and Training

1. **Freediving-Specific Capabilities:**
   - Modern dive computers track depth, surface intervals, and freedivers' ascent/descent speed.
   - Threshold alarms for depth and time prevent hypoxia and shallow-water blackouts.

2. **Physiological Tracking:**
   - Heart rate and oxygen saturation sensors track vital data throughout dives to keep divers within their limits.

3. **Post-Dive Analytics:**
   - Dive computers integrated with mobile apps record and analyze everything from total dive time and recovery intervals to performance trends.

4. **Ergonomic Designs:**
   - Compact and lightweight devices reduce drag, which, with a diver's equipment, is less in the way.

B. Advanced Wetsuits: Warmth, Flexibility, and Sustainability

1. **Thermal Insulation:**
   - Good-quality neoprene in modern wetsuits, like Yamamoto 45, provides excellent insulation without losing too much flexibility.

2. **Smooth-Skin Technology:**
   - The smooth-skin outer layers reduce water resistance when a diver passes through the water.

3. **Custom Fit:**
   - The made-for-order wetsuit fits a diver perfectly, offering superior thermal retention, comfort, and hydrodynamics.

4. **Eco-Friendly Alternatives:**
   - Plant-based materials and recycled components have also been increasingly employed in producing wetsuits to minimize environmental effects.

C. High-Efficiency Fins: Power with Precision

1. **Carbon Fiber and Composite Materials:**
   - Light, rigid fins that allow for the highest propulsion using the least possible energy preserve oxygen supplies and minimize fatigue.

2. **Modular Designs:**
   - Divers can customize their fins by matching blades with the foot pocket that best suits their needs and diving conditions.

3. **Improved Biomechanics:**
   - The blades' specific angulation and ergonomic foot pockets optimize energy transfer for smoother, more efficient movements.

D. Low-volume masks and Snorkels

1. **Optimized for Depth:**
   - Low-volume masks require minimal air for equalization and are thus the best in deep dives.

2. **Hydrodynamic Snorkels:**
   - Sleek designs minimize drag while allowing comfortable breathing during surface preparation and recovery.

E. Buoyancy and Safety Gear

1. **Safety Buoys:**
   - Provide the necessary platforms with provisions for storing gear and flags to increase visibility in open water.

2. **Weight Systems Adjustable:**
   - Allow divers to adjust their weight to achieve negative buoyancy and effectiveness and control both during descents and ascents.

3. **Rescue Systems:**
   - Passive flotation devices monitor a panic signal and help bring unconscious divers to the surface.

2. Training Tools and Techniques: Building Strength and Safety

These are the technological innovations in free diving for better performance and safety:

A. Virtual Reality and Augmented Reality Training

1 **Simulated Environments:**
   - VR systems can simulate an underwater environment and train divers to equalize, relax, and perform techniques for static apnea.

2. **Dynamic Feedback:**
   - Using augmented reality overlays to see real-time metrics while training includes finning efficiency and body posture.

B. Breath Training Devices

1. **Respiratory Muscle Strengthening:**
   - Tools like PowerBreathe increase lung capacity and strength in the diaphragm, thus enhancing breath control and efficiency.

2. **Real-Time Monitoring:**
   - Oximeters and CO_2 sensors will monitor physiological responses to ensure that any progress in training apnea is safe.

C. Digital Tools for Training

1. **Freediving Apps:**
   - Apps like Dive+ and FreedivePro allow divers to log dives, analyze performance metrics, and create customized apnea tables.

2. **Wearables:**
   - Fitness trackers for freedivers also track heart rate variability, oxygen levels, and recovery times.

D. Specialized Pool Training Equipment

1. **Weighted Sleds:**
   - Simulate depth in controlled environments, enabling divers to practice equalization techniques and adaptation to depth.

2. **Resistance Bands:**
   - Strengthen the muscles used in finning and develop endurance for dynamic and static apnea.

3. Advanced Freediving Techniques Supported by Technology

Technological tools have enabled divers to perfect and master advanced techniques, unlocking new performance levels.

A. Hydrodynamics
- Improved gear design reduces drag, allowing divers to conserve energy and oxygen for longer bottom times.

B. Equalization

1. **Mastering Mouth-Fill Technique:**
   - Training devices help divers achieve precise control over this advanced equalization method for deep dives.

2. **Pressure Sensors:**
   - Provide real-time feedback on middle-ear pressure, helping divers refine equalization techniques.

C. CO_2 and O_2 Tolerance

1. **Custom Apnea Protocols:**
   - Training apps create personalized apnea tables based on physiological data.

2. **Dynamic Adaptation:**
   - Simulated drills mimic real situations to reinforce resiliency in a changing environment.

4. Freediving Safety Innovations: Reducing the Risks

The sport of free diving has adopted a raft of new technologies designed to reduce the risk factor.

A. Wearable Monitors
- Devices monitor vital signs while diving and alert for early hypoxia or excessive CO_2 buildup.

B. Dive Line Sensors
- Monitor depth and time, warning safety teams when approaching unsafe limits.

C. Emergency Response Systems
- Safety buoys automatically detect emergencies and release flotation devices to help distressed divers.

5. Freediving and the Environment

Advances in freediving are increasingly designed to be more sustainable, causing minimal impact on marine ecosystems.

A. Eco-Friendly Gear

Wetsuits, fins, and accessories made from sustainable materials reduce waste and carbon footprints.

B. Sustainable Practices

1. **Reef-Safe Sunscreen:**
   - Safeguards coral reefs from chemicals that destroy them.

2. **Plastic-Free Diving:**
   - Divers use reusable containers and avoid single-use plastics.

6. The Future of Freediving Technology

As technology continues to evolve, the future of freediving will increasingly integrate high-end tools with sustainable practices.

A. Artificial Intelligence (AI)

1. **Performance Optimization:**
   - AI-driven applications analyze dive data and provide tailored training recommendations.

2. **Marine Life Identification:**
   - AI algorithms will identify species and monitor changes in biodiversity with the help of underwater imagery.

B. Smart Wearables
- The integrated suits and masks will track physiological and environmental data in real-time.

C. Advanced Materials
- Nanotechnology research will make the gear lighter, stronger, and more sustainable.

D. Collaboration in Research
- Freedivers will also continue partnering with marine scientists, making further valuable contributions to biodiversity, climate change, and habitat restoration.

7. Freediving to Advance Conservation and Exploration

Freedivers hold an essential position in the spheres of ocean conservation and exploration. They do it by assisting marine science with technology.

A. Data Gathering
- Divers contribute to monitoring coral reefs, tracking species, and documenting water quality for research.

B. Public Engagement
- Freedivers use high-quality visuals and storytelling in a way that moves them and inspires ocean care around the world.

8. Conclusion

Technological innovations in equipment and methodologies have transformed freediving, making this sport much safer, more performative, and sensitive to the marine environment. From the ingenuity of design in dive computers to AI-driven training tools, the freediver can explore depth with more excellent economy and awareness. As freediving continues to evolve, it will be important not only in the redefinition of human potential but also in preserving marine ecosystems and fostering sustainable practices so that the underwater world can continue to amaze and inspire future generations.

Ethical Considerations for the Future of Freediving: A Comprehensive Framework

It is more than a sport; it links human possibilities with nature. As freediving continues to evolve and becomes increasingly sophisticated, so will the sport's ethics have to evolve marine ecosystems, be inclusive, and be sustainable. The face of freediving is constantly changed by ever-changing ecological challenges, technologies, and communities, bringing positive change within the sport.

1. Freedivers' Responsibility towards Marine Ecosystems

Freedivers have an intimate and peculiar relationship with the sea; their conduct directly affects the ecosystems they dive into. Therefore, ethical concerns should focus on noninvasive interaction and the protection of underwater habitats.

A. Non-Interference with Marine Life

1. **Respect for Natural Behaviors:**
   - Freedivers must observe marine species without changing their behaviors or natural environment. They should avoid touching, chasing, and feeding the organisms, as these actions can cause stress or injure wildlife.

2. **Promoting Biodiversity Conservation:**
   - Divers must not enter areas that interfere with marine life in breeding, feeding, or along their migration routes.

3. **Minimal Disturbance:**
   - No artificial lighting and noise as it may distract night-active species and sensitive ecosystems.

B. Habitat Preservation

1. **Physical Damage Avoidance:**
   - Exercise reasonable buoyancy control and swim efficiently to avoid unplanned contact with coral reefs or seagrass beds.
   - Use access and exit routes to prevent disturbing the topography of the seabed.

2. **Ecological Practices:**
   - Apply reef-safe sunscreens free from poisonous chemicals like oxybenzone and octinoxate since they were linked to the bleaching of coral reefs.

2. Sustainability in Freediving

With significant growth in this sport globally, freediving also faces questions of sustainability. There is now an incredible urge for a far more ethical manner of conducting this sport through improved practices aimed at minimizing impact and ensuring marine life conservation.

A. Responsible Tourism

1. **Eco-Friendly Operators:**
   - Support operators with a serious commitment to sustainability by limiting group size, not creating waste, and following the no-touch policy.

2. **Carbon Footprint Reduction:**
   - This includes estimating a reduction in travel emissions by using local operators who can combine travel trips with conservation activities, such as clean-ups, workshops, or other related workshops.

B. Conservation Advocacy Protection of MPAs:

1. **Protecting Marine Protected Areas (MPAs):**
   - MPAs are implemented, developed, and managed to protect biodiversity hotspots.

2. **Active Engagement:**
   - Participate in activities like restoring coral reefs, cleaning up underwater, or monitoring biodiversity to give back to the ecosystems that sustain the sport.

C. Sustainable Gear and Technology

1. **Eco-Friendly Equipment:**
   - Such equipment shall be made from recycled or sustainable material to reduce environmental impact.

2. **Waste Reduction:**
   - Replace single-use plastics with reusable ones: water bottles, dive bags, and packaging.

3. Responsible Use of Technology in Competitive Freediving

With technology increasingly being used in the sport of freediving, ethical considerations in its development and use must balance safety and performance without compromising environmental integrity.

A. Safety Before Exploitation

1. **Give Importance to Skill Development:**
   - Divers must learn techniques and not rely on technology to push the limits.

2. **Avoid Exploitative Practices:**
   - Technology should be used responsibly to document marine life and environments without destroying and exploiting species commercially.

B. Transparent Data Usage

1. **Collaboration with Scientists:**
   - Share responsibly with researchers the data obtained from expeditions in free diving, considering precision and integrity.

2. **Public Accessibility:**

- Make nonsensitive discoveries freely available and allow international cooperation to save marine life.

4. Equality in Freediving

It should be open to people of every class, caste, creed, and color, respecting local customs and culture.

A. Cultural Sensitivity

1. **Respect to Indigenous Practices:**
   - Freedivers should respect indigenous peoples, such as the Ama in Japan or the Bajau Laut in Southeast Asia, for whom diving has traditionally been a part of their lives.

2. **Involvement of Local Communities:**
   - Employ local guides and operators with the promise of financial gain and cultural exchange.

B. Promotion of Diversity

1. **Training Programs Accessible:**
   - Underrepresented groups, including women, youth, and low-income individuals, will be offered sliding-scale fees, scholarships, or free workshops.

2. **Adaptive Freediving:**
   - Programs and equipment that allow people with disabilities to take part in the sport of freediving confidently and safely.

5. Competitive Freediving Ethics

Competitions and record attempts in freediving should be organized so that ethical considerations make safety, equity, and concern for the environment paramount.

A. Safety of the Athletes

1. **Stringent Safety Protocols:**
   - Appropriate safety divers, advanced life-support equipment, and emergency contingency plans must cover all competitions.

2. **Mental Health Support:**
   - Competitors are encouraged to make available psychological resources to help athletes cope with performance pressure and post-competition recovery.

B. Environmental Responsibility

1. **Low-Impact Events:**
   - Use eco-friendly venues and limit environmental disruptions during competitions.

2. **Conservation Integration:**
   - Incorporate educational talks, clean-ups, or restoration projects into event programming.

6. Freediving as a Tool for Marine Conservation

This is where freedivers may contribute to preserving and restoring marine ecosystems through advocacy, citizen science, and education.

A. Citizen Science and Data Collection

1. **Marine Monitoring:**
   - Record the diversity of species, coral health, and pollution levels to contribute to scientific research and policy decisions.

2. **Climate Change Insights:**
   - Observe visible signs of climate change, such as coral bleaching or species migration patterns, and prepare reports for the relevant bodies.

B. Storytelling and Awareness

1. **Visual Documentation:**
   - The rest of the world is stirred to protect and respect the ocean by using photography and videography in storytelling.

2. **Educational Outreach:**
   - Provide workshops and in-school programs, discussing responsible ways of freediving and the concepts supporting preserving marine life.

7. The Freediver's Ethical Check List

Category	Key Actions
Respect Marine Life	Observe without interfering; avoid touching or feeding animals.
Promote Sustainability	Support eco-friendly operators; use sustainable gear.
Engage in Conservation	Participate in cleanups, reef restoration, and biodiversity monitoring.
Use Technology Responsibly	Prioritize safety; avoid exploiting marine resources or ecosystems.
Foster Inclusivity	Encourage diverse participation; develop programs for underrepresented groups.
Minimize Event Impacts	Ensure competitions are environmentally sustainable and culturally sensitive.

8. How Freediving Shapes Global Conservation

Freediving goes beyond the sport to global conservation and education.

A. Global Action Inspired
- Freedivers are ambassadors for marine ecosystems, inspiring others through experiences to care for the ocean.

B. Framing Future Policy
- The collaboration of the freedivers with policy and NGOs magnifies their observations into actionable conservation strategies.

9. Conclusion

The ethics concerning the future of freediving will responsibly continue this sport by balancing human achievement with environmental and cultural integrity. Freedivers must be guardians of the underwater world: They should respect marine ecosystems, promote sustainability, and advocate inclusivity. If all of these principles are pursued, freediving will stand a better chance of continuing to inspire and empower people to contribute to preserving the ocean for future generations.

Freediver Code of Conduct and Ethics: All-Inclusive Manual on Safety, Ethics, and Responsibility

Freediving represents physical strength, mental toughness, and a deep connection with the underwater world. As this sport evolves and technology improves, the need for a sound ethical foundation also increases. The Code of Conduct of Freedivers stipulates guidelines for best practices for protecting marine environments for the community's well-being. This shows that freedivers contribute positively to the sport they practice, the ocean they dive in, and the society around them.

1. Safety: The Cornerstone of Freediving

Safety is the most integral part of freediving. Proper training, adherence to safety protocols, and respect for one's limitations ensure a safe experience for everyone.

A. Individual Responsibility

1. **Training and Certification:**
   - Attend formal freediving classes, including an overview of holding breath, equalization techniques, and rescue methods.
   - Higher advanced certification will be required if your experience or depth goals improve.

2. **Physical and Mental Readiness:**
   - Be in good physical and mental health, and your body and mind should be prepared for the stresses of the dive. Do not drive after drinking alcohol, using drugs, or taking medications that decrease judgment or reaction time.

3. **Progressive Development:**
   - Increase depth and time slowly to allow the body to adapt to the increased pressure and lengthen apnea gradually.

B. The Buddy System

1. **Always Dive with a Buddy:**
   - Freediving solo is the most dangerous sport in existence. A buddy helps when something goes wrong.

2. **Clear Communication**
   - Pre-dive agreed signals and emergency procedures ensure that communication will work properly under the water.

3. **Mutual Vigilance**
   - The safety divers need to be ever watchful of dives, especially the ascents when shallow-water blackouts might happen.

C. Emergency Preparation

1. **Rescue Training:**
   - Learn various rescue techniques, practice the blackout treatment, and adequately provide surface support.

2. **First Aid and CPR:**
   - Maintain current certifications in first aid, including CPR and oxygen administration.

3. **Safety Equipment:**
   - You are expected to carry the essential equipment for any dive- a safety buoy, whistle, signaling devices, and a first aid kit.

2. Ethics in Freediving

Freediving is an intensive sport that requires awareness of interaction with the marine environment, technology, and other divers.

A. Care for Marine Environments

1. **Non-Invasive Interaction:**
   - Never touch, chase, or feed marine animals. Doing so can cause stress and injury and disrupt their natural behaviors.

2. **Habitat Protection:**
   - Be considerate when making movements to avoid accidentally damaging coral reefs, seagrass beds, or other sensitive habitats.
   - Do not remove any souvenirs or disturb the underwater environment.

3. **Eco-Friendly Behaviors:**
   - Use reef-safe sunscreens and do not add pollutants or waste into the water.

B. Responsible Use of Technology

1. **Responsible Documentation:**
   - Use underwater photography and videography to increase awareness of marine conservation without disturbing wildlife.

2. **Data Integrity:**
   - Freedivers participating in citizen science initiatives should ensure data integrity and ethical dissemination of information collected during dives.

3. **Skill Over Devices:**
   - Do not be overly dependent on devices. Freediving is an art that blossoms by a person's skill, control, and intuition.

C. Respect for Fellow Freedivers

1. **Inclusivity:**
   - We should include all divers, regardless of their level, whether male or female, old or young or what culture they represent.

2. **Teamwork and Mentorship:**
   - Knowledge-sharing, experience, and sharing, working together for safe communal growth and security in freediving.

3. **Non-Competitive Ethics**
   - Do not practice aggressive, destructive competitiveness in competitions or training at any time.

3. Accountability for the Marine Environment

Freedivers often attest to the beauty and fragility of marine environments. Their proximity to nature also puts them at the forefront of efforts to conserve oceans.

A. Supporting Marine Conservation

1. **Support Marine Protected Areas (MPAs):**
   - Responsible diving in MPAs includes diving within existing rules, if any, concerning other marine animals.

2. **Participate in restoration projects:**
   - Restore and give something to the sea world by planting new coral reefs in coral bleaching spots.

3. **Raise Awareness of the Cause:**
   - Share personal experiences and observations to create awareness about the importance of ocean conservation.

B. Sustainable Practices

1. **Eco-Friendly Gear:**
   - Handle and use only such equipment made of recycled or biodegradable material.

2. **Minimal Waste:**
   - Bring a refillable water bottle, bags, and containers to minimize plastic waste during dives.

3. **Low-Impact Tourism:**
   - Select operators abiding by sustainable tourism rules, including controlling group sizes and refraining from visiting too-populated sites.

4. Freediving Competitions and Events

Ethical considerations are crucial because freediving competitions and events prioritize safety, fairness, and environmental responsibility.

A. Athlete Safety

1. **Rigorous Safety Measures:**
   - Organizers must provide trained safety teams, medical professionals, and appropriate emergency equipment.

2. **Mental Health Support:**
   - Competitors should have access to resources for managing stress, performance pressure, and post-event recovery.

B. Environmental Stewardship

1. **Eco-Friendly Events:**
   - Host events with minimal environmental impact, such as using renewable energy sources, reducing waste, and avoiding sensitive habitats.

2. **Community Engagement:**
   - Include conservation activities in the event programs, such as cleaning up beaches and other educational activities.

5. Inclusivity and Accessibility in Freediving

Freediving should be a sport for all, overcoming participation barriers by becoming more diverse.

A. Accessibility Initiatives

1. **Adaptive Freediving Programs:**
   - Develop training and equipment to enable divers with disabilities to access this sport on equal grounds.

2. **Financial Accessibility:**
   - Scholarships or reduced fees to allow access to under privileged groups.

B. Respect for Culture and Cooperation

1. **Local Involvement:**
   - Support the indigenous people and the local involvement by considering the existing traditional practices and ocean knowledge.

2. **Celebrate Diversity:**
   - Encourage and let the voices of all participants who belong to each culture, female, male, and other orientations in the sport be heard.

6. Check List - Code of Conduct for a Freediver

Category	Ethical Practice
Safety	Always dive with a buddy and stay within personal limits.
Respect for Marine Life	Observe without touching, chasing, or feeding animals.
Environmental Care	Leave no trace; participate in conservation initiatives.
Ethical Technology Use	Balance reliance on tools with skill mastery; document responsibly.
Inclusivity	Promote diversity and accessibility in freediving programs.
Competition Ethics	Prioritize safety, fairness, and environmental sustainability in events.
Advocacy and Education	Share knowledge to inspire ocean conservation and sustainable practices.

7. The Greater Good of Freediving

Freediving is so much more than the achievements of individuals; its connection with the ocean can offer a route to global change, empowering people to take action.

A. Creating Conservation
- Through storytelling, freedivers inspire environmental stewardship by relating experiences of beauty and fragility from marine ecosystems.

B. Building Global Communities
- A worldwide community of freedivers might form a platform from which people unite through a shared aspiration: to practice sustainability, exchange culture, and find mutual accountability for the well-being of the seas.

8. Conclusion

The Freediver Code of Conduct presents the holistic perspective of responsible behavior and ethics concerning freediving. Safety in focus, respect toward marine life, fostering inclusiveness, and promoting the cause of conservation: freedivers can ensure sustainable development in this sport, with protection for nature they love. It is not just about going into the ocean deep but protecting, respecting, and celebrating everything underwater for generations to come.

Freediving Community Code and Ethics Practices: A Full Guide to Safety, Ethics, and Sustainability

Freediving is a sport, a way of living, and connecting with the sea. The freediving community worldwide must adopt one code of conduct and a set of ethics, as this sport has become so popular and complex. This Freediving Community Code sets safety, inclusion, and marine environmental protection to inspire conservation on common grounds. By following these fundamental principles, the freediving community will be contributing to the sustainable development of this sport while at the same time preserving those ecosystems that sustain it.

1. Safety: The Foundation of Freediving Practices

Safety is at the very core of freediving.

A broad commitment to safety for all in this sport means regard for people's well-being and setting specific standards for conduct.

A. Individual Accountability in Safety

1. **Training and Awareness:**
   - Take complete, certified courses in freediving that teach critical skills related to breathing control, equalization techniques, and rescue procedures.
   - Keep updated on all the evolutions in freediving techniques, improvements in safety matters, and equipment.

2. **Preparation and Physical and Psychological Conditioning:**
   - Regular physical exercise and sport contribute to cardiovascular fitness, flexibility, and the development of lungs,
   - Be prepared psychologically for dives: cool-headedness, avoiding tension factors affecting judgment, and proper decision-making process.

3. **Gradual Progression:**
   - With experience and confidence comes depth and length but without unnecessary risks.

B. The Buddy System

1. **Shared Responsibility:**
   - Dive always with a buddy, each responsible for the other.

2. **Pre-Dive Communication:**
   - Establish specific hand signals and emergency procedures before entering the water.

3. **Buddy Awareness:**
   - Practice being the diver and then the safety observer, watching for the first signs of distress, especially during ascents.

C. Emergency Preparedness

1. **Rescue Skills:**
   - Regularly practice rescue drills, including blackout response and methods for recovering an unconscious diver from the surface.

2. **Equipment Essentials:**
   - Safety buoys, whistles, and signaling devices in case of an emergency to alert others.

3. **First Aid Preparation:**
   - CPR and oxygen administration: Keep current with certification and act efficiently in case of a medical accident.

2. Marine Life Interaction - Ethics

Because of this privilege, the freediver is privileged to enter the underwater world and is bound to become its custodian regarding conservation.

A. Care for Marine Life

1. **Non-Invasive Observations:**
   - Observe marine life without touching, chasing, or altering the natural behavioral patterns of the animals.

2. **Not to Feed Wildlife:**
   - Feeding disturbs ecosystems and, in most circumstances, harms the animals fed by creating dependencies on humans.

3. Protection of Endangered Species:
- Avoid entering areas reported or known as breeding or resting grounds of sensitive or endangered species.

B. Habitat Preservation

1. **Minimizing Impact:**
- Have positive buoyancy and controlled fin movement to avoid touching coral reefs or stirring up sediment.

2. **Environmentally Friendly Products::**
- Use and practice biodegradable, reef-safe sunscreens, and never throw pollutants into the marine environment.

3. **Sustainable Gear:**
- Choose gear made of recycled or sustainable material to reduce the sport's ecological footprint.

C. Conservation Advocacy

1. **Active Participation:**
- Participate in locally organized, easy events such as underwater clean-ups, coral reef rehabilitation, and seagrass planting.

2. **Educational Outreach:**
- Relate experiences and observations made to help raise awareness for marine conservation.

3. **Support Marine Protected Areas (MPAs):**
- Support MPA's expansion and follow the rules in diving.

3. Diversity and Inclusion in the Sport of Freediving

A freediving freediving is diverse, inclusive, and provides equitable access.

1. **Adaptive Freediving:**
   - Freediving training ramps and equipment are necessary to provide the sport for divers with disabilities so they can safely.

2. **Financial Accessibility:**
   - Scholarships or free workshops should be offered, and community programs should be implemented to allow the under-resourced community to go freediving.

B. Cultural Diversity

1. **Respect Tradition:**
   - Interact responsibly with freediving's cultural heritage communities, such as the Ama of Japan and the Bajau Laut of Southeast Asia.

2. **Local Collaboration:**
   - Act with local guides and operators to support sustainable tourism and exchange.

C. Fostering Gender Equality

1. **Representative Leadership:**
   - Ensure women have equal opportunity to compete in, lead, and hold positions within freediving, training programs, and decision-making positions.

2. **Encourage Participation:**
   - Provide an opportunity to get involved in the sport without being threatened by practices of discrimination and harassment. Safe spaces will be provided for women and under-represented groups to get involved in the sport of free diving.

4. Competitive Event Freediving - Freediving Ethical

Competitions are events that pit human abilities against nature. Questions relating to fair play practices, including marine environments, are essential for many reasons.

A. Safety of Athletes

1. **Safety Measures**
   - Trained safety divers and advanced medical equipment with detailed emergency response plans at events.

2. **Mental Health**
   - Competition Stress and Pressure: Provide resources to the athletes to deal with competitive stress and pressure.

B. Environmental Responsibility

1. **Sustainable Event Management:**
   - Organize events so minimal waste is minimized, renewable energy sources are used wherever possible, and fragile ecosystems are avoided.

2. **Inclusion of Conservation Activities:**
   - The programs include conservation workshops, beach clean-ups, or marine biodiversity talks.

C. Fair Competition

1. **Rules:**
   - Rules must be well-defined and consistent for every competitor.

2. **Equal Opportunities:**
   - Competitors of all backgrounds and calibers are given equal access to training and resources.

5. Responsible Use of Freediving Technology

As technology improves freediving performance and safety, freediving must be done to consider ethical and environmental concerns.

A. Skill Over Reliance
- More emphasis has to be put on freediving without over-dependency on technological assistance.

B. Ethical Documentation
- Underwater cameras and cameras after drone use are great for documenting marine life.

C. Support Research and Conservation
- Share data collected with researchers and conservation organizations to advance marine science and protection.

6. Freediving toFreedivingarine Ecosystems Conservation

Freedivers have this incredible platform to inspire marine conservation through advocacy, education, and personal stories.

A. Creating Awareness
- Social media, photography, and videography showcase the beauty of marine ecosystems and highlight environmental threats.

B. Engaging Youth and Communities
- Workshops, lectures, and dive programs should be arranged to grow the next wave of ocean stewards.

C. Partnerships with Other NGOs
- Cooperate with other protectionist organizations to widen your sphere of influence on behalf of marine life.

7. Freediving Community of Conduct Checklist

Category	Key Action
Safety	Dive with a buddy, maintain fitness, and adhere to limits.
Respect for Marine Life	Avoid interference, use eco-friendly products, and minimize impact.
Inclusivity	Promote diversity, provide access for all, and respect cultural traditions.
Ethical Competitions	Prioritize fairness, safety, and sustainability in events.
Technology Use	Balance skill development with technology and document responsibly.
Conservation Advocacy	Participate in restoration projects, cleanups, and education initiatives.

8. The Future of Freediving and Freediving Ethical Responsibility

The sport's future depends on how the community embraces an ethic that balances personal achievement with environmental and social responsibility.

A. To Drive Global Conservation
- Apart from that, freedivers can be ambassadors to the ocean as a catalyst for action on climate change, plastic pollution, and the loss of biodiversity.

B. Building a United Community
- In freediving, everyone is integral to this big-world model, just as everything in the ocean is unique and should be protected.

C. Sustaining Ocean Stewardship
- It mentors the next generation in the community, gives them a sense of responsibility, and will continue beyond today so that the sport of freediving is for good.

9. Conclusion

The Freediving CoFreedivingde aims to bring practitioners closer to the sport with much responsibility. The only way that guarantees a continuing future- which also holds within its marine ecosystems- is by basing the activities of freedivers upon the principles of safety, respect in aquatic environments, diversity, and conservation principles. It is much more than any sport; it covers aspects of interest when discovering, caring for, or celebrating these miracles of the oceans.

Inspiring Biography & Achievements

Best Male Freedivers: Pioneers and Record-Breakers in Freediving

Recently, this form of diving has attracted many adventurers and athletes who are enthusiastic about learning more about it. Much of its establishment is due to brilliant individuals who, through their achievements, raised the standards in depth, breath-holding time, and dynamic movement through the water. The following is a detailed review of accomplishments, approaches, and philosophies from the world's top male freedivers, each with something different to bring to the sport.

1. Alexey Molchanov (Russia)

Specialization: Deep Freediving Constant Weight and Free Immersion

Achievements:
- He has set **world records** in the deepest CWT dive, **133 meters**, thus far in 2023.
- Has been regularly on top of major international competitions in **Vertical Blue**.
- Son of the late Natalia Molchanova, one of the best freedivers in history, continues her legacy and innovations.

Techniques:
- **Monofin Skills:** Has perfect technique and gets the most propulsion for the least energy expended.
- **Equalization Skills:** Masters different equalization techniques for extreme depths, such as the Frenzel and mouthfill.

- **Mental Preparation:** Trained in relaxation and visualization techniques, keeping him focused during challenging dives.

Contributions:
- He initiated the **Molchanov Training System,** an all-rounded freediving curriculum used today by all levels of freedivers worldwide.
- Advocates for a scientific and systematic approach to the sport of freediving, a combination of physical conditioning, mental training, and advanced breathing techniques.

2. William Trubridge (New Zealand)

Specialization: Constant Weight Without Fins (CNF)

Achievements:
- He set numerous world records in CNF, his deepest dive at **102 meters** in 2023.
- Founder of **Vertical Blue,** one of the most prestigious annual freediving competitions, held in Dean's Blue Hole, Bahamas.
- He is also known for his environmental advocacy in marine conservation through free diving.

Techniques:
- **Arm and Leg Coordination:** Perfected arm strokes and leg kicks synergy to minimize energy expenditure.
- **Streamlined Movement:** Ensures minimal drag by maintaining precise body alignment throughout the freedive.
- **Mental Discipline:** Outstanding is outstanding mental strength, using mindfulness and breathing techniques for all difficulties.

Philosophy:
- Sees freediving as a bridge that connects humankind with the ocean, pointing to a more spiritual and ecological approach to this sport.

3. Herbert Nitsch (Austria)

Specialization: NoLimits (NLT) Variable Weight (VWT)

Achievements:
- Holder of the title **"Deepest Man on Earth"** for his **No-Limits dive to 214** meters in 2007.
- Set over **30 world records** in various freediving disciplines, including Free Immersion and Constant Weight.
- Survived extreme decompression sickness after attempting a NoLimits dive to 253 meters.

Techniques:
- **Equalization:** Equalization at extreme depths is possible for the first time fast and efficiently with Equalization.
- **Sled Control:** Mastered sled-assisted descents and controlled lift-assisted ascents for NoLimits dives.
- **Mental Focus:** Meditation and visualization combine to keep calm during the most challenging dives.

Legacy:
- His performances in NoLimits diving have improved technique and safety within the freediving community.

4. Umberto Pelizzari (Italy)

Specialization: Multi-Disciplinary Freediving (CWT, FIM, NLT)

Achievements:
- Held several **world records** in various disciplines: Constant Weight, Free Immersion, and no limits beyond **150 meters**.
- He was a forerunner of the modern era in freediving and an example to an entire generation of athletes.

Techniques:
- He developed the first instructional programs integrating traditional freediving techniques with modern science.
- **Smoothing:** Perfects body position for maximum efficiency in a dive's active and passive phases.
- **Relaxation:** Fully promotes mental and physical relaxation to maximize utilization of oxygen.

Contributions:
- He has written renowned books about freediving and continuously educates upcoming free divers worldwide.

5. Guillaume Néry

Specialization: Constant Weight (CWT) and Variable Weight (VWT)

Achievements:
- He was the world record holder in Constant Weight at **126 meters**. He is also known for creating several underwater artistic films that incorporate the worlds of art and free diving. I have also won multiple medals at various world championships, showing consistency and mastery.

Techniques:
- **Artistic Approach:** This approach combines athleticism with the concept of art, making freediving even more accessible and inspiring for many people.
- **Relaxation:** The whole attitude is conducted with a flow state in diving; mentally and physically, the performance will be optimal.

Philosophy:
- Supporting freediving as such a meditation process, focusing on harmony within the underwater environment.

6. Goran Golak (Croatia)

Specialization: Static Apnea and Dynamic Apnea

Achievements:
- The multiple-time world record holder in the **pool disciplines**, such as static apnea and dynamic apnea.
- He is widely recognized for his **23-minute pure oxygen breath hold** and excellent CO_2 tolerance.
- Dominates in both pool and open water events in international freediving competitions.

Techniques:
- **Superior Breath Control:** Learn how to relax and hold your breath longer to extend static apnea times.
- **Aerobic and Anaerobic Training:** A combination of endurance and strength training for better results.

7. Davide Carrera (Italy)

Specialization: Constant Weight and Free Immersion

Achievements:
- Reached depths beyond **110 meters** in Constant Weight, showing skill in deep freediving.
- Combines freediving with ecology, using ocean exploration to promote marine life conservation

Techniques:
- **Spiritual Approach:** Meditates and trains himself on mindfulness; he competes this way.
- **Hydrodynamics:** Graceful, flowing movements to conserve energy.

8. Carlos Coste (Venezuela)

Specialization: Free Immersion and Variable Weight

Achievements:
- First freediver to surpass **100 meters in Free Immersion**, setting a historic milestone.
- Multiple world records in Variable Weight and Constant Weight disciplines.

Techniques:
- **Strength and Precision:** He combines physical power with technical finesse during ascents.
- **Equalization:** He uses advanced methods to maintain consistency at extreme depths.

9. BrankoPetrović Serbia

Specialization: Static Apnea

Achievements:
- He holds world records in Static Apnea, with times over **12 minutes** without pure oxygen, is the most dominant competitor in competitive pool freediving, and is unparalleled in his breath-hold ability.

Techniques:
- Mental Relaxation: Advanced techniques of overcoming the urge to breathe.
- CO_2 Tolerance: Focuses on adapting to high carbon dioxide levels through structured training.

10 Martin Št pánek (Czech Republic)

Specialization: Constant Weight, Free Immersion, and Variable Weight

Achievements:
- Establish multiple **world records** in each discipline, including beyond **120 meters.**
- Dedicated instructor and mentor to a lot of freedivers all over the world, with complete training programs.

Techniques
- Safety First Philosophy: It's a philosophy of minimizing risks by proper technique and preparation.
- Training Regimens: Transforms scientific knowledge into practical applications for performance enhancement.

Conclusion

The best male freedivers have reconstituted human limits in the water with outstanding performance, including physical, mental, and technical abilities. Their performances have raised the bar higher and inspired the global freediving community. Any aspiring freediver can learn a lot from them by learning their techniques, philosophies, and training methods, thus improving performance or gaining deeper contact with the world underwater. Training with dedication and respect for the ocean, these athletes remind us of the incredible feats the human body and mind are capable of.

Top Female Freedivers: Champions, Innovators, and Record Breakers

Female free divers have achieved incredible things, time and again extending the limits of human possibilities underwater. These ladies have been the face of the sport due to their physical prowess, mental toughness, pioneering techniques, record-breaking, inspiring others, and ocean conservation advocacy. A better version of the overview will delve into the lives, achievements, and techniques of the most influential female freedivers.

1. Natalia Molchanova (Russia)

Specialization: MultiDisciplinary Freediving (CWT, CNF, STA, FIM)

Achievements:
- Considered the best female freediver of all time, having acquired **41 world records** in different disciplines, something nobody has achieved up to date.
- Reached a dive in **Constant Weight (CWT)** to **101 meters**, the first woman ever to break the 100-meter barrier.
- Held a record in Static Apnea with a breath-hold of more than **9 minutes**.
- Dominant in FIM and CNF, she had set various records for depth and pool categories.

Techniques:
- **Fluid Movement:** Pioneered ways to save more energy using only smooth and controlled movements in the water.
- **Holistic Approach:** In-depth physical training has been perfectly combined with yoga and meditation, which is the right way to achieve inner peace.
- **Equalisation Mastery:** Using a more advanced Frenzel equalization technique and the mouthfill of air during deep dives.

Legacy:
- She founded the Molchanova School of Freediving, through which she has trained numerous divers worldwide.

- Encourages her son, Alexey Molchanov, to continue her work to progress global freediving training systems.
- A legend whose methods and philosophy inspire both amateur and professional freedivers.

2. Alessia Zecchini (Italy)

Specialization: Constant Weight (CWT), Variable Weight (VWT)

Achievements:
- Multitime world record holder, including **Constant Weight CWT** to **123 meters**, performed at Vertical Blue in 2023.
- He still regularly wins international competitions, including the most prestigious ones: **Vertical Blue** and **World Freediving Championships**.
- He has been consistently breaking records in depth disciplines, becoming one of the most popular freedivers of modern times.

Techniques:
- Monofin Precision: Great with a monofin in propulsion, using strength and flexibility.
- Relaxation Under Pressure: This is a method of relaxation during deep dives to prevent oxygen waste and equalize control.
- Position and Streamlining: Position impeccable, drag reduced, efficiency enhanced.

Philosophy:
- There is a need to push one's limit within safety protocols.
- Competition coupled with the love for the ocean by using freediving to bring awareness to marine ecosystems.

3. Alenka Artnik (Slovenia)

Discipline: Constant Weight (CWT)

Achievements
- Established a world record in the **Constant Weight (CWT)** category, reaching **122 meters** in 2020; she and Alessia Zecchini have beaten the record since then.

- Medals in international freediving competitions, such as Vertical Blue, often show consistency and determination.
- She became a freediving sensation worldwide in a few years, joining the ranks of the sport's best.

Techniques:
- **Efficient Free Fall:** She optimizes her descent by mastering relaxation and streamlining during free fall.
- **Mental Conditioning:** Relies heavily on visualization and meditation to stay calm and focused during dives.
- **Equalization Expertise:** Experienced in mouthfill equalization, which is of extreme depths.

Philosophy:
- She sees freediving as a journey to her 'self,' believing every dive brings her closer to that part of herself and the ocean.
- She enjoys championing mental health and strength from within, encouraging people around her to fight personal demons with this sport.

4. Hanako Hirose (Japan)

Specialization: Free Immersion (FIM), Constant Weight (CWT)

Achievements:
- Held multiple world records in **free immersion (FIM) over 90 meters.**
- She was often placed within the top ranks in various freediving competitions for her steadfast performances.
- She is considered "poetry in motion" due to her style, which is both graceful and efficient.

Techniques:
- **Smooth Pulling:** Developed perfect hand-over-hand to minimize energy use and increase efficiency.
- **Body Alignment:** Remains in a streamlined position throughout the dive and minimizes drag.
- **Relaxation Mastery:** Works on achieving a meditative state while diving to achieve better performances.

Philosophy:
- It focuses on freediving with joy and peace, encouraging divers to be connected with their bodies and water.

5. Sayuri Kinoshita (Japan)

Specialization: Dynamic Apnea, Constant Weight Without Fins (CNF)

Achievements:
- Set a world record in the event of **Constant Weight Without Fins (CNF)** with **72 meters**, showing great technique and endurance simultaneously.
- Successive champion, breaking records in disciplines like **Dynamic Apnea (DYN)** and **Dynamic No Fins (DNF)**.
- Helped lift Japan to the international ranks in freediving, catalyzing a new generation.

Techniques:
- **Precision and Rhythm:** Flawless movement patterns in pool disciplines brought maximum distance with every breath-hold.
- **Mental Toughness:** High CO_2 levels were overcome with advanced relaxation techniques.

Legacy:
- She left an indelible mark in freediving and is remembered by many as an athlete who combined competitive greatness with humility and kindness.

6. Sofia Gómez Uribe (Colombia)

Specialization: Constant Weight (CWT), Free Immersion (FIM)

Achievements:
- Multiple American records, including a **Free Immersion (FIM)** dive to **86 meters**.

- Gained international recognition for freediving in South America and became a role model for young divers in the region.
- Melds athletic success with a strong voice for ocean conservation and environmental awareness.

Techniques:
- **Precise Equalization:** Masters equalization at intermediate depths, ensuring smooth descents.
- **Energy Conservation:** Balances power and relaxation to optimize efficiency during dives.

Philosophy:
- Believes in using freediving as a catalyst for change to promote sustainability in marine life conservation.

7. Marianna Gillespie (Russia)

Specialization: Static Apnea (STA), Dynamic Apnea (DYN)

Achievements:
- Various world records in the pool disciplines include holding one's breath with Static Apnea (STA) for over **8 minutes.**
- Highly talented in **Dynamic Apnea (DYN),** always among the world's best during international competitions.

Techniques:
- **Advanced Breath Control:** Uses CO_2 tolerance drills and relaxation techniques to extend breath-hold durations.
- **Streamlining:** Focuses on hydrodynamics to maximize the distance covered in dynamic events.

8. Mirela Kardasevic (Croatia)

Specialization: Dynamic Apnea, Static Apnea

Achievements:
- Hold several national and international records in **Dynamic Apnea (DYN)** and **Dynamic No Fins (DNF).**

- She has a strong reputation for her endurance and ability to push through discomfort, especially in the pool disciplines.

Techniques:
- **Hydrodynamic positioning:** Ensures maximum efficiency by maintaining a streamlined body position.
- **Mental Focus:** Trains for staying relaxed during prolonged breath holds, even in intense competition environments.

9. Jessica Lu (China)

Specialization: Constant Weight (CWT), Dynamic Apnea

Achievements:
- Over **90 meters** of **Constant Weight** multiple Asian records.
- Versatility describes this athlete in pool or depth disciplines since he will not stop until the deed is done.

Techniques:
- **Monofin Precision:** Combining Power and Finesse for Maximum Propulsion.
- **Equalization and Relaxation:** She lets her mind fall into a deep state of clarity to better cope with pressure changes.

10. Fatima Korok (Hungary)

Specialization: Free Immersion (FIM), Static Apnea

Achievements:
- Holds the European record in **Free Immersion,** reaching depths of over **85 meters.**
- Known for her serene demeanor and meditative approach to freediving.

Techniques:
- **Smooth and Relaxed Pulling:** Focuses on fluidity and efficiency in Free Immersion.
- **Mental Clarity:** Uses breathing exercises and visualization to maintain focus.

11. Marina Kazankova (Russia)

Specialization: No-Limits (NLT), Dynamic Apnea, and Underwater Performing Arts

Achievements:
- Multiple world records in **No-Limits (NLT)** and **Dynamic Apnea (DYN)**, with a **103-meter No-Limits dive.**
- Integration of freediving into the arts of performing underwater, cinema, and theater.
- I participated in international freediving competitions and was ranked among the best athletes.

Techniques:
- **Sled Diving Expertise:** Operated weighted sleds in No-Limits dives for a controlled descent with safety.
- **Dynamic Precision:** Has an excellent record in streamlined position and efficiency in the pool disciplines
- **Artistic Movements:** She incorporates fluid, almost dance-like motions into her dives, fusing athleticism and art.

Philosophy:
- She views freediving as both a sport and an art. When diving, she tells stories and takes her audience on a journey under the sea.
- An advocate for using freediving to engage with nature and express humanity's creativity.

Legacy:
- Marina also emphasized the visual arts and storytelling in freediving, highlighting the beauty of the underwater world that is often overlooked.
- Being a marine conservationist, she promotes and spreads awareness about the necessity of protecting the ocean through this medium.

12. Nataliia Zharkova (Ukraine)

Specialization: Dynamic Apnea (DYN, DNF), Static Apnea (STA), and Pool Disciplines

Achievements:
- Multiple **world records** holder in **Dynamic Apnea (DYN)** and **Dynamic Apnea Without Fins (DNF)**-continuously pushing the limits in the pool disciplines.
- Had a record **DNF swim of 215 meters**. Few human beings have such stamina and precision.
- Consistently ranked among the top athletes in major international freediving competitions, including world championships and regional events.

Techniques:
- **Dynamic Efficiency:** Places emphasis on streamlined body positioning and precise propulsion for maximizing distance per breath.
- **Mental Toughness:** Advanced relaxation and visualization techniques to help him overcome high CO_2 levels and mental fatigue.
- **Breath Control:** Employs meticulous breath preparation and recovery strategies to optimize oxygen use and recovery between attempts.

Philosophy:
- Believes freediving is a sport, a journey of self-discovery, and mental resilience.
- Advocates for precision and control, seeing freediving as an art form combining technique and grace.

Legacy:
- Currently one of the most accomplished pool freedivers, Nataliia has raised the profile of the Dynamic Apnea disciplines and encourages others to pursue them through competitive freediving.
- Her devotion to training and competition has entrenched her position as an exemplary figure among aspiring freedivers worldwide.

Conclusion

Records were broken, and women freedivers' achievements inspired a global community. In that sense, they proved what a person can do to themselves and others through hard work, innovation, and being linked with the ocean. From being an athletic success through advocacy in ocean conservation to their personal stories that moved them further, these champions will forever change the sport of freediving while linking us with the deep.

Historic Legends in Freediving: Pioneers and Icons of the Sport

Legendary freedivers are the pioneers and icons of the sport. It connects man and the underwater world with a dive while holding his breath. Its rich history links the ancient traditions of man to the modern achievements that have created legendary figures, redefining human limits and inspiring hundreds while helping globalization take place within this sport. Much more than athletes-ambassadors of marine conservation, speakers for the freediving community, and explorers of human potential.

1. Enzo Maiorca (Italy)

Era: 1960s–1980s

Achievements:
- Nicknamed "The Lord of the Deep," Enzo Maiorca is amongst a couple of pioneer freedivers into whose hands extreme deep waters opened modern freediving.
- He started the series of records on in-depth disciplines, including both No Limits and Constant Weight, most of the time taking precedence from/after records among famous record divers at his time.
- Maiorca reached a depth of over 100 meters that no one could have imagined, but they did so to inspire the freediving world.

Legacy:
- Big Blue filmed a competition between Maiorca and Jacques Mayol, an action-drama about competitive free diving.

- Except for his records, Maiorca was deeply concerned about ocean conservation. Using his celebrity platform to spread protection for marine ecosystems has always been his passion.
- He preached this form of diving, considerations on sustainable practices, and respect for marine life, thus setting the code of conduct for further generations of divers.

2. Jacques Mayol (France)

Era: 1950s–1980s

Achievements:
- Jacques Mayol became the first person to free-dive 100 meters, overcoming psychological and physiological barriers.
- Mayol was one of the first to introduce yoga, meditation, and breathing control into this form of freediving. This approach emphasizes the interrelation of mind and body because of success in results underwater.
- On exit, Mayol completely revolutionized free diving, proving that clarity of mind and relaxation are as important as physical capability.

Legacy:
- Nicknamed "The Dolphin Man," Mayol's deep connection to marine life, particularly dolphins, symbolized Mayol's holistic approach to freediving.
- His life and philosophies inspired the film The Big Blue, which propelled freediving right into the minds of the public consciousness and introduced most viewers to this sport.
- Environmentalism and philosophic writings-just like his book, Homo Delphinus-remain a source of inspiration today for those many free divers who plunge not just in sport but deep within themselves in their sport of free diving.

3. Audrey Mestre (France)

Era: 1990s–2002

Achievements:
- No-limits freediving record dives at 130 meters made Audrey Mestre the figure of most importance within the sport.
- Her momentary bravery, precision, and years spent perfecting herself in extreme conditions deep free dives were conducted made her a constant subject of reminiscence.

Legacy:
- Mestre died during a record dive of 171 meters of the substantial perils faced within extreme free diving.
- She was a grim reminder that adherence to safety, preparation, and capricious underwater worlds counts for everything.
- She informed and spoke about safety in free diving, presented changes in equipment, and updated the procedures for emergencies.

4. Tarek Omar (Egypt)

Era: 1980s–2000s

Achievements:
- Considered one of the founders of modern Egyptian and wider Arab freediving, Tarek Omar spread the sport throughout the region.
- More training and coaching of the divers helped them lay a better foundation for having a solid, freediving culture, first in Egypt and then in the surrounding countries.

Legacy:
- Taught and introduced to many walks of life regarding this sport helped the sport get further in shape.
- One of those few selected who indeed champion community building and making freediving as inclusive as it can be inspired a generation ahead in the future of this sport in the Middle East.

5. Pipin Ferreras (Cuba)

Era: 1990s–2000s

Achievements:
- Pipin Ferreras was the forerunner in No Limits freediving and smashed a series of world records to contribute to developing new limits of human depth achievements.
- With charisma and ambitious features, Ferreras became the sport's face in the Americas.

Legacy:
- The story of his relationship with Audrey Mestre and her tragic death during an attempt at setting the record put an international spot in view regarding both the beauty and danger of this sport.
- Ferreras contributes to the sport in many ways, including improving training and safety and creating inspiring films and documentaries about free diving.

6. Jacques Piccard (Switzerland)

Era: 1960s

Achievements:
- Although never having been a competitive freediver, Jacques Piccard was an oceanographer whose work with deep-sea exploration inspired generations of free divers.
- His dive into the Mariana Trench in the bathyscaphe Trieste unveiled the mystery of the deep ocean and increased humanity's knowledge of marine environments.

Legacy:
- Indirectly, Piccard influenced the freedivers to venture into the underwater world, yet with much respect for the ecosystems.
- His contribution to oceanography underlined the interrelation of exploration, science, and conservation.

Conclusion

These historical legends of freediving represent a mix of athleticism, innovation, and deep respect for the underwater world. These pioneers and icons have not only pushed the limits of human potential but also inspired a community of millions worldwide to connect with the ocean in meaningful and sustainable ways. The records, philosophies, and conservation mark the indelible stamp these figures have left on the sport, reminding us of the beauty and fragility of this underwater world. Their legacy keeps inspiring all divers and non-divers alike as one celebration of resilience, curiosity, and respect that defines free diving.

Appendix

The appendix contains general resources, tools, and information that might assist a freediver in training, safety, and communion with the underwater world. The references are from highly reputed freediving organizations and research experts.

Appendix A: Freediving Terms

- **Apnea:** The act of not breathing voluntarily, common to all the complimentary diving disciplines.
- **Barotrauma:** Injuries to body parts that contain air due to pressure differences during ascents and descents.
- **CO_2 Tolerance:** During Apnea, one's human body can sustain higher carbon dioxide levels.
- **CWT:** Constant Weight; in this freediving discipline, the freediver makes a descent and ascent unaided with the same weight.
- **STA - Static Apnea:** In this form of discipline, the athlete gets a maximum breath hold while remaining stationary in the water.
- **Equalization:** Equalizing the inner air pressure against the rising external water pressure while going down.

Recommended Reference: Freediving Manual: Learn How to Freedive, Advanced Techniques for Beginners by Mike McGuire.

Appendix B: Freediving Safety Checklist

1. **Pre-Dive Preparation:**
   - **Equipment Check:** Ensure the mask, fins, wetsuit, and dive computer are working correctly
   - **Dive Plan:** Establish maximum depth, bottom time, and emergency signals with your buddy.

- **Hydration and Rest:** No alcohol or heavy meals 24 hours before diving.

2. **During the Dive:**
   - Relaxation: To be relaxed, with calm and controlled breathing before and during the dive.
   - Safety Procedure: Buddy is in sight all the time during the dive.
   - Depth Awareness: To be within my limit and never beyond what training has prepared me for.

3. **After the Dive Recovery:**
   - recover breathing properly to deoxygenize the body safely;
   - log the dive for analysis. Depth, time, and fatigue fatigue.

Further Reading: Manual of Freediving by Umberto Pelizzari and Stefano Tovaglieri.

Appendix C: Training Templates

1. **Beginners Weekly Training Plan :**
   - Day 1: CO_2 sensitivity tables (dynamic Apnea or static Apnea).
   - Day 2: Cardio-vascular training - swimming/ running.
   - Day 3: In the pool, do dynamic Apnea with fins drill.

2. **Advanced Weekly Training Program**
   - Day 1: Open water - depth training in equalization
   - Day 2 Flexibility exercise, Yoga, and diaphragm stretch
   - Day 3: In the pool, Static Apnea drill O_2 and CO_2 tables

Recommended Resource: Apnea Academy training programs.

Appendix D: Useful resource on freediving

1. **Books:**
   - Homo Delphinus: The Dolphin Within Man Jacques Mayol.

- Deep: Freediving, Renegade Science, and What the Ocean Tells Us about Ourselves by James Nestor.

2. **Websites:**
   - **AIDA International:** Global governing body for freediving.
   - **Apnea Academy:** Freediving education and training programs.
   - **Molchanovs Freediving System:** Advanced training methods and gear.

3. **Mobile Applications:**
   - Apnea Trainer: CO_2 and O_2 tolerance tables.
   - Freedive Log: Logbook for tracking depth, time, and performance.
   - Dive+: Real-time analysis and post-dive metrics.

Appendix E: Freediving Organizations and Certifications

1. **Global Freediving Organizations:**
   - **AIDA International:** Internationally recognized certifications from beginner to advanced levels.
   - **CMAS Freediving:** Very strict freediving and instructor certifications.
   - **PADI Freediver Program:** One of the more well-known certification paths from beginner to professional.

2. **Certification Pathways:**
   - **Beginner:** Basic Freediver or Freediver Level 1.
   - **Intermediate:** Advanced Freediver or Freediver Level 2.
   - **Professional:** Freediving Instructor and Instructor Trainer programs.

Recommended Reference: AIDA Official Guidelines and PADI Freediving Manuals.

Appendix F: Iconic Freediving Locations

1. **Blue Hole, Dahab (Egypt):**
   - Accessible, with perfect conditions both for training and record attempts.

2. **Dean's Blue Hole (Bahamas):**
   - The world's most bottomless blue hole is a paradise for world records and elite competitions.
3. **Deep Dive Dubai DDD (UAE):**
   - The deepest pool in the world guarantees that highly prepared freedivers will have the best conditions in a controlled environment to perfect their techniques.
4. **Kona Coast (Hawaii):**
   - It is known for its crystal-clear waters, plenty of marine life, and excellent conditions for freediving.

Suggested Reading: The Freediver's Guide to Iconic Dive Spots by Freedive Magazine.

Appendix G: Marine Conservation Resources

1. **Conservation Groups:**
   - Reef Check Foundation: Community-based monitoring of reef health.
   - Mission Blue: A global mission to protect marine ecosystems by establishing Hope Spots.
   - Project AWARE: Works for ocean conservation and supports policy.
2. **Sustainable Practices for Freedivers:**
   - Use of eco-friendly diving gear; avoid single-use plastics.
   - Advocacy and involvement in localized marine protections and reef restoration efforts.

A Recommended Resource: Wallace J. Nichols's Blue Mind explains the emotional and ecological importance of the ocean.

Appendix H: Common Freediving Challenges and Solutions

1. **Equalization Issues:**
   - Practice the Frenzel and Valsalva techniques on land before diving.

- Incorporate flexibility exercises targeting the neck and diaphragm.

2. **Mental Barriers:**
   - Use visualization and meditation to overcome fear and anxiety.
   - Break depth goals into smaller, manageable milestones.

3. **CO_2 and O_2 Tolerance:**
   - Gradually increase breath-hold times using tolerance tables.
   - Ensure proper rest and hydration before intensive training sessions.

Recommended Reference: *Freediving for Beginners and Intermediate Freedivers* by Mateusz Malina

www.ingramcontent.com/pod-product-compliance
Lightning Source LLC
Chambersburg PA
CBHW061253230426
43665CB00027B/2930